MULTICULTURAL EDUCATION SERIES

James A. Banks, Series Editor

For a complete list of series titles, please visit www.tcpress.com/MCE

(continued)

Seeing Whiteness

The Essential Essays of Robin DiAngelo

Robin DiAngelo

Series Foreword by James A. Banks

TEACHERS COLLEGE PRESS

TEACHERS COLLEGE | COLUMBIA UNIVERSITY
NEW YORK AND LONDON

Published by Teachers College Press,® 1234 Amsterdam Avenue, New York, NY 10027

Cover stucco texture by Henry & Co via Pexels.

Library of Congress Cataloging-in-Publication Data

Names: DiAngelo, Robin, 1956– author.
Title: Seeing whiteness : the essential essays of Robin Diangelo / Robin
    DiAngelo ; Foreword by James A. Banks.
Description: New York, NY : Teachers College Press, [2023] |
    Series: Multicultural education series | Includes bibliographical references and index.
Identifiers: LCCN 2023017067 | ISBN 9780807768556 (hardcover) |
    ISBN 9780807768549 (paperback) | ISBN 9780807781821 (ebook)
Subjects: LCSH: Social justice and education. | DiAngelo, Robin, 1956–. |
    White people—Race identity. | Race relations. | Racism in education. |
    Educational sociology. | Education—Political aspects.
Classification: LCC LC192.2 .D53 2023 | DDC 306.43—dc23/eng/20230718
LC record available at https://lccn.loc.gov/2023017067

ISBN 978-0-8077-6854-9 (paper)
ISBN 978-0-8077-6855-6 (hardcover)
ISBN 978-0-8077-8182-1 (ebook)

Printed on acid-free paper
Manufactured in the United States of America

In my experience of 24 years of facilitating racial justice work, I have found that it is not helpful to put together in the same room folks who have had racism aimed at them all their lives and folks who haven't had to think about it very much, if at all. The latter group, white people, need a place to start thinking and feeling about it, a space for using prajña (insight) to discover how white conditioning, through no choice of their own, has been embedded in their ego. There is no white person in North America who does not have white conditioning.

Robert Horton, Co-Founder, The UNtraining:
Healing Personal & Social Oppressions

Contents

Series Foreword

Robin DiAngelo brings more than 2 decades of deep reflection, insights, and powerful experiences working as a diversity trainer and teacher educator to this informative, prescient, and engaging book. It is being published at a challenging and toxic time in the United States. The national reckoning that occurred after the murder of George Floyd by police officer Derek Chauvin in Minneapolis in 2020 and the killings of other Blacks by police—such as Breonna Taylor in Louisville, Kentucky, in 2020—have triggered angry, concerted, organized, and influential reactions by conservative political and cultural leaders. Christopher F. Rufo, a conservative activist at the Manhattan Institute, spearheaded a movement that mobilized parents against the teaching of race in schools by falsely claiming that schools were teaching critical race theory (Fortin, 2021). By March 19, 2022, 13 bills that restrict how teachers and students interact about topics related to race had become law in 11 states (*New York Times* Editorial Board, 2022).

The right has appropriated the term "woke" and is using it as a cudgel to attack and delegitimize social justice and equity initiatives in schools and other institutions (Goldberg, 2023). Governor Ron DeSantis of Florida, while testing the waters to become a Republican presidential candidate in 2024, arrogantly stated, "Florida is where woke goes to die" (Blow, 2023; Dixon & Fineout, 2023). Florida rejected a pilot version of an AP course on African American history developed by the College Board (Bouie, 2023; Hartocollis & Fawcett, 2023; Mervosh, 2022).

This book is a crucial counter-narrative to the detrimental conservative initiatives that are endangering the progress that has been made in reducing structural and institutional racism and promoting equity and social justice in the United States since the 1960s and 1970s. DiAngelo's insightful and robust analysis of institutional and structural racism in American society is especially needed and appropriate in these arduous times. Whites will benefit greatly from this book because they are victimized and misled by institutional and structural racism because of the false consciousness, misconceptions, and illusions about the United States and the world that it perpetuates. DiAngelo provides a framework for whites to respond to two essential questions: "What does it mean to be white in a society that is deeply divided and unequal by race?" and "How can I develop more transformative practices and use my position to challenge systemic racism?" (p. 3).

DiAngelo reveals the myths and misconceptions about whiteness that prevent many white Americans from developing a sophisticated understanding of how their actions and beliefs contribute to the codification and perpetuation of white supremacy and prohibit them from comprehending its detrimental consequences for the United States and the world. The 20th anniversary of the U.S. invasion of Iraq is now being observed. Most of the people who advised President George W. Bush about the war were white males (Draper, 2023). They viewed the world from a nationalist and white perspective and encouraged Bush to invade Iraq. This phenomenon was a manifestation of how institutionalized white racism can restrict comprehension of the "other"—cultures and peoples—and lead to destructive and lethal actions (Garcia-Navarro, 2023).

The focus of this book on helping white educators to comprehend structural and institutional racism is a timely and significant contribution to the Multicultural Education Series. The major purpose of the Multicultural Education Series is to provide preservice educators, practicing educators, graduate students, scholars, and policymakers with an interrelated and comprehensive set of books that summarizes and analyzes important research, theory, and practice related to the education of ethnic, racial, cultural, and linguistic groups in the United States and the education of mainstream students about diversity. The dimensions of multicultural education, developed by Banks and described in the *Handbook of Research on Multicultural Education* (Banks, 2004), *The Routledge International Companion to Multicultural Education* (Banks, 2009), and the *Encyclopedia of Diversity in Education* (Banks, 2012), provide the conceptual framework for the development of the publications in the series. These dimensions are content integration, the knowledge construction process, prejudice reduction, equity pedagogy, and an empowering institutional culture and social structure.

The books in the Multicultural Education Series provide research, theoretical, and practical knowledge about the behaviors and learning characteristics of students of color (Conchas & Vigil, 2012; Lee, 2007), language minority students (Gándara & Hopkins, 2010; Valdés, 2001; Valdés et al., 2011), low-income students (Cookson, 2013; Gorski, 2018), multiracial youth (Joseph & Briscoe-Smith, 2021; Mahiri, 2017), and other minoritized population groups, such as students who speak different varieties of English (Charity Hudley & Mallinson, 2011) and LGBTQ youth (Mayo, 2022).

An important message of this book is that to become culturally responsive and effective practitioners, educators need to comprehend the complex ways in which structural and institutional racism influences their attitudes, perceptions, and behaviors. Other books in the Multicultural Education Series that focus on *institutional and structural racism* and ways to reduce it include Özlem Sensoy and Robin DiAngelo (2017), *Is Everyone Really Equal? An Introduction to Key Concepts in Social Justice Education* (2nd ed.); Gary Howard (2016), *We Can't Teach What We Don't Know: White Teachers, Multiracial Schools* (3rd ed.); Zeus Leonardo (2013), *Race Frameworks: A Multidimensional Theory of Racism and Education*; Daniel Solórzano and Lindsay Pérez Huber (2020), *Racial Microaggressions: Using Critical Race Theory in Education to Recognize and Respond to Everyday Racism*; and Gloria Ladson-Billings (2021), *Critical Race Theory in Education: A Scholar's Journey.*

Most readers will find DiAngelo's concept of "white fragility" illuminating, compelling, and useful. She defines it as

> a state in which even a minimum amount of racial stress becomes intolerable, triggering a range of defensive moves. These moves include the outward display of emotions such as anger, fear, and guilt, and behaviors such as argumentation, silence, and leaving the stress-inducing situation. (p. 129)

DiAngelo details vivid and telling examples of white fragility she has experienced in diversity workshops. In some of these examples, the expression of white fragility by one or more white participants in the workshop results in the workshop experience being diverted from its goals and becoming centered on dealing with the anger of one or more white participants. This can result in the marginalization of the experiences of people of color in the workshop. Another manifestation of white fragility is the mandates issued by states that prohibit the teaching of lessons about race that make white students feel uncomfortable or guilty (Wallace-Wells, 2021).

I am pleased to welcome Robin's second book in the Multicultural Education Series. Her first book in the series, which is co-authored by Özlem Sensoy, *Is Everyone Really Equal? An Introduction to Key Concepts in Social Justice Education* (2nd ed., 2017), is a bestseller that has been warmly received by teacher education students and educational practitioners. I invited Özlem and Robin to write this book when they were my doctoral students at the University of Washington. I was delighted when Robin's book *White Fragility: Why It's So Hard for White People to Talk About Racism*, published by Beacon in 2018, became a *New York Times* bestseller. I hope this, her second book in the Multicultural Education Series, will have a wide and influential audience because of its merits and timeliness, and because of the ominous challenges that multicultural and educational equity initiatives are experiencing in the United States and around the world (Banks, 2023).

—James A. Banks

REFERENCES

Banks, J. A. (2004). Multicultural education: Historical development, dimensions, and practice. In J. A. Banks & C. A. M. Banks (Eds.), *Handbook of research on multicultural education* (pp. 3–29). Jossey-Bass.

Banks, J. A. (Ed.). (2009). *The Routledge international companion to multicultural education*. Routledge.

Banks, J. A. (2012). Multicultural education: Dimensions of. In J. A. Banks (Ed.), *Encyclopedia of diversity in education* (Vol. 3, pp. 1538–1547). Sage.

Banks, J. A. (Ed.). (2023). *Global migration and civic education: Research, policy, and practice*. Routledge.

Blow, C. M. (2023, February 15). The 'wicked wisdom' of Ron DeSantis. *The New York Times*. https://www.nytimes.com/2023/02/15/opinion/ron-desantis-black-history.html?searchResultPosition=2

Bouie, J. (2023, January 29). Ron DeSantis likes his culture wars for a reason. *The New York Times*. https://www.nytimes.com/2023/01/24/opinion/desantis-florida-culture-w.html?searchResultPosition=1

Charity Hudley, A. H., & Mallinson, C. (2011). *Understanding language variation in U.S. schools*. Teachers College Press.

Conchas, G. Q., & Vigil, J. D. (2012). *Streetsmart schoolsmart: Urban poverty and the education of adolescent boys*. Teachers College Press.

Cookson, P. W., Jr. (2013). *Class rules: Exposing inequality in American high schools*. Teachers College Press.

DiAngelo, R. (2018). *White fragility: Why it's so hard for white people to talk about racism*. Beacon.

Dixon, M., & Fineout, G. (2023, January 3). 'Where woke goes to die': DeSantis, with eye toward 2024, launches second term. *Politico*. https://www.politico.com/news/2023/01/03/desantis-2024-second-term-00076160

Draper, R. (2023, March 20). Iraq, 20 years later: A changed Washington and a terrible toll on America. *The New York Times*. https://www.nytimes.com/2023/03/20/us/politics/iraq-20-years.html?searchResultPosition=1

Fortin, J. (2021, November 8). Critical race theory: A brief history. *The New York Times*. https://www.nytimes.com/article/what-is-critical-race-theory.html

Gándara, P., & Hopkins, M. (Eds.). (2010). *Forbidden language: English language learners and restrictive language policies*. Teachers College Press.

Garcia-Navarro, L. (2023, March 20). Americans have mostly forgotten the Iraq war. I haven't. *The New York Times*. https://www.nytimes.com/2023/03/20/opinion/iraq-war-20th-anniversary.html?searchResultPosition=1

Goldberg, M. (2003, March 10). The right's obsession with wokeness is a sign of weakness. *The New York Times*. https://www.nytimes.com/2023/03/10/opinion/republican-woke-focus.html?searchResultPosition=3

Gorski, P. C. (2018). *Reaching and teaching students in poverty: Strategies for erasing the opportunity gap* (2nd ed.). Teachers College Press.

Hartocollis, A., & Fawcett, E. (2023, February 1). The College Board strips down its A.P. curriculum for African American studies. *The New York Times*.

https://www.nytimes.com/2023/02/01/us/college-board-advanced-place ment-african-american-studies.html?searchResultPosition=3

Howard, G. (2016). *We can't teach what we don't know: White teachers, multiracial schools* (3rd ed.). Teachers College Press.

Joseph, R. L., & Briscoe-Smith, A. (2021). *Generation mixed goes to school: Radically listening to multiracial kids.* Teachers College Press.

Ladson-Billings, G. (2021). *Critical race theory in education: A scholar's journey.* Teachers College Press.

Lee, C. D. (2007). *Culture, literacy, and learning: Taking bloom in the midst of the whirlwind.* Teachers College Press.

Leonardo, Z. (2013). *Race frameworks: A multidimensional theory of racism and education.* Teachers College Press.

Mahiri, J. (2017). *Deconstructing race: Multicultural education beyond the color-bind.* Teachers College Press.

Mayo, C. (2022). *LGBTQ youth and education: Policies and practices* (2nd ed.). Teachers College Press.

Mervosh, S. (2022, August 27). Back to school in DeSantis's Florida, as teachers look over their shoulders. *The New York Times.* https://www.nytimes.com /2022/08/27/us/desantis-schools-dont-say-gay.html?searchResultPosi tion=2

New York Times Editorial Board. (2022, March 19). America has a free speech problem. *The New York Times.* https://www.nytimes.com/2022/03/18/opinion /cancel-culture-free-speech-poll.html?searchResultPosition=1

Sensoy, Ö., & DiAngelo, R. (2017). *Is everyone really equal? An introduction to key concepts in social justice education* (2nd ed.). Teachers College Press.

Solórzano, D., & Huber, L. P. (2020). *Racial microaggressions: Using critical race theory in education to recognize and respond to everyday racism.* Teachers College Press.

Valdés, G. (2001). *Learning and not learning English: Latino students in American schools.* Teachers College Press.

Valdés, G., Capitelli, S., & Alvarez, L. (2011). *Latino children learning English: Steps in the journey.* Teachers College Press.

Wallace-Wells, B. (2021). How a conservative activist invented the conflict over critical race theory. *The New Yorker.* https://www.newyorker.com/news/annals -of-inquiry/how-a-conservative-activist-invented-the-conflict-over-critical -race-theory

Seeing Whiteness

Introduction

Following the videotaped police execution of George Floyd in the summer of 2020, a global reckoning in race relations took place. The Black Lives Matter movement gained widespread international support. Concepts such as systemic racism and white supremacy were taken up in mainstream discourse. Organizations and corporations professed a commitment to antiracism and rewrote their mission statements. The simplistic idea that racism consists of occasional and isolated acts of intentional meanness was challenged and complicated. More white people began to see that racism operates well beyond the individual or personal level; racism is a system that is woven into the fabric of society. Due to the systemic nature of racism, by every measure, across every institution, Black, Indigenous, and Latinx people are consistently at the bottom in outcomes and access, from maternal and infant mortality rates to income, homeownership, health outcomes, and life expectancy. Omissions and false narratives in the traditional ways of teaching Western history have reinforced mainstream narratives that these outcomes are due to failings on the part of people of color. But as Ibram X. Kendi illustrates in *How to Be an Antiracist*, there are only two overall ways to explain the persistent racial inequality between white people and people of color: Either white people are superior, or racism is systemic. During the summer of 2020, more white Americans were beginning to explain racial inequality with the latter, understanding that while everyone has bias and everyone discriminates, the bias of those who control the institutions is backed with legal authority and institutional power. This is the critical element that differentiates individual racial prejudice and discrimination from systemic racism—the historical accumulation and ongoing use of institutional power and authority to support that prejudice and to enact discriminatory behaviors across the whole of society. Since the founding of the United States, those who control the institutions have been and continue to be overwhelmingly white. This awareness has moved many white people from asking *if* we are part of systemic racism to *how* we are part of it.

The level of callous racial brutality made visible in the video of George Floyd's murder in a society that rarely shows us experiences other than our own was a rare sight in white America, and many white Americans were deeply moved by bearing witness. To be white is to be like a fish in the water of systemic racism, swimming with a current that moves us along, enhancing the impact of our efforts. At the same time, by virtue of its very nature, our whiteness is rarely acknowledged. One of our first tasks as white people is to learn to see what we have been deeply trained not to see: the water in which we have been socialized and that shapes every aspect of our lives. We live within a racial hierarchy that places us at the top and gives us structural advantage across all institutions. To challenge the inequity of this system, we need to understand how it developed, how it operates today, and how we have been socialized to participate in it.

However, a brief glimpse is not enough to sustain on-going engagement and falling back into the comfort of the status quo is highly seductive. While we may take heart in how many white people were involved in the awakening and activism we saw in the summer of 2020, predictably, much of that focus has faded and many who were initially involved have done nothing further. Their apathy has been reinforced by the swift structural backlash banning books, misrepresenting Critical Race Theory, and removing courses that acknowledge the existence of racism, both past and present. As Carol Anderson has argued in *White Rage: The Unspoken Truth of Our Racial Divide*, every inch of Black progress has been met with a backlash of white rage and this backlash is evident today.

For more than 20 years, I have been researching and writing about whiteness and white racial identity, working to help white people see—and continue to see—how whiteness shapes our lives. I have done so from the position of an insider to whiteness—as a white person myself speaking directly to other white people. I have written more than 20 peer-reviewed articles, some of which have been published in well-known education journals such as the *Harvard Educational Review, Race & Ethnicity in Education,*

Multicultural Perspectives, and *Equity & Excellence in Education*. In addition, I have published two textbooks, one of which was co-written with Özlem Sensoy and won the 2012 Critics' Choice Book Award from the American Educational Studies Association (AESA) for outstanding contribution to scholarship in the Social Foundations of Education field and the 2018 Society of Professors of Education Book Award. I have written three non-academic books on white racial identity, two of which have been *New York Times (NYT)* bestsellers: *White Fragility: Why It's So Hard for White People to Talk About Racism* and *Nice Racism: How Progressive White People Perpetuate Racial Harm*. *White Fragility* spent 3 years on the *NYT* Best Sellers List and at the time of this publishing has been translated into 12 languages. This record demonstrates my ability to communicate key concepts in both academic and mainstream discourse.

Here, I pull together 2 decades of my research and publications on the specific role that white people play in either upholding or challenging systemic racism. I provide the conceptual framework necessary for white people to answer two essential questions: What does it mean to be white in a society that is deeply divided and unequal by race? and How can I develop more transformative practices and use my position to challenge systemic racism? Readers of color may also find this collection helpful for navigating whiteness in daily life. People of color cannot avoid understanding white consciousness to some degree if they are to be successful in this society, yet little in dominant culture acknowledges their perspectives or validates their frustrations when they interact with white people. I hope that this exploration affirms the cross-racial experiences of people of color and provides some useful insight.

A Note About Repetition: While each chapter speaks to a specific aspect of whiteness and its manifestations, the overall theoretical framework the analysis is drawn from is the same. Before readers can understand a specific manifestation, they must understand the foundation of white supremacy from which it issues. Because each chapter was written as a stand-alone, readers will note that many chapters repeat aspects of the theoretical setup and describe the same set of dynamics common to white socialization. Chapter 6 is the foundational article "White Fragility," originally published in the *International Journal of Critical Pedagogy*. Chapter 7 is a shorter, non-academic version of that original article, intended to be accessible to readers outside of academia.

A Note About Language: Readers should also note that language is dynamic and changes over time. Many marginalized groups that are generally recognized today were erased in the past due to a lack of language to attest to and validate their existence. Oftentimes, the language that was available was so demeaning that there was no way to use it without further reinforcing deep biases. The chapters here were written across a span of 2 decades and reflect the language and terms that were understood at the time of the original writing as the most appropriate. If writing a similar analysis today, I might use different terms.

ONE

My Class Didn't Trump My Race
Using Oppression to Face Privilege

I grew up poor and white. Although my class oppression has been relatively visible to me, my race privilege has not. In my efforts to uncover how
race has shaped my life, I have gained deeper insight by placing race in the
center of my analysis and asking how each of my other group locations has
socialized me to collude with racism. In so doing, I have been able to address in greater depth my multiple locations and how they function together to hold racism in place. Thus, my exploration of what it means to be
white starts with what it means to be poor, for my understanding of race
is inextricably entwined with my class background. I now make the distinction that I grew up poor and white, for my experience of poverty would
have been different had I not been white. For white people who experience
oppression in other areas of our lives (such as class, gender, religion, or
sexual orientation), it can be difficult to center a location through which
we experience privilege. When leading discussions in equity-oriented
courses, I find that white students often resist centering racism in their
analysis, feeling that to do so invalidates the positions in which they experience oppression. These students also feel that these oppressions make
them "less" racially privileged. However, rather than ameliorating my race
privilege, my oppressed class location was a primary avenue through which
I came to understand what being white meant. As I work to unravel my
internalized racial dominance, I have found two key questions useful:

Originally published as "My class didn't trump my race: Using oppression to face privilege." *Multicultural Perspectives, 8*(1), 51–56. Copyright © 2006 National Association for Multicultural Education, reprinted by permission of Taylor & Francis Ltd, http://www.tandfonline.com on behalf of National Association for Multicultural Education.

1. How does internalized dominance function collectively for white people, regardless of our other social locations?
2. How did I learn racism specifically through my class (or other) oppression?

I was born to working-class parents; my father was a construction worker and my mother was a switchboard operator. When I was 2, my parents divorced and my mother began to raise us on her own; at that point we entered into poverty. I have never understood people who say, "We were poor but we didn't know it because we had lots of love." Poverty hurts. It isn't romantic or some form of "living simply." Poor people are not innocent and childlike. The lack of medical and dental care, the hunger, and the ostracization are concrete. The stress of poverty made my household much more chaotic than loving.

We were evicted frequently and moved four or five times a year. There were periods when oatmeal was the only food in our house. I had no health or dental care during my childhood, and today all of my front teeth are filled because by the time I was 10 they had visible holes. If we got sick, my mother would beat us, screaming that we could not get sick because she could not afford to take us to the doctor. We occasionally had to live in our car, and I was left with relatives for 8 months while my mother tried to secure housing for us. My teacher once held my hands up to my 4th-grade class as an example of poor hygiene and, with the class as her audience, told me to go home and tell my mother to wash me.

I used to stare at the girls in my class and ache to be like them—to have a father, to wear pretty clothes, to go to camp, to be clean, and to get to sit with them. I knew we didn't have enough money and that meant that I couldn't join them in school or go to their houses or have the same things they had. But the moment the real meaning of poverty crystallized for me came when we were visiting another family. As we were leaving, I heard one of their daughters ask her mother, "What is wrong with them?" I stopped, riveted. I too wanted to know. Her mother held her finger to her lips and whispered, "Shhh, they're poor." This was a revelatory moment for me. The shock came not just in the knowledge that we were poor but that it was exposed. There was something wrong with us, indeed, and it was something that was obvious to others and that we couldn't hide, something shameful that could be seen but should not be named. It took me many years to gain a structural analysis of class that would help shift this sense of shame.

I begin this narrative with my class background because it so deeply informs my understanding of race. From an early age I had the sense of being an outsider; I was acutely aware that I was poor, that I was dirty, that I was not normal, and that there was something "wrong" with me. But I also knew that I was not Black. We were at the lower rungs of society, but there was always someone on the periphery, just below us. I knew that "colored" people existed and that they should be avoided. I can remember many occasions when I reached for candy or uneaten food laying on the street and was admonished by my grandmother not to touch it because a "colored person" may have touched it. The message was clear to me; if a colored person touched something it became dirty. The irony here is that the marks of poverty were clearly visible on me: poor hygiene, torn clothes, homelessness, hunger. Yet through comments such as my grandmother's, a racial Other was formed in my consciousness, an Other through whom I became clean. Race was the one identity that aligned me with the other girls in my school.

I left home as a teenager and struggled to survive. As I looked at what lay ahead, I could see no path out of poverty other than education. The decision to take that path was frightening for me; I had never gotten the message that I was smart, and academia was a completely foreign social context. But once I was in academia, I understood that a college degree is not conferred upon those who are smarter or who try harder than others; it comes through a complex web of intersecting systems of privileges that include internal expectations as well as external resources. In academia, racism, a key system that I benefit from, helped to mediate my class-based disadvantages.

Upon graduation, with my degree in sociology and a background in adult education, I answered a call for diversity trainers from a state department that had lost a civil rights lawsuit and been mandated to provide 16 hours of diversity training to all their employees. They needed 40 diversity trainers to train 3,000 people. Looking back from where I am now, I see how naïve I was when I started that contract. I thought that being "liberal" qualified me because, after all, racists were people who didn't have an open mind. I had an open mind and was thus not a racist, my reasoning went; these employees just needed help opening their minds too. As happens all too often, those in the position to hire me (primarily other white people) did not have the ability to assess the qualifications of someone leading discussions on race, and I was hired, along with 39 other people from a range of backgrounds.

I was completely unprepared for the depth of hostility and the disconnection from racial realities that I encountered from white people in these trainings. It was unnerving to be in a room composed exclusively of white employees and hear them bitterly complain that because of affirmative action, white people could no longer get jobs. That white employees would feel free to express this hostility to my co-leader of color (who was racially isolated in the room) was another piece of the puzzle I was yet to put together. Even more significantly, the training teams were always interracial, and the very dynamics that I sought to enlighten my participants on were actively manifesting between my co-trainers and myself. Over time, I began to see racial dynamics more clearly, and after many years in the field, along with much personal work and some very patient mentors, I became more grounded in the dynamics of racialized knowledge construction. These trainings provided an extraordinary opportunity to observe first-hand the processes by which a white racial identity is socially constructed and privileged, and the mechanisms by which white people receive and protect that privilege. I also reflected on my own responses to the ways in which I was being racially challenged, for unlike the middle-class culture of academia that I found foreign, the culture of whiteness was so normalized for me that it was barely visible. I had my experience of marginalization to draw from in understanding racism, which helped tremendously, but as I became more conversant in the workings of racism, I came to understand that the oppression I experienced growing up poor didn't protect me from learning my place in the racial hierarchy.

Since those early days, I have led dialogues on race with police officers, social workers, and teachers, and in both the private and government sectors. I recently completed my dissertation on how white student teachers reproduce racism in interracial dialogues about race. As I look at the world now, I see racism as ever-present and multidimensional. I realize that poor and working-class white people don't necessarily have any less racism than middle- or upper-class white people; our racism is just conveyed in different ways and we enact it from a different social location than the middle or upper classes.

As I reflect back on the early messages I received about being poor and being white, I now realize that my grandmother and I needed people of color to cleanse and realign us with the dominant white culture that our poverty had separated us from. I now ask myself how the classist messages I internalized growing up lead me to collude in racism. For example, as a child who grew up in poverty, I received constant reminders that I was stupid, lazy, dirty, and a drain on the resources of hard-working people. I internalized these messages, and they worked to silence me. Unless I work to uproot them, I am less likely to trust my own perceptions or feel like I have a "right" to speak up. I may not attempt to interrupt racism because the social context in which it is occurring intimidates me. My fear on these occasions may be coming from a place of internalized class inferiority, but in practice my silence colludes with racism and ultimately benefits me by protecting my white privilege and maintaining racial solidarity with other white people. This solidarity connects and realigns me with white people across other lines of difference, such as the very class locations that have silenced me in the first place. I am also prone to use others to elevate me, as in the example with my grandmother. So although my specific class background mediated the way I learned racism and how I enact it, in the end it still socialized me to collude with the overall structure.

It is my observation that class dictates proximity between white people and people of color. Poor white people are most often in closest proximity to people of color because they tend to share poverty. I hear the term "white trash" frequently. It is not without significance that this is one of the few expressions in which race is named for white people. I think the proximity of the people labeled as white trash to people of color is why; race becomes marked or "exposed" by virtue of a closeness to people of color. In a racist society, this closeness both highlights and pollutes whiteness. Owning-class people also have people of color near them because people of color are often their domestics and gardeners—their servants. But they do not interact socially with people of color in the same way that poor white people do. Middle-class white people are generally the furthest away from people of color. They are the most likely to say that "there were no people of color in my neighborhood or school. I didn't meet a Black person until I went to college" (often adding "so I was lucky because I didn't learn anything about racism"). Looking specifically at how class shaped my racial identity has been very helpful to me in attempting to unravel the specific way I manifest my internalized racial superiority.

I am no longer poor. Although I still carry the marks of poverty, those marks are now only internal. But the marks limit me in more than what I believe I deserve or where I think I belong; they also interfere with my ability to stand up against injustice, for as long as I believe that I am not as smart or as valuable as other white people, I won't challenge racism. I believe that in order for white people to unravel our internalized racial dominance, we have two interwoven tasks. One is to work on our own internalized oppression—the ways in which we impose limitations on ourselves based on the societal messages we receive about the inferiority of the lower-status groups we belong to. The other task is to face the internalized dominance that results from being socialized in a racist society—the ways in which we consciously or unconsciously believe that we are more important, more valuable, more intelligent, and more deserving than people of color.

I cannot address the interwoven complexity of other white people's social locations. However, after years facilitating dialogues on race with thousands of white people from a range of class positions (as well as varied gender, sexual orientation, religious, and ability positions), and bearing witness to countless stories and challenges from people of color about my own racism and that of other white people, I have come to see some very common patterns of internalized dominance. These patterns are shared across other social positions due to the bottom-line nature of racism: Regardless of one's other locations, white people know on some level that being white in this society is "better" than being a person of color, and this, along with the very real doors whiteness opens, serves to mediate the oppression experienced in those other social locations. In the next section of this chapter, I will identify several of these patterns of internalized dominance that are generally shared among white people.

WE LIVE SEGREGATED LIVES

Growing up in segregated environments (schools, workplaces, neighborhoods, media images, historical perspectives, etc.), we are given the message that our experiences and perspectives are the only ones that matter. We receive this message day in and day out, and it is not limited to a single moment; it is a relentless experience. Virtually all of our teachers, history books, role models, and movie and book characters are white like us. Further, as white people, we are taught not to feel any loss about the absence of people of color in our lives. In fact, the absence of people of color is what defines our schools and neighborhoods as "good." And we get this message regardless of where we are oppressed in other areas of our lives. Because we live primarily segregated lives in a white-dominated society, we receive little or no authentic information about racism and are thus unprepared to think critically or complexly about it. Although segregation is often mediated somewhat for poor urban (and other) white people who may live near and have friendships with people of color on the microlevel, segregation is still operating on the macrolevel and informing our collective perspectives and what is deemed the most valuable or "official" knowledge.

White people from the lower classes who may have more integrated lives on the microlevel still receive the message that achievement means moving out of poverty and away from the neighborhoods and schools that define us. Upward mobility is the great class goal in the United States, and the social environment gets tangibly whiter the higher up one goes, whether it be in academia or in management. Whiter environments, in turn, are marked as the most socially and economically valuable. Reaching toward the most valuable places in society thus entails leaving people of color behind.

WE ARE TAUGHT IN OUR CULTURE TO SEE OUR EXPERIENCE AS OBJECTIVE AND REPRESENTATIVE OF REALITY

The belief in objectivity, coupled with setting white people up as outside of culture and thus the norm for humanity, allows us to see ourselves as universal humans who can represent all of human experience. People of color can only represent their own racialized experience—that is, Robert Altman is a film director whose work is expected to relate to everyone, and Spike Lee is a Black film director whose films are from "the Black" perspective. But there is no objective, neutral reality. Human objectivity is not actually possible, but as long as we construct the world as if it is, and then ascribe it only to ourselves, we keep white experience and people centered and people of color in the margins.

WE ARE RAISED TO VALUE THE INDIVIDUAL AND TO SEE OURSELVES AS INDIVIDUALS, RATHER THAN AS PART OF A SOCIALIZED GROUP

Individualism allows us to present ourselves as having "just arrived on the scene," unique and original, outside of socialization and unaffected by the relentless racial messages we receive. This also allows us to distance ourselves from the actions of our group and demand that we be granted the benefit of the doubt (because we are individuals) in all cases. Thus, we get very irate when we are "accused" of racism, because as individuals, we are "different" from other white people and expect to be seen as such. We find intolerable any suggestion that our behavior or perspectives are typical of our group as a whole, and this ensures that we cannot deepen our understanding of racism.

Seeing ourselves as individuals erases our history and hides the way in which wealth has accumulated over generations and benefits us, as a group, today. Further, being an individual is a privilege only afforded to white people. By focusing on ourselves as individuals, white people are able to conceptualize the racist patterns in our behavior as "just our personality" and not connected to intergroup dynamics. For example, I might be an extrovert and cut people off when I am engaged in a discussion. I can say, "that is just my personality, I do that to everyone. That is how we talked at the dinner table in my family." But the moment I cut off a person of color, it becomes racism because the history and the impact of that behavior for both of us is different. The freedom to remain oblivious to that fact, with no sense that this obliviousness has any consequences of importance, is white privilege (racism).

If we use the line of reasoning that we are all individuals and social categories such as race, class, and gender don't matter and are just "labels" that stereotype us, then it follows that we all end up in our own "natural" places. Those at the top are merely a collection of individuals who rose under their own individual merits, and those at the bottom are there due to individual lack. Group membership is thereby rendered inoperative and racial disparities are seen as essential rather than structural. Thus, the discourse of individuality is not only connected to the discourse of meritocracy but also with the Darwinism of the "bell curve." It behooves those of us oppressed in other places to understand group membership, for the discourse of individuality may benefit us in terms of racial privilege but ultimately holds all of our oppressions in place.

IN OUR DOMINANT POSITIONS WE ARE ALMOST ALWAYS RACIALLY COMFORTABLE AND EXPECT TO REMAIN SO

We can often choose if and when we will put ourselves into racially uncomfortable situations, and for most of our lives we have been advised not to do it because it is "dangerous." Thus, racial comfort becomes not only an expectation, but something to which we feel entitled. If racism is brought up and we become uncomfortable, then something is "wrong" and we blame the person who triggered our discomfort (usually a person of color). Because racism is necessarily uncomfortable, insisting that we remain comfortable guarantees we will never really face it or engage in authentic dialogue with others about it.

White people often confuse comfort with safety and state that we don't feel safe when what we really mean is that we don't feel comfortable. This trivializes our history of savage brutality toward people of color and perverts the reality of that history. Because we don't think complexly about racism, we don't ask ourselves what safety means from a position of dominance, or the impact on people of color for white people to complain about their safety when merely talking about racism.

WE FEEL THAT WE SHOULD BE JUDGED BY OUR INTENTIONS RATHER THAN THE EFFECTS OF OUR BEHAVIOR

A common white reasoning is that as long as we didn't intend to perpetuate racism, then our actions don't count as racism. We focus on our intentions and discount the impact, thereby invalidating people of color's experiences and communicating that the effects of our behavior on them are unimportant. We then spend great energy explaining to people of color why our behavior is not racism at all. This invalidates their perspectives while enabling us to deny responsibility for making the effort to understand enough about racism to see our behavior's impact in both the immediate interaction and the broader, historical context.

WE BELIEVE THAT IF WE CAN'T FEEL OUR SOCIAL POWER, THEN WE DON'T HAVE ANY

White social power is so normalized that it is outside of our conscious awareness. Yet we often expect that power is something that one can feel, rather than something one takes for granted. The issue of social power is where a lower-class location often becomes confused with a lack of racial privilege. For example, in discussions on race I often hear white working-class men protest that they don't have any social power. They work long and grueling hours, often in jobs in which they have no long-term security, and come home feeling beaten and quite disempowered. These men can often not relate to the concept of holding social power. But if being able to feel racial privilege is required before white people can acknowledge its reality, we will not be able to see (and thus change) it. The key to recognizing power is in recognizing normalcy—what is not attended to or in need of constant navigation. These men are indeed struggling against social and economic barriers, but race is simply not one of them; in fact, race is a major social current running in their direction and not only moving them along but helping them navigate their other social struggles. Not feeling power is not necessarily aligned with how others perceive or respond to us, or our relationship to social and institutional networks.

WE THINK IT IS IMPORTANT TO PRETEND NOT TO NOTICE RACE

The underlying assumption of a color-blind discourse is that race is a defect and it is best to pretend that we don't notice it. But if we pretend we don't notice race, we cannot notice racism. If we don't notice racism, we can't understand or interrupt it in ourselves or others. We have to start being honest about the fact that we do notice race (when it isn't white) and then pay attention to what race means in our everyday lives. White people and people of color do not have the same racial experience, and this has profound and tangible consequences that need to be understood if we want to stop colluding with racism.

WE CONFUSE NOT UNDERSTANDING WITH NOT AGREEING

Because of the factors discussed previously, there is much about racism that white people don't understand. Yet, in our racial arrogance, we have no compunction about debating the knowledge of people who have lived, breathed, and studied these issues for many years. We feel free to dismiss these informed perspectives rather than have the humility to acknowledge that they are unfamiliar to us, reflect further on them, or seek more knowledge. We trivialize others' intelligence and expertise and counter with simplistic platitudes that often begin with "People just need to. . . ."

People from the lower classes often have the opportunity to learn more about the perspectives of people of color through their more likely proximity to them. Yet the conflicting messages we receive within our own families and the myriad messages we receive from the larger culture contradict these perspectives and do not support us in either seeking them out or valuing them.

WE WILL BE THE JUDGE OF WHETHER OR NOT RACISM HAS OCCURRED

Because of our social, economic, and political power within a white supremacist culture, we are in the position to legitimize people of color's assertions of racism. Yet we are the least likely to see, understand, or be invested in validating those assertions and being honest about their consequences. We construct racism as specific acts that individuals either do or don't do, and we think we can simply look at a specific incident and decide if "it" happened. But racism is infused in every part of our society, our beings, and our perspectives. It is reinforced every day in countless and often subliminal ways. It cannot be pulled out into specific moments, and our inability to think complexly about racism, as well as our investment in its benefits, makes us the least qualified to assess its manifestations.

RACISM HAS BEEN CONSTRUCTED AS BELONGING TO EXTREMISTS AND BEING VERY BAD

Racism is a deeply embedded, multidimensional, and internalized system that all members of this society are shaped by. Yet dominant culture constructs racism as primarily in the past and only currently occurring as isolated acts relegated to individual bad people (usually living somewhere in the South, or "old"). Although many white people today sincerely believe that racism is a bad thing, our abhorrence of racism coupled with a superficial conceptualization of it causes us to be highly defensive about any suggestion that we perpetuate it. Many white people (and liberal white people in particular) think that we can deal with racism in our heads (and without ever interacting with people of color) by deciding that we have not been affected because we don't want to have been affected.

A superficial understanding of racism coupled with a desire to distance ourselves from being perceived as "bad" is further complicated by resentments we may feel about places in our lives where we suffer from other forms of social injustice. It is often very difficult for white people who have not been validated for the oppression they experience elsewhere to keep their attention on a form of oppression from which they benefit. But I have found that when I explore how classism and other oppressions I experience set me up to participate in racism, I am more able to interrupt the manifestation of both in my life. By placing racism in the center of my analysis, I have been able to begin to unravel my other group socializations and how they work together to support social hierarchies.

INTERRUPTING INTERNALIZED DOMINANCE

I have found that a key to interrupting my internalized racial dominance is to defer to the knowledge of people whom I have been taught, in countless ways, are less knowledgeable and less valuable than I am. I must reach for humility and be willing to not know. I may never fully understand the workings of racism, as I have been trained my entire life to perpetuate racism while denying its reality. I do not have to understand racism for it to be real, and my expectation that I could is part of my internalized dominance. Reaching for racial humility as a white person is not the same for me as being mired in class shame.

My class position is only one social location from which I learned to collude with racism. For example, I have also asked myself how I learned to collude with racism as a Catholic and a woman. How did it shape my sense of racial belonging, of racial correctness, to be presented with God, the ultimate and universal authority, as white? How did the active erasure of Jesus's race and ethnicity shape my racial consciousness? How did the universalization of Catholicism as the true religion for all peoples of the world engender racial superiority within me when all the authorities within that religion were white like myself? At the same time, how did my conditioning under Catholicism not to question authority lead me to silently collude with the racism of other white people?

As a white woman, how did I internalize racial superiority through the culture's representation of white women as the embodiment of ultimate beauty? What has it meant for me to have a key signifier of female perfection—whiteness—available to me? How have images of white women in the careers deemed valuable for women shaped my goals? How has mainstream feminism's articulation of white women's issues as universal women's issues shaped what I care about? At the same time, what has it meant to live under patriarchy and to be taught that as a woman I am less intelligent, that I should not speak up, that I should defer to others and at all times be nice and polite? How have all of these messages ultimately set me up to collude in the oppression of people of color? By asking questions such as these I have been able to gain a much deeper and more useful analysis of racism, and rather than finding that centering racism denies my other oppressions, I find that centering racism has been a profound way to address the complexity of all my social locations.

TWO

✕✕✕✕✕✕✕✕✕✕✕✕✕✕✕✕✕✕✕✕✕✕✕

Why Can't We All Just Be Individuals? Countering the Discourse of Individualism in Antiracist Education

In my years as a white person co-facilitating antiracism courses for primarily white audiences in a range of academic, corporate, and government institutions across the United States, Canada, and the United Kingdom, I have come to believe that the discourse of individualism is one of the primary barriers preventing well-meaning (and other) white people from understanding racism. Individualism is such a deeply entrenched discourse that it is virtually immovable without sustained effort. A recent interaction may illustrate the depth of this narrative.

I was co-facilitating a mandatory workplace training titled Race & Social Justice. Two key components of this training are my presentation, as a white person, on the dynamics of white privilege, and my co-facilitator's presentation, as a person of color,[1] on the dynamics of internalized racial oppression. Included in my presentation is a list of common barriers for white people in seeing racism. One of these barriers is that we see ourselves as individuals, outside of social groups. I had just finished presenting this list and had called for a break, during which a white woman, "Sue," who had been sitting next to a white man, "Bill," approached me and declared, "Bill and I think we should all just see each other as individuals." Although in my

Originally published as "Why Can't We All Just Be Individuals?: Countering the Discourse of Individualism in Anti-racist Education." *InterActions: UCLA Journal of Education and Information Studies,* 6(1). Retrieved from: http://www.escholarship.org/uc/item/5fm4h8wm

work moments like this occur frequently, they continue to disorient me on two interconnected levels. First, I had just stated that seeing each other as individuals was a perspective only available to the dominant group. Yet Sue's statement implied I had never heard or considered this most simple and popular of "solutions" to racism, much less just raised and critiqued it. I was left wondering, yet again, what happens cognitively for many white people in forums such as this that prevents them from actually hearing what is being presented. Second, why did she, as a white person, feel confident to declare the one-sentence "answer" to a profoundly complex and perennial dilemma of social life? Why not consider my background in the field and instead engage me in a dialogue on the matter, or ask me to explain my point in more depth? I did my best to reiterate my previous position, but to no avail. By the afternoon break, Sue had walked out.

So what was Sue and Bill's point? In my experience, when white people insist on individualism in discussions about racism, they are in essence saying:

> My race has not made a difference in my life, so why do we have to talk about race as if it mattered? It is talking about race as if it mattered that divides us. I don't see myself as a member of a racial group; you shouldn't see me that way either. In fact, by saying that my group membership matters, you are generalizing. Generalizing discounts my individuality; unless you know me, you can't profess to know anything about my life and all of the ways I am unique relative to anyone else. Further, as an individual I am objective and view others as individuals and not as members of racial groups. For example, if I were hiring, I would hire the best person for the job no matter what their race was. Racism will disappear when we all see each other as individuals. In fact, it has disappeared because I already see everyone as individuals—it's just misguided people such as yourself who refuse to see everyone as an individual and thus keep racism alive.

Obviously I disagree with these familiar dominant claims, as they stand in the face of all evidence to the contrary, both research-based evidence of racial discrimination and disparity on every measure (see Copeland, 2005; Hochschild & Weaver, 2007; Micceri, 2009; Wessel, 2005) and visible evidence of ongoing patterns of segregation in education, economics, and housing.

The purpose of this paper is to offer a critical analysis of how the discourse of individualism, rather than ameliorating racism, actually functions to obscure and maintain racism's manifestation in our lives. In countering these claims in depth, my goal is to provide a more comprehensive challenge to the dominant discourse of individualism that inevitably surfaces in antiracist work, for the more deeply we can interrogate this discourse, the more effectively we might challenge it. In order to challenge dominant discourse, one must be able to think critically about it, to see what the discourse obscures and how it functions to normalize inequitable power relations (Billig, 2001; Fairclough, 1989). To this end, I will start with a theoretical overview of discourse, critical discourse analysis, and the discourse of individualism, followed by an explication of eight key dynamics of racism that this discourse obscures. I will conclude with my thoughts on why a critique of individualism is so difficult for many white people to entertain, and how we might reconceptualize individualism in service of challenging racism.

THEORIES OF DISCOURSE

Discourse analysis is a useful tool in explicating racism because it allows for a nuanced analysis of the socially and historically informed discourses that are available for negotiating racial positions (Gee, 1999; Van Dijk, 1993). Discourse analysis can reveal processes of racism that otherwise would be difficult to establish, or that would be formally denied by the majority of participants (Van Dijk, 1992). In this section I provide a brief overview of the methodology of discourse analysis, and specifically overview the discourse of individualism.

In theories of discourse, language is not conceptualized as a "pure" or neutral transmitter of a universal reality or truth (Allen, 1996). Rather, language is conceptualized as the historically and culturally situated means by which we construct reality or truth, and thus is dependent on the historical and social moment in which it is expressed (Billig, 2001; Cameron et al., 1992; Fairclough, 1989; Foucault, 1972; Gee, 1999). Meaning is made through the specific frameworks that are culturally, historically, and ideologically available to a specific social group at a specific moment in space and time (Billig, 2001). For example, the concept of Individualism would have been incomprehensible before the Enlightenment, and the concept of distinct human races incomprehensible before European colonialism (Mills, 1999). Gee (1999) states that "Meaning is not general and abstract, not something that resides in dictionaries, or even in general symbolic representations inside people's heads. Rather, it is situated in specific social and cultural practices, and it is continually transformed in those practices" (p. 63). Justin Johnson (2005) explains discourse as "an institutionalized way of speaking that determines not only what we say and how we say it, but also what we do not say. Discourses provide a unified set of words, symbols, and metaphors that allow us to construct and communicate a coherent interpretation of reality" (p. 1). It is not possible to escape discourse because we cannot make sense of our social relations without the meaning-making frameworks that discourses provide. Fairclough (1989) states that "whenever people speak or listen or write or read, they do so in ways that are determined socially and have social effects" (p. 23).

Yet discourse is not simply a socio-historically specific meaning-making framework. Discourse, because it constructs social relations and social positioning, is infused with relations of unequal power. Fairclough (1989) argues that discourse is shaped by relations of power and invested with ideologies; ideology—taken-for-granted assumptions infused throughout a society—is the prime means of manufacturing consent to these power relations. Fairclough states, "The idea of 'power behind discourse' is that the whole social order of discourse is put together and held together as a hidden effect of power" (p. 55). Discourses are acquired within and licensed by specific social and historically shaped practices representing the values and interests of specific groups of people. As Billig (2001) explains, "Each act of utterance . . . carries an ideological history. An ideology comprises the ways of thinking and behaving within a given society which make the ways of that society seem 'natural' or unquestioned to its members" (p. 217). In this way, ideology is the "common sense" of the society that functions in various ways to render unequal social relations as natural or inevitable (Billig, 2001; Fairclough, 1989). Discourses that become dominant do so because they serve the interests of those in power. A discourse may initially surface as a challenge to power, such as Martin Luther King's call for a "color-blind" society, but if they resonate with the masses in a way that threatens dominant interests, they are often co-opted and reinterpreted by and in service of dominant interests, as is unquestionably the case with color-blind discourse (Bonilla-Silva, 2006; Schofield, 2004; Su, 2007). Thus, to study discourse is to study power and ideology.

THE DISCOURSE OF INDIVIDUALISM

The discourse of individualism is a specific set of ideas, words, symbols, and metaphors—a storyline or narrative—that creates, communicates, reproduces, and reinforces the concept that each of us is a unique individual and that our group memberships, such as our race, class, or gender, are not important or relevant to our opportunities (Flax, 1999). In explaining the discourse of individualism, Flax (1999) notes that there is an irreconcilable tension within U.S. life. The legitimacy of our institutions depends upon the concept that all citizens are equal. At the same time, we each occupy distinct raced (and gendered, classed, etc.) positions that profoundly shape our life chances in ways that are not voluntary or random. In order to manage this tension, we use the discourse of individualism. This discourse posits that there are no intrinsic barriers to individual success, and that failure is not a consequence of systematic structure but of individual character. It also conveys that success is independent of privilege, that one succeeds through individual effort, and that there are no favored starting positions that provide competitive advantage (Flax, 1999).

The discourse of individualism is a claim that we all act independently from one another and that we all have the same possibility of achievement and are unmarked by social positions such as race, class, and gender (Bonilla-Silva, 2006). As Mills (1999) states, however, "The reality is that one can pretend the body does not matter only because a particular body ... [white] is being presupposed as the somatic norm" (p. 53). The discourse of individualism posits race as irrelevant. In fact, claiming that race is relevant to one's life chances is seen as limiting one's ability to stand on one's own; standing on one's own is both the assumption and the goal of individualism (Flax, 1999). Because it obscures how social positioning impacts opportunity, the discourse of individualism is a dominant discourse that functions ideologically to reinforce and reproduce relations of unequal power.

CRITICAL DISCOURSE ANALYSIS

Discourse analysis is the study of language and the making of meaning in action and in social contexts. It is a method of investigating the back-and-forth dialogues that constitute social action, along with patterns of signification and representation that constitute culture (Davies & Harre, 1990; Gee, 1999; Wetherell et al., 2001). Discourse analysis is attentive to the usages of language and how those usages position speakers in relation to others, both physically present others and larger categories of others (i.e., social groups; Gee, 1999). As with other forms of meaning, discourse analysts do not conceptualize language about the self as a transparent or neutral transmitter of one's core ideas or personhood. Rather, language about the self is conceptualized as historically and socially situated, the language itself creating what it means to be a person. Critical discourse analysis specifically focuses on the discursive reproduction of social inequality (Van Dijk, 1993). In differentiating critical discourse analysis from other forms, Van Dijk (1993) states that "Although there are many directions in the study and critique of social inequality, the way we approach these questions and dimensions is by focusing on *the role of discourse in the (re)production and challenge of dominance*" (p. 249, emphasis in original). Dominance is defined here as the exercise of social power by elites, institutions, or groups that results in reproducing, maintaining, and justifying social inequality. The reproduction process includes the implicit support, enactment, representation, legitimation, denial, mitigation, or concealment of dominance. Critical discourse analysts focus on the structures, strategies, or other properties of text, talk, verbal interaction, or communicative events that play a role in these modes of reproduction. Van Dijk (1993), in describing critical discourse analysis, states:

> This does not mean that we see power and dominance merely as unilaterally "imposed" on others. On the contrary, in many situations, and sometimes paradoxically, power and even power abuse may seem "jointly produced," e.g. when dominated groups are persuaded, by whatever means, that dominance is "natural" or otherwise legitimate. Thus, although an analysis of strategies of resistance and challenge is crucial for our understanding of actual power and dominance relations in society, and although such an analysis needs to be

included in a broader theory of power, and counter-power and discourse, our critical approach prefers to focus on the elites and their discursive strategies for the maintenance of inequality. (p. 250)

White people are the racial elite in the United States (Dyer, 1997; Feagin, 2000; Leonardo, 2009; Lipsitz, 1998; Mills, 1999; Morrison, 1992; Roediger, 2008), and thus this analysis explicates the discourse of individualism as an ideology of dominance. Indeed, in order to relate the discourse of individualism to the reproduction of dominance and inequality, we need to examine in detail how this discourse functions: How does it position social actors and groups in relation to one another? What does it explain or legitimize in terms of power relations, and how?

Relationally, the discourse of individualism does more than posit that opportunity is equal and people arrive at their achievements through hard work alone, thus positioning dominant group members in a favorable light. It simultaneously obscures structural barriers and positions members of social groups who have achieved less in an unfavorable light. Van Dijk (1993) states that

> The justification of inequality involves two complementary strategies, namely the positive representation of the own group, and the negative representation of the Others. Arguments, stories, semantic moves and other structures of such discourse consistently and sometimes subtly, have such implications, for instance in everyday conversations, political discourse, textbooks or news reports (Van Dijk, 1987a, 1991, 1993a). Thus, models are being expressed and persuasively conveyed that contrast us with THEM. (p. 263, capitalization in original)

Although on the surface suggesting that we are all "just individuals" may appear to represent everyone equally (i.e., as an individual) and therefore not function as unequal group representation, dominant society, relying on the discourse of individualism, must also apply it on a macro level to explain persistent patterns in achievement and outcomes. This is the level at which we see individualism positioning groups at the top of the social hierarchy (in the case of race, white people) as a collection of outstanding (and unraced) individuals who value hard work, education, and determination.

Simultaneously, groups of color who have been consistently denied institutional access and thereby have not consistently achieved at the group level (Conley, 1999; Meizhu et al., 2006) lack these values and ethics. Of course, it also functions at the micro level to invalidate an individual person of color's experiences of structural racism. If society acknowledged that social group memberships such as race, class, and gender mattered, structural inequality would need to be addressed, not dismissed. Thus, as Fairclough (1989) states, "power is won, held, and lost in social struggles. We might say that . . . discourse is the site of power struggles—for control over orders of discourse is a powerful mechanism for sustaining power" (p. 74). This helps explain why discourses are so passionately contested—why Sue and others for whom the racial status quo appears to be working are so invested in individualism (in this case, because as a dominant discourse it upholds current social structures that favorably benefit and represent white people), and why I and others who see the status quo as inequitable are so invested in challenging it.

WHAT DYNAMICS OF RACISM DOES THE DISCOURSE OF INDIVIDUALISM MASK?

Before I discuss the specific dynamics of racism that the discourse of individualism masks, I want to be clear about how racism is defined here. Although people use the terms "racism" and "prejudice" interchangeably as if they mean the same thing, they do not (Bell, 1997; Hilliard, 1992). Prejudice is learned prejudgment. It operates on the individual level and all people have prejudice; it is not possible to avoid absorbing misinformation circulating in the culture about social groups to which we do not belong (Harro, 2001; Sensoy & DiAngelo, 2009; Tatum, 2001). However, scholars define racism as race prejudice plus the social and institutional power to enforce that prejudice throughout the culture (Augoustinos & Reynolds, 2001; Bonilla-Silva, 2006; Dei et al., 2004; Fine, 1997; Frankenberg, 1997; Hilliard, 1992; Hyland, 2009; Jones, 1997). Akintunde (1999) states, "Racism is a systemic, societal, institutional, omnipresent, and epistemologically embedded phenomenon that pervades every vestige of our reality" (p. 1). For example, in the United States, which is the primary context for this analysis, only white people have the collective group power to benefit from their racial prejudices in ways that privilege all members of their racial group regardless of intentions (McIntosh, 2004; Trepagnier, 2006; Weber, 2009). Therefore, in the U.S. context, only white people can be racist because the term refers to holding social and institutional power.

In this section, I review eight key dynamics of racism that the discourse of individualism masks or reinforces. First, however, let me be clear: I am not denying that we are all individuals in general. Rather, I am arguing that white insistence on individualism in regard to racism in particular prevents cross-racial understanding, denies the salience of race and racism in our lives, and serves to reinforce and maintain racist relations. It is important to note that processes underlying racist ideologies and discourse production are largely not explicit. That is, there is no need to assume that discourses that support racist relations are intentional or even conscious. As Van Dijk (1993) states, "Intentionality is irrelevant in establishing whether discourses or other acts may be interpreted as being racist" (p. 262).

Dynamic One: Denies the Significance of Race and the Advantages of Being White

Scientific research has shown that there are no biological or genetically distinct races as we have traditionally understood them (Sundquist, 2008). The differences we can observe, such as hair texture, skin tone, and facial features, occur at the most superficial genetic level. There are actually many more genetic differences among members of what we think of as a racial group than there are across racial groups. These superficial differences are due to adaptations to geography (e.g., more melanin in the skin protects those who live in warmer climates; Madrigal & Barbujani, 2007; Winlow, 2006). Given these findings, we now understand race to be socially constructed; its meaning and boundaries change over time and are deeply affected by current social and political dynamics (Ossorio & Duster, 2005; Sundquist, 2009). In other words, race is not about difference, it is about the meaning a society assigns to difference, in this case the superficial differences of physical appearance.

Despite its scientific insignificance at a genetic level, race has profound meaning as a social category. There are consistent, predictable patterns related to one's life outcomes based on the racial group society assigns to people. On every measure—health, education, interaction with the criminal justice system, income, and wealth—there is disparity between white people and people of color, with people of color consistently relegated to the bottom and white people holding consistent advantage (Meizhu et al., 2006; Picower, 2009; Weber, 2009). Regardless of the intentions of white people, and regardless of the other social groups they may belong to, such as class, gender, sexual orientation, religion, ability, and so forth, white people as a group benefit from a society in which racism (white advantage) is deeply embedded (DiAngelo, 2006b). These benefits are referred to as "white privilege." White privilege is a sociological concept referring to advantages enjoyed and taken for granted by white people that cannot be enjoyed and taken for granted by people of color in the same context (government, community, workplace, schools, etc.; A. Johnson, 2005; Tatum, 2003). White people need not hold consciously racist beliefs or intentions in order to benefit from being white (see McIntosh, 2004). Insistence on seeing everyone as an individual and ignoring the significance of group membership denies the reality that not all individuals have the same access to resources based on whether they are perceived as white or a person of color.

Dynamic Two: Hides the Accumulation of Wealth Over Generations

Seeing ourselves as individuals erases our history and hides the way in which wealth has accumulated over generations and benefits us, as a group, today. Our country was founded on the exploits of slavery (as well as genocide), and racism did not end when slavery ended. Legal exclusion of people of color, in addition to illegal acts of terrorism against them such as lynching, continued all the way through the 1960s. For example, people of color were denied Federal Housing Act (FHA) loans in the 1950s that allowed a generation of white people to attain middle-class status through homeownership (Wise, 2005). Homeownership is critical in the United States because it is how the "average" person builds and passes down wealth, providing the starting point for the next generation (Yeung & Conley, 2008). People of color were systematically denied this opportunity, and today the average white family has eight times the wealth of the average Black or Latino family (Conley, 1999; Federal Reserve Board, 2007). Excluding people of color from mechanisms of society that allow the building of wealth continues today through illegal but common practices such as higher mortgage rates, more difficulty getting loans, real estate agents steering them away from "good" neighborhoods, discrimination in hiring, and unequal school funding (Johnson & Shapiro, 2003; Oliver & Shapiro, 1995). Insisting on individualism hides the reality of white advantage at every level of our past and present society through superficial and simplistic platitudes such as "I didn't own slaves so I have not benefited from racism."

Dynamic Three: Denies Social and Historical Context

Discourses are an interrelated "system of statements which cohere around common meanings and values . . . [that] are a product of social factors, of powers and practices, rather than an individual's set of ideas" (Hollway, 1984, p. 231). These statements are embedded in a matrix of past statements, stories, and meanings—they connect to, expand, extend, and refer back to discourses already circulating in the culture. If they did not connect to existing discourse, we could not make sense of them. Removing these historical dimensions from the analysis prevents an understanding of all that has occurred in the past (Mills, 1999). Insisting on individualism denies that we are products of our historical lineage and prevents us from understanding how the past bears upon the present and how it has led us to the current conditions in which we find ourselves. When white people shift the discussion to one of individual experience, these experiences are posited as if they occurred in a socio-historical vacuum (DiAngelo & Allen, 2006). The individual is thereby positioned as a unique entity—one that appears to have emerged from the ether, untouched by socio-historic conditioning—rather than as a social, cultural, and historical subject. To be able to think critically about the phenomenon of racism, we must be able to think socio-historically about it. Individualism falsely positions us as existing outside of social history.

For example, beyond the accumulation of wealth discussed in point two, there are nonmonetary social benefits accrued from whiteness that were honed and ratified through U.S. history. Harris (1993) discusses whiteness as a form of property that confers social and legal status, resource, and privilege. McIntosh (2004) uses the metaphor of a knapsack to describe these social benefits: "White privilege is like an invisible weightless knapsack of special provisions, maps, passports, codebooks, visas, clothes, tools, and blank checks" (p. 1). These provisions include the everyday racial comfort of being seen as "normal"; a sense of racial belonging in the media, textbooks, and on college campuses; feeling racially welcome in virtually any situation and environment deemed "valuable" by mainstream society (e.g., in the "good" schools and neighborhoods); and having advantage over people of color on every measure including health and health care, the criminal justice system, education, and net worth (Picower, 2009). Individualism denies this social and historical context of privilege.

Dynamic Four: Prevents a Macro Analysis of the Institutional and Structural Dimensions of Social Life

Insisting that we should just see ourselves as individuals prevents us from seeing and addressing persistent social and historical patterns of inequality based on social group membership. Group membership is traced to consistently inequitable outcomes on every indicator of quality of life, and these outcomes are well documented and predictable (Bonilla-Silva, 2006; Jensen, 2005; Weber, 2009). Limiting our analysis to the micro or individual level prevents a macro or "big picture" assessment. It also reinforces the conceptualization of racism as individual acts of meanness that only some "bad" people commit. At the micro level, we cannot assess and address the macro dimensions of society that help hold racism in place, such as practices, policies, norms, rules, laws, traditions, and regulations (Kincheloe, 1999). For example, in the United States, people of color have been barred by laws and by discrimination from participating in government wealth-building programs that benefit white Americans (Conley, 1999; Wise, 2005). Individualism keeps our focus on isolated exceptions to the rules and allows us to deny the significance of the rules themselves, who makes the rules, and who the rules serve. Consider, for example, the ways in which schools are funded through the property tax base of the community they are situated in. Given that due to systematic and historical racism, youth of color disproportionately live in poor communities and their families rent rather than own, youth of color are penalized through this policy, which ensures that poor communities will have inferior schools (Kozol, 2005). In turn, this practice ensures that middle- and upper-class students, who are more likely to be white, will get a superior education and have less competition in the future workplace—an example of both institutional racism and its result, individual white privilege. In the face of all the possible creative options for funding schools to ensure that every child gets equal access to quality education, the current method of funding and the social acceptance of this tradition are examples of institutional racism.

Other examples of institutional racism that reinforce the ways that schools reproduce inequality include mandatory culturally biased testing; "ability" tracking; a primarily white teaching force with the power to determine which students belong in which tracks; cultural definitions of intelligence, what constitutes it, and how it is measured; and standards of good behavior that reflect dominant white norms (Kunjufu, 2005; Lee, 2005; Oakes, 2008). All of these dynamics work together and function as institutional racism. Rather than serving as the great equalizer, schools function in actual practice to reproduce racial inequality (Abu El-Haj & Rubin, 2009; Apple, 2004; Gillborn, 2008; Kincheloe & Steinberg, 2006).

Individualism also allows white people to exempt ourselves personally from these patterns and the resulting network of race-based advantage (Jensen, 2005; McIntosh, 2004). In other words, as a white person, if I personally do not agree with receiving advantages, individualism allows me to deny that I receive them, as if a desire that resides in my head can effectively ward off the society in which I am embedded. Of course, even if it were possible to simply decide not to benefit from racial advantages, it would require at least two criteria: (1) admit that I benefit from racial privilege and (2) become conscious of the myriad ways I act on that privilege and stop acting on it. While the first criterion is relatively straightforward, the second entails a lifetime of reflection and study and still it remains dubious that it is possible to become conscious of all that we are unconscious of, or to interrupt the totality of the mechanisms of society (Sullivan, 2006). As McIntosh (2004) muses, "I think whites are carefully taught not to recognize white privilege. . . . I have come to see white privilege as an invisible package of unearned assets that I can count on cashing in each day, but about which I was 'meant' to remain oblivious" (p. 1). Even if we could effectively counter our deeply socialized oblivious-ness, both criteria are still limited to the individual and do not prevent the myriad ways in which society grants privilege to white people automatically and at both individual and institutional levels, regardless of their personal desires.

Dynamic Five: Denies Collective Socialization and the Power of Dominant Culture (Media, Education, Religion, etc.) to Shape Our Perspectives and Ideology

Individualism allows us to present ourselves as unique and original, outside of socialization and unaffected by the relentless racial messages we receive on a daily basis from films, advertising, textbooks, teachers, relatives, shared stories, silence, the absence of information, segregated schools and neighborhoods, and countless other dimensions of social life. Individualism, which places us outside of culture and history, is further developed and refined through modern-day advertising and consumerism, which depends on this conceptualization (Holtzman, 2000). Individualism helps us maintain the illusion that we are unaffected by media, and that our consumer choices reflect our unique tastes and preferences. At the same time, we believe that the brands we have been conditioned to use represent us and make us special (Kilbourne, 1999). Advertisers certainly see us as group members with specific and predictable patterns, and have effectively built a multibillion dollar industry on these patterns (Heath, 2001). Advertisers need us to see ourselves as individuals who are unaffected by the culture around us in order to maintain the illusion of free choice. The irony of advertising, of course, is that this sense of free choice is necessary precisely in order to manipulate group behavior (Kilbourne, 1999).

White denial of ourselves as socialized group members, deeply affected by images and discourses that circulate in the culture, is also necessary to hold domination in place, for it ensures that these discourses will affect our relations while remaining unexamined (Apple, 2004; Van Dijk, 1992). Individualism prevents white people from being able to think critically about the messages we receive. If we cannot think critically about these messages, we cannot challenge them and our racial conditioning continues unchecked. Individualism exempts people from the forces of socialization and reinforces the idea of personal objectivity.

Dynamic Six: Functions as Neo-Color-Blindness and Reproduces the Myth of Meritocracy

If we use the line of reasoning that we are all individuals and social categories such as race, class, and gender do not matter and are just "labels" that stereotype and limit us, then it follows that we all end up in our own "natural" places. Those at the top are merely a collection of individuals who rose under their own individual merits, and those at the bottom are there due to individual deficiencies. Group membership is thereby rendered inoperative and racial disparities are seen as the result of essential character attributes rather than the result of consistent structural barriers. Via individualism, it is either "just a fluke" that those at the top are a very homogeneous collection of individuals, or else white, middle- and upper-class men and sometimes women are consistently "the cream of the crop" (Bonilla-Silva, 2006; Brown, 2005). According to individualism, white privilege is not a factor because we do not see color anyway (i.e., color-blindness); we see each person as a unique individual and we treat him or her as such. This ideology is particularly popular with white teachers (Sleeter, 1993). Thus, the discourse of individualism not only upholds the myth of meritocracy that success is the result of ability and hard work but also upholds the belief in the overall superiority of those at the top (Bonilla-Silva, 2006; Wise, 2005). Individualism naturalizes the social order and relations of inequality (Billig, 2001).

Unfortunately, many studies show that we do not actually see each person as a unique individual, even when that is our intention (see, e.g., Bertrand & Mullainathan, 2004; Darity & Mason, 1998; Goldin & Rouse, 2000). A common statement from those who profess individualism and are opposed to programs to support underrepresented candidates is that they would hire the best person for the job regardless of their color (Bonilla-Silva, 2006). Yet we may believe we are not seeing (or at least ignoring) a candidate's race but we are not actually doing that in practice. For example, in a 2005 study, 5,000 fictitious resumes were sent in response to help-wanted ads. Typically white-sounding names (e.g., Emily Walsh or Greg Baker) were randomly assigned to half the resumes and typically African American–sounding names to the other half (e.g., Lakisha Washington or Jamal Jones). White-sounding applicants received 50% more callbacks, regardless of the industry, occupation, or employer size (Wessel, 2005). The resume screeners would likely state that they were not responding to the resumes based on race, and possibly would not be consciously aware that they were. However, the names triggered unconscious racial frameworks that resulted in the resumes being interpreted differently. The screeners are not a special group—dominant culture socializes all of us collectively into racial frameworks that favor white people (Van Ausdale & Feagin, 2002).

Anyone who has had a conversation about race or hiring in the workplace has likely heard the common assumption that all people of color got their jobs (unfairly) via affirmative action programs. In my years as a workplace diversity trainer, I have rarely heard a white person assume that the person of color really was the most qualified. More common is a deep-seated resentment that the person got the job that rightfully belonged to the white person doing the complaining. The assumption is that people of color are inherently unqualified for jobs that are of interest to white people (Bonilla-Silva, 2006). This reveals the core contradiction between our desire to see ourselves as people who would hire the most qualified person regardless of race if there were one, and the deeply internalized belief that the only qualified people are white.

Dynamic Seven: Individualism, as Well as Universalism, Is Only Culturally Available to the Dominant Group

White people are taught to see their perspectives as objective and representative of reality (Dyer, 1997). The belief in objectivity, coupled with positioning white people as outside of race, and thus the norm for humanity, allows white people to view themselves as universal humans who can represent all of human experience. Within this construction, people of color can only represent their own racialized experience. Dyer (1997) states, "The claim to power is the claim to speak for the commonality of humanity. Raced people can't do that—they can only speak for their race. But non-raced people can, for they do not represent the interests of a race" (p. 2). Universalism is evidenced through an unracialized identity or location that functions as a kind of blindness, an inability to think about whiteness as an identity or as a "state" of being that would or could have an impact on one's life. In this position, the significance of being white is not recognized or named by white people, and a universal reference point is assumed (Frankenberg, 2001). I refer to this as the discourse of universalism, and it functions similarly to the discourse of individualism, but instead of declaring that we all need to see each other as individuals (everyone is different), the person declares that we all need to see each other as human beings (everyone is the same) (DiAngelo, 2006a). Of course, we are all humans and I am not critiquing universalism in general, but when applied to racism, universalism has similar effects as individualism. Once again, the significance of race and the advantages of being white are denied. Further, universalism assumes that white people and people of color have the same reality, the same experiences in the same context (i.e., "I feel comfortable in this primarily white classroom, so you must too"), the same responses from others, and—like individualism—assumes that the same doors are open (Ellsworth, 1997).

White people invoke these seemingly contradictory discourses—we are either all unique or we are all the same—interchangeably (DiAngelo, 2004). Both discourses work to deny white privilege and the significance of race. Further, on the cultural level, being an individual or being a human outside of a racial group is a social position only afforded to white people. In other words, people of color are almost always seen as "having a race" and described in racial terms (e.g., "a Black man," "a Black film director"), whereas white people are rarely defined by race (e.g., "a man," "a film director"), thereby allowing white people to see themselves as objective and nonracialized (Dyer, 1997; Mills, 1999; Schick, 2004). In turn, being seen (and seeing ourselves) as individuals outside of race frees white people from the psychic burden of race in a wholly racialized society (Frankenberg, 2001; Morrison, 1992). Race and racism become their problem, not ours (Jensen, 2005; Wise, 2007).

Dynamic Eight: Makes Collective Action Difficult

Given the ideology of individualism, we see ourselves as different from one another and expect others to see us as different too. Not having a group consciousness, white people often respond defensively when associated with other white people, feeling unfairly generalized and "accused" of benefiting from racism (Picower, 2009). Individualism prevents us from seeing ourselves as responsible for or accountable to other white people as members of a shared racial group who collectively profit from racism. Individualism allows white people to distance themselves from the actions of their racial group and demand to be granted the benefit of the doubt, as individuals, in all cases (DiAngelo, 2006a). As individuals, we are not each other's problems and we leave people of color in the position to challenge other white people. Challenging white people is much more difficult for people of color to do, for when people of color challenge white people they are often dismissed with a variety of accusations, including playing the race card, having a chip on their shoulder, seeing race in everything, or being oversensitive or angry (Applebaum, 2003; Bonilla-Silva, 2006). When white people break racial solidarity and speak up to challenge racism, while it is difficult and rife with social risks, we are still seen as more credible, more objective, and the resistance is less painful because it does not trigger a lifetime of racial invalidation (Schick, 2004; Sue, 2003). Given that white people hold social and institutional power and benefit from racism, racism is essentially a white problem and we need to take collective action for and among ourselves (Akintunde, 1999; Katz, 2003; Wise, 2007).

WHY COULDN'T SUE AND BILL HEAR ME?

Many white people, such as Sue and Bill, depend on the model of individualism to maintain racial equilibrium by inscribing their racial innocence and positioning themselves as standing outside of hierarchical social relations. At stake are very real resources that have concrete effects on people's lives. Also at stake is our very identity—a sense of ourselves as fair, open-minded, and hard-working. Thus, white people who are explicitly opposed to racism, as I believe Sue and Bill are, often organize their efforts around a denial of the racially based privileges they hold that reinforce racist disadvantage for others (Marty, 1999). What is particularly problematic about this contradiction is that white moral objection to racism so often increases white resistance to acknowledging complicity with it and thereby works to protect and maintain it. The discourse of individualism allows a way out of this contradiction. If we can sustain a denial of ourselves as members of groups, social inequity and its consequences become personally moot (Trepagnier, 2006), and so too does any imperative to change this inequity.

There is another dimension of the interaction I had with Sue that is a function of white fragility: the lack of humility in providing "the answer" to racism. In the context of racism and white privilege, white racial humility must be developed and is thus a psychosocial skill. Because most white people have not been trained to think with complexity about racism, and because it benefits white dominance not to do so, we have a very limited understanding of it (Kumashiro, 2009; LaDuke, 2009). We are the least likely to see, comprehend, or be invested in validating people of color's assertions of racism and being honest about their consequences (King, 1991). At the same time, because of white social, economic, and political power within a white-dominant culture, white people are the group in the position to legitimize people of color's assertions of racism. Being in this position engenders a form of racial arrogance, and in this racial arrogance, white people have little compunction about debating the knowledge of people who have thought deeply about race through research, study, peer-reviewed scholarship, deep and ongoing critical self-reflection, interracial relationships, and lived experience (Chinnery, 2008). This expertise is often trivialized and countered with simplistic platitudes, such as "people just need to see each other as individuals" or "see each other as humans" or "take personal responsibility."

White lack of racial humility often leads to declarations of disagreement when in fact the problem is that we do not understand. White people generally feel free to dismiss informed perspectives rather than have the humility to acknowledge that they are unfamiliar, reflect on them further, seek more information, or sustain a dialogue (DiAngelo & Sensoy, 2009). My co-facilitator and I do not claim that we were the sole authorities on racism in Sue and Bill's workshop, and we do not ask for blind allegiance from participants. But we can, and did, ask participants to be willing to grapple with the concepts we presented, rather than strive to maintain the perspectives they already held.

It would be disingenuous for me to offer suggestions beyond this analysis on how to engage the Sues and Bills we encounter in our antiracist endeavors, as this is difficult, complex, and oftentimes deeply discouraging work. What I have found, however, is that the more sustained analysis of this discourse that I can provide from an antiracist framework, the more I have been able to critically engage resistant white people. To that end, I offer this analysis to provide a concise yet complex list of dynamics individualism obscures, in hopes that it may be useful to others engaged in antiracist work.

CONCLUSION

The disavowal of race as an organizing factor is necessary to support current structures of inequity and domination for, without it, the correlation between the distribution of social resources and unearned white privilege would be plainly evident (Billig, 2001; Flax, 1999; Mills, 1999). The visibility of structural inequality destabilizes the claim that privilege is simply a reflection of hard work and virtue. Therefore, inequality must be hidden or justified as resulting from lack of effort (McIntosh, 2004; Ryan, 2001). Individualism accomplishes both of these tasks. Flax (1999) argues that when the individual is considered the basic unit of society, the problem of race is understood within the rubric of inclusion or exclusion. In other words, there are no structural barriers; the issue at hand is simply a matter of including or "letting one in." Inclusion is made possible by demonstrating individual worth and is displayed through such virtues as decency, discipline, and hard work. If one proves worthy via these virtues, they may be included. If they do not prove worthy, their exclusion is rationalized as the result of their own poor choices or lack of virtues. This approach allows no possibility for questioning the reference point from which that worth is judged. The dominant narrative, supported by these normative rules, stipulates that the social context is representative, objective, and fair.

One day, individualism may be the "answer" to racism, realized, but it is precisely because that day is not a reality that the discourse of individualism is so pernicious. Given that individualism is not a current racial reality, positioning oneself as operating from it, as Sue and Bill did, is patently false and delusional, and can only function to support and protect white privilege (King, 1991). While white privilege plays out somewhat differently for white people depending on the intersections of our other identities, such as class, gender, religion, sexual orientation, or ability, it is still always at play. For example, as a woman who grew up in poverty, I learned my place in the racial order differently than a middle-class white woman learned hers, but I still learned it— we were below other white people, but always above people of color (DiAngelo, 2006a).

My class position is only one social location from which I learned to collude with racism. It is the task of each of us to explore how white privilege and racism inform our lives. To this end, the constructive use of individualism for white people is to ask ourselves how racism and white privilege have played out specifically for us based on all of our other identities and experiences. Rather than discovering that acknowledging the collective dimensions of white experience denies my individuality, it has been a profound way to address the unique complexity of all my social identities. It is through this conceptualization of the individual—an entity rooted in the larger matrix of socio-historical location and power relations—that I wish to engage Sue and Bill.

NOTE

1. Race is a deeply complex sociopolitical system whose boundaries shift and adapt over time (Bonilla-Silva, 2006). As such, I recognize that "white" and "people of color" are not discrete categories, and that within these groupings are other levels of complexity and difference based on the various roles assigned by dominant society at various times (i.e., Asian vs. Black vs. Latino). However, for the purposes of this limited analysis, I use these terms to indicate the two general, socially recognized divisions of the racial hierarchy in the United States.

REFERENCES

Abu El-Haj, T., & Rubin, B. (2009). Realizing the equity-minded aspirations of detracking and inclusion: Toward a capacity-oriented framework for teacher education. *Curriculum Inquiry, 39*(3), 435–463.

Akintunde, O. (1999). White racism, white supremacy, white privilege, and the social construction of race: Moving from modernist to postmodernist multiculturalism. *Multicultural Education, 7*(2), 2–8.

Allen, D. (1996). Knowledge, politics, culture, and gender: A discourse perspective. *Canadian Journal of Nursing Research, 28*(1), 95–102.

Apple, M. (2004). *Ideology and curriculum* (3rd ed.). Routledge.

Applebaum, B. (2003). Social justice, democratic education and the silencing of words that wound. *Journal of Moral Education, 32*(2), 151–162.

Augoustinos, M., & Reynolds, K. J. (Eds.). (2001). *Understanding prejudice, racism, and social conflict.* Sage.

Bell, L. (1997). Theoretical foundations for social justice education. In M. Adams, L. Bell, & P. Griffin (Eds.), *Teaching for diversity and social justice: A sourcebook* (pp. 3–15). Routledge.

Bertrand, M., & Mullainathan, S. (2004). Are Emily and Greg more employable than Lakisha and Jamal? A field experiment on labor market discrimination. *American Economic Review, 94*(4), 991–1013.

Billig, M. (2001). Discursive, rhetorical and ideological messages. In M. Wetherell, S. Taylor, & S. J. Yates (Eds.), *Discourse theory and practice: A reader* (pp. 210–221). Sage.

Bonilla-Silva, E. (2006). *Racism without racist: Color-blind racism and the persistence of racial inequality in the United States* (2nd ed.). Rowman & Littlefield.

Brown, M. (2005). *Whitewashing race: The myth of a color-blind society.* University of California Press.

Cameron, D., Frazer, E., Harvey, P., Rampton, M., & Richardson, K. (1992). *Researching language: Issues of power and method.* Routledge.

Chinnery, A. (2008). Revisiting "The Master's Tools": Challenging common sense in cross-cultural teacher education. *Equity & Excellence in Education, 41*(4), 395–404.

Conley, D. (1999). *Being Black, living in the red: Race, wealth and social policy in America.* University of California Press.

Copeland, V. C. (2005). African Americans: Disparities in health care access and utilization. *Health & Social Work, 30*(3), 265–270.

Darity, W. A., & Mason, P. L. (1998). Evidence on discrimination in employment: Codes of color, codes of gender. *The Journal of Economic Perspectives*, *12*(2), 63–90.

Davies, B., & Harre, R. (1990). Positioning: The discursive production of selves. *Journal of the Theory of Social Behavior*, *20*, 43–65.

Dei, G. J., Karumanchery, L. L., & Karumanchery-Luik, N. (2004). *Playing the race card: Exposing white power and privilege*. Peter Lang.

DiAngelo, R. (2004). *Whiteness in racial dialogue: A discourse analysis* [Unpublished dissertation]. University of Washington, Seattle.

DiAngelo, R. (2006a). My race didn't trump my class: Using oppression to face privilege. *Multicultural Perspectives*, *8*(1), 51–56.

DiAngelo, R. (2006b). The production of whiteness in education: Asian international students in a college classroom. *Teachers College Record*, *108*(10), 1960–1982.

DiAngelo, R., & Allen, D. (2006). "My feelings are not about you": Personal experience as a move of whiteness. *InterActions: UCLA Journal of Education and Information Studies*, *2*(2), article 2.

DiAngelo, R., & Sensoy, Ö. (2009). "We don't want your opinion": Knowledge construction and the discourse of opinion in the equity classroom. *Equity & Excellence in Education*, *42*(4), 443–455.

Dyer, R. (1997). *White*. Routledge.

Ellsworth, E. (1997). Double binds of whiteness. In M. Fine, L. Weis, C. Powell, & L. Wong (Eds.), *Off white: Readings on race, power, and society* (pp. 259–269). Routledge.

Fairclough, N. (1989). *Language and power*. Longman Group.

Feagin, J. (2000). *Racist America: Roots, current realities, and future reparations*. Routledge.

Federal Reserve Board. (2007). *Survey of consumer finances*. Retrieved from www.federalreserve.gov/PUBS/oss/oss2/scfindex.html

Fine, M. (1997). Introduction. In M. Fine, L. Weis, C. Powell, & L. Wong (Eds.), *Off white: Readings on race, power and society* (pp. vii–xii). Routledge.

Flax, J. (1999). *American dream in Black and white: The Clarence Thomas hearings*. Cornell University Press.

Foucault, M. (1972). *The archeology of knowledge*. Pantheon.

Frankenberg, R. (1997). Introduction: Local whitenesses, localizing whiteness. In R. Frankenberg (Ed.), *Displacing whiteness: Essays in social and cultural criticism* (pp. 1–33). Duke University Press.

Frankenberg, R. (2001). The mirage of an unmarked whiteness. In B. B. Rasmussen, E. Klinenberg, I. J. Nexica, & M. Wray (Eds.), *The making and unmaking of whiteness* (pp. 72–96). Duke University Press.

Gee, J. P. (1999). *An introduction to discourse analysis: Theory and method.* Routledge.

Gillborn, D. (2008). *Racism and education: Coincidence or conspiracy?* Routledge.

Goldin, C., & Rouse, C. (2000). Orchestrating impartiality: The impact of blind auditions on female musicians. *The American Economic Review, 90*(4), 715–741.

Harris, C. (1993). Whiteness as property. *Harvard Law Review, 106*(8), 1707.

Harro, B. (2001). The cycle of socialization. In M. Adams, W. Blumenfeld, R. Castañeda, H. Hackman, M. Peters, & X. Zúñiga (Eds.), *Readings for diversity and social justice* (pp. 15–21). Routledge.

Heath, R. (2001). *The hidden power of advertising.* NTC Publications.

Hilliard, A. (1992). *Racism: Its origins and how it works* [Paper presentation]. Mid-West Association for the Education of Young Children, Madison, WI.

Hochschild, J., & Weaver, J. (2007). The skin color paradox and the American racial order. *Social Forces, 86,* 643–670.

Hollway, W. (1984). Gender differences and the production of subjectivity. In J. Henriques, W. Hollway, C. Urwin, C. Venn, & V. Walkerdine (Eds.), *Changing the subject* (pp. 227–263). Methuen.

Holtzman, L. (2000). *Media messages.* M. E. Sharpe.

Hyland, N. (2009). Opening and closing communicative space with teachers investigating race and racism in their own practice. *Action Research, 7*(3), 335–354.

Jensen, R. (2005). *The heart of whiteness: Confronting race, racism and white privilege.* City Lights.

Johnson, A. (2005). *Privilege, power and difference.* McGraw-Hill.

Johnson, H., & Shapiro, T. (2003). Good neighborhoods, good schools: Race and the "good choices" of white families. In A. W. Doane & E. Bonilla-Silva (Eds.), *White out: The continuing significance of racism* (pp. 173–187). Routledge.

Johnson, J. (2005). *What is discourse?* Retrieved April 22, 2008, from http://www.stolaf.edu/depts/cis/wp/johnsoja/works/index.html

Jones, J. M. (1997). *Prejudice and racism* (2nd ed.). McGraw-Hill.

Katz, J. (2003). *White awareness: Handbook for anti-racism training.* University of Oklahoma Press.

Kilbourne, J. (1999). *Can't buy my love: How advertising changes the way we think and feel.* Simon & Schuster.

Kincheloe, J. (1999). The struggle to define and reinvent whiteness: A pedagogical analysis. *College Literature, 26*(3), 162.

Kincheloe, J., & Steinberg, S. (2006). An ideology of miseducation: Countering the pedagogy of empire. *Cultural Studies/Critical Methodologies, 6*(1), 33–51.

King, J. (1991). Dysconscious racism: Ideology, identity, and the miseducation of teachers. *The Journal of Negro Education, 60*(2), 133–146.

Kozol, J. (2005). *Shame of the nation: The return to apartheid schooling in America.* Three Rivers Press.

Kumashiro, K. (2009). *Against common sense: Teaching and learning toward social justice.* Routledge.

Kunjufu, J. (2005). *Keeping Black boys out of special education.* African American Images.

LaDuke, A. (2009). Resistance and renegotiation: Preservice teachers interactions with and reactions to multicultural education course content. *Multicultural Education, 16*(3), 37–44.

Lee, S. (2005). *Up against whiteness: Race, school and immigrant youth.* Teachers College Press.

Leonardo, Z. (2009). *Race, whiteness and education.* Routledge.

Lipsitz, G. (1998). *The possessive investment in whiteness: How white people profit from identity politics.* Temple University Press.

Madrigal, L., & Barbujani, G. (2007). Partitioning of genetic variation in human populations and the concept of race. In M. Crawford (Ed.), *Anthropological genetics: Theory, methods, and applications* (pp. 28–30). Cambridge University Press.

Marty, D. (1999). White antiracist rhetoric as apologia: Wendell Berry's *The Hidden Wound.* In T. Nakayama & J. Martin (Eds.), *Whiteness: The communication of social identity* (pp. 51–68). Sage.

McIntosh, P. (2004). White privilege and male privilege: A personal account of coming to see correspondence through work in women's studies. In M. Anderson & P. Hill Collins (Eds.), *Race, class, and gender: An anthology* (pp. 94–105). Wadsworth.

Meizhu, L., Robles, B., & Leondar-Wright, B. (2006). *The color of wealth: The story behind the U.S. racial wealth divide.* New Press.

Micceri, T. (2009, February). *How we justify and perpetuate the wealthy, white, male academic status quo through the use of biased admissions requirements*

[Paper presentation]. Florida Association for Institutional Research Annual Conference, Cocoa Beach, FL.

Mills, C. (1999). *The racial contract.* Cornell University Press.

Morrison, T. (1992). *Playing in the dark.* Random House.

Oakes, J. (2008). Keeping track: Structuring equality and inequality in an era of accountability. *Teachers College Record, 110*(3), 700–712.

Oliver, M., & Shapiro, A. (1995). *Black wealth/white wealth: A new perspective on racial inequality.* Routledge.

Ossorio, P., & Duster, T. (2005). Race and genetics: Controversies in biomedical, behavioral, and forensic sciences. *American Psychologist, 60*(1), 115–116.

Picower, B. (2009). The unexamined whiteness of teaching: How white teachers maintain and enact dominant racial ideologies. *Race Ethnicity and Education, 12*(2), 197–215.

Roediger, D. (2008). *How race survived U.S. history: From settlement and slavery to the Obama phenomenon.* Verso.

Ryan, W. (2001). Blaming the victim. In P. Rothenberg (Ed.), *Race, class, and gender in the United States: An integrated study* (pp. 572–582). Worth.

Schick, C. (2004). Disrupting binaries of self and other: Anti-homophobic pedagogies for student teachers. In J. McNinch & M. Cronin (Eds.), *"I could not speak my heart": Education and social justice for gay and lesbian youth* (pp. 243–254). Canadian Plains Research Center.

Schofield, J. (2004). The colorblind perspective in schools: Cause and consequences. In J. A. Banks & C. A. M. Banks (Eds.), *Multicultural education: Issues & perspectives.* Wiley.

Sensoy, Ö., & DiAngelo, R. (2009). Developing social justice literacy: An open letter to our faculty colleagues. *Phi Delta Kappan, 90*(5), 345–352.

Sleeter, C. (1993). How white teachers construct race. In C. McCarthy & W. Crichlow (Eds.), *Race identity and representation in education* (pp. 157–171). Routledge.

Su, C. (2007). Cracking silent codes: Critical race theory and education organizing. *Discourse: Studies in the Cultural Politics of Education, 28*(4), 531–548.

Sue, D. W. (2003). *Overcoming our racism: The journey to liberation.* Jossey-Bass.

Sullivan, S. (2006). *Revealing whiteness: The unconscious habits of racial privilege.* Indiana University Press.

Sundquist, C. (2008). The meaning of race in the DNA era: Science, history and the law. *Temple Journal of Science, Technology & Environmental Law, 27*(2), 231–265.

Sundquist, C. (2009). Science fictions and racial fables: Navigating the final frontier of genetic interpretation. *Harvard Black Letter Law Journal, 25,* 57–93.

Tatum, B. (2001). Defining racism: Can we talk? In P. Rothenberg (Ed.), *Race, class, and gender in the United States: An integrated study* (5th ed., pp. 100–107). Worth.

Tatum, B. (2003). *"Why are all the Black kids sitting together in the cafeteria?" A psychologist explains the development of racial identity.* Basic Books.

Trepagnier, B. (2006). *Silent racism: How well-meaning white people perpetuate the racial divide.* Paradigm.

Van Ausdale, D., & Feagin, J. (2002). *The first R: How children learn race and racism.* Rowman & Littlefield.

Van Dijk, T. A. (1992). Discourse and the denial of racism. *Discourse & Society,* 3(1), 87–118.

Van Dijk, T. A. (1993). Principles of critical discourse analysis. *Discourse & Society,* 4(2), 249–283.

Weber, L. (2009). *Understanding race, class, gender and sexuality: A conceptual framework.* Oxford University Press.

Wessel, D. (2005). Racial discrimination: Still at work in the U.S. *The Wall Street Journal Online.* Retrieved May 26, 2005, from http://www.careerjournal.com/myc/diversity/20030916-wessel.html

Wetherell, M., Taylor, S., & Yates, S. J. (Eds.). (2001). *Discourse theory and practice: A reader.* Sage.

Winlow, H. (2006). Mapping moral geographies: W. Z. Ripley's races of Europe and the United States. *Annals of the Association of American Geographers,* 96(1), 119–141.

Wise, T. (2005). *Affirmative action: Racial preference in Black and white.* Routledge.

Wise, T. (2007). *White like me: Reflections on race from a privileged son.* Soft Skull Press.

Yeung, W., & Conley, D. (2008). Black–white achievement gap and family wealth. *Child Development,* 79(2), 303–324.

THREE

"My Feelings Are Not About You"
Personal Experience as a Move of Whiteness

ROBIN DIANGELO AND DAVID ALLEN

The concepts of personal experience and speaking from experience have figured prominently in a number of educational practices oriented toward social justice (Chor et al., 2003). Antiracism work within teacher education, for example, has traditionally proposed guidelines for class discussions and dialogue. These guidelines, intended to foster a climate in which a range of perspectives can be affirmed, often consist of confidentiality, the practicing of critical self-reflection, and consideration of multiple perspectives. One guideline addresses the practice of personalized knowledge, in which students speak for themselves and from their own experience. This guideline is meant to prevent students from universalizing their perspectives (e.g., "Everybody knows that . . .") and to encourage awareness of positionality and the racialized locations from which we each speak.

History has taught us, however, that any resistive practice can come to serve the very interests it was developed to oppose. For example, affirmative action discourse is now being used to support white males; men who hold jobs previously held by women are characterized as having "broken a glass ceiling" (Editorial Board, 2005). This chapter examines one situation in which a resistive practice has come to serve the interests it was designed to oppose: In interracial discussions of racism, the practice of speaking from experience was used by white people (and primarily white women) to inoculate their

Originally published as DiAngelo, R. J, & Allen, D. (2006). "My Feelings Are Not About You": Personal Experience as a Move of Whiteness. *InterActions: UCLA Journal of Education and Information Studies*, 2(2). http://dx.doi.org/10.5070/D422000577. Retrieved from https://escholarship.org/uc/item/6dk67960

claims against interrogation or critique. We refer to this strategy as the discourse of personal experience (as performed by white people) and have not seen this discourse discussed in the whiteness literature within the field of education. In this chapter we will explore how this discourse of personal experience, as performed by white participants in our study, functioned in an interracial dialogue about race with white student teachers and students of color. Our goals are twofold: to explicate how the discourse of personal experience functioned to hold white racism and privilege in place, and to unsettle the discursive authority that this discourse offers. After briefly reviewing the theoretical literature, we analyze the results of one study of interracial dialogue, using a poststructural and discourse-oriented methodology.

THE THEORY OF EXPERIENCE

The notion of experience has an extensive pedigree in education. John Dewey's work, for example, which emphasizes experiential learning, continues to inspire and shape educational debate. More recently, hermeneutic traditions such as Hans-Georg Gadamer's have re-articulated various perspectives on experience and education (Kerdeman, 2003). Educational research, especially qualitative methodologies, has spawned myriad publications on the experiences of teachers or students or organizations with the hope of casting light on the complexities of everyday practice. Reviewing this body of literature is beyond the scope of this chapter. Instead, we will focus on two issues: (1) the development of experience as a way to counter authoritarian and expert-based knowledge claims, and (2) recent criticism of the assumptions about and utility of concepts of experience. We suggest ways to preserve some of its benefits (e.g., keep people talking about their own lives and not making claims about other groups) while resisting it as a way to end constructive dialogue and critique.

Ideas of experience have been most extensively elaborated upon in feminist theory and practice, especially in recent years (Bannerji, 1992; Chay, 1993; Kruks, 2001; Mardorossian, 2002; Mohanty, 1992; Mulinari & Sandell, 1999). In feminism, valuing experience is a response to authoritarian knowledge claims that dismiss women's accounts of their own lives as biased (subjective), unreliable (hysterical), or trivial (idiosyncratic and private). As a resistive practice, valuing experience collapses two different rationales for privileging first-person accounts: one epistemological and one political. The epistemological role of experience itself assumes two forms—a modest claim that women's accounts should be considered useful data about social life and, ironically, a transcendental claim that such accounts are privileged or fundamental sources of insight (Allen & Cloyes, 2005; Foss & Foss, 1994). The political rationale is usually congruent with the modest epistemological claim: Women's accounts (or the accounts of any marginalized group) deserve serious attention and should not be overridden by accounts of more privileged groups (which are often framed not as accounts but as truth) (Allen & Cloyes, 2005; Stone-Mediatore, 1998). A more radical rationale for privileging these accounts is the epistemological claim that they have greater "truth" status. Attributing greater truth to marginalized accounts stems from Hegel's Master–Slave dialectic. Hegel argued that slaves had to understand both their own world and that of their masters, while the latter had no need to understand the daily life of slaves (Bellamy & Leontis, 1993).

These radical epistemological and political rationales have been extensively critiqued. Epistemological privilege is difficult to sustain; marginalized groups and individuals can certainly hold mistaken or unproductive understandings of social life (Hardin, 2003; Scott, 1992). Furthermore, deconstructionist orientations have decried the tendency toward essentialism in such accounts (e.g., whose interpretation counts as privileged?). Categories such as woman or African American are power and knowledge classifications that are already caught up in the practices being opposed by the radical traditions. Hence, deconstructionists argue, they cannot be used without reproducing at least some of the politics that produced them in the first place (Allen, 1996; Richard, 1996). Scholars following democratic and dialogic traditions have also criticized this privileging as simply replacing one authoritarian account with another.

THE LANGUAGE OF EXPERIENCE

Discursively oriented critics have raised concerns about how experience functions in various forms of discourse (Mardorossian, 2002). Perhaps the most influential of these critics is historian Joan Scott, who argues that experience is constituted linguistically and thus needs to be explained historically. For example, how did someone come to encounter the world within any particular vocabulary or framework (Scott, 1992)? Critical scholars have noted that research claims about experience often conflate notions of experience as witness testimony (e.g., what happened to someone?) and experience as confession (making public the private contents of one's mind or soul). The latter move is deeply embedded in the individualism and Cartesianism that—according to discursive psychologists— characterize Western notions of self (Allen & Cloyes, 2005; Martin, 2002). As Cartesianism posits, when one's language—one's ideas—are seen as existing in the mind and finding expression (being pressed out into public space), then the mind becomes nonsocial, private, and inaccessible to anyone outside of the individual. We will return to this argument when we analyze how white participants in a racially diverse group addressing racism positioned experience in their own performances. To prepare for that discussion, we now turn to the more specific context of whiteness and antiracist educational practices.

WHITENESS AND ANTI-RACIST EDUCATION

Whiteness scholars within the field of education seek to unravel the racialized intersection between social position, knowledge construction, and power (Apple, 1997; Macedo & Bartolome, 1999; Nieto, 2002; Sleeter, 1993; Tatum, 2001). In highlighting the power basis of knowledge construction, John Fiske (1989) asserts:

> Knowledge is never neutral. It never exists in an empiricist, objective relationship to the real. Knowledge is power, and the circulation of knowledge is part of the social distribution of power. The discursive power to construct a commonsense reality that can be inserted into cultural and political life is central in the social relationships of power. (pp. 149–150)

Interrogating whiteness has emerged from the frequent failure of education initiatives to adequately identify where change needs to occur.

Many traditional solutions to inequitable educational outcomes have been directed toward the problems of racialized "others" and to the challenges of implementing culturally relevant pedagogy; few have addressed the workings of the dominant culture itself (Banks, 1995). Cynthia Levine-Rasky (2000) calls this misidentification of the problem "the focus on the space between 'us' and 'them'" (p. 272). To conceptualize whiteness not as a fixed and unified variable, but rather as a set of practices, reveals the performative dimension of racialization. By exposing power dynamics, a discourse on whiteness attempts to show not just how whiteness oppresses people of color, but how whiteness elevates white people (McIntosh, 1988). The elevation of white people over others is constantly being contested by marginalized groups and must be actively maintained by dominant culture. As Michelle Fine (1997b) states, "Whiteness, like all colors, is being manufactured, in part, through institutional arrangements. Schools and work, for example, do not merely manage race; they create and enforce racial meanings" (p. 58). But because race is negotiated, rather than fixed, it is also unstable and susceptible to acts of resistance and contestation (Flax, 1998; Frankenberg, 2001).

A major goal of a discourse on whiteness within education is to make apparent what is often transparent or obscured, including the circuits of power in racialized intergroup dynamics (Fine, 1997b). Identifying the production of whiteness is an attempt to break open one of these circuits, exposing aspects of its operation. This provides an opportunity to track the flow of power and potentially interrupt it, for whiteness maintains its dominance in part through invisibility (Flax, 1998). The study discussed in this chapter was designed to track power—to examine empirically how whiteness was performed under contestation via an intergroup dialogue on racism among future teachers. We anchored the study in poststructuralist perspectives on discourse.

DISCOURSE ANALYSIS

Discourse analysis is the study of language as action in social contexts. It is a method of investigating the back-and-forth dialogues that constitute social action, along with the patterns of signification and representation that constitute culture (Davies & Harre, 1990; Gee, 1999; Wetherell et al., 2001). James Gee (1999) states that "Meaning is not general and abstract, not something that resides in dictionaries, or even in general symbolic representations inside people's heads. Rather, it is situated in specific social and cultural practices, and it is continually transformed in those practices" (p. 63). Discourse analysis is attentive to the uses of language and how those uses position speakers in relation to others, both those who are physically present and those who belong to larger categories of others (i.e., social groups). Language is conceptualized as historically and socially situated, and discourse analysis is concerned with how ideologies are communicated and what the multiple effects of that communication might be (Evans, 2002).

Discourse analysis is a useful tool for explicating how the discourse of personal experience supports whiteness, because it allows for a nuanced analysis of the socially and historically informed practices that are available for negotiating racial positions. Discourse analysis can reveal processes of racism that otherwise would be difficult to establish, or that would be formally denied by the majority of participants (Van Dijk, 1993). In differentiating discourse analysis from other frameworks for studying inequality, Teun Van Dijk (1993) states that "Although there are many directions in the study and critique of social inequality, the way we approach these questions and dimensions is by focusing on *the role of discourse in the (re)production and challenge of dominance*" (p. 3, emphasis in original). In other words, we are interested in the social processes by which white people produce and maintain their racial position and power in situations in which their position is being challenged. Better understanding of how this process works may enable teachers and others to shape group conversations to destabilize, rather than reinforce, white privilege.

METHODOLOGY

This study involved observing and videotaping four intergroup dialogues on racism among future elementary and secondary school teachers (for more information on the methodology used in this study, see DiAngelo, 2004). A number of key components in an interracial dialogue on race are relevant to this study. In contrast to similar discussions taking place in a classroom setting, the explicit agenda of these dialogues was to talk about race—therefore, the focus on race was not competing with other topics or processes. Our goal was to observe the ways in which white participants perform racially in these dialogues—how the mechanisms of discourse get "recruited, 'on-site,' to 'pull off' specific social activities and identities (membership in various social groups and institutions)" (Gee, 1999, p. 1).

These racial dialogues removed a number of key obstructions that typically manifest in classrooms: a white social taboo that precludes talking directly about race; a power differential between students and teachers that can motivate participants to attempt to perform correctly; pedagogical practices, such as lectures, that can thwart discussion; and physical logistics that make it easier for participants to hide, for example, behind tables and in back rows. To minimize these obstructions as much as possible, the study was designed as a series of facilitated dialogues (Weiler, 1995). Two trained and experienced facilitators from different social locations (one identified as a woman of color and the other as a white woman) guided the discussion and led exercises designed to bring reactions and reflections about race to the surface (Nagda et al., 1995). Using an interracial team of facilitators also allowed researchers to observe how participant responses to the facilitators varied by racial location.

PARTICIPANT SELECTION

Participants were recruited primarily from the teacher education program (TEP) at a major research university in a large urban area in the northwestern United States. A third-party email was sent to all TEP master's students, both first- and second-year cohorts, inviting them to participate in a research study involving a series of facilitated interracial dialogues on race. Students' area of study or discipline was not important because the analysis was tied to a wider, macro-level analysis of how whiteness functions overall in U.S. society (Dyer, 1997; Fine, 1997a; Frankenberg, 2001; Roediger, 1998; Sleeter, 1993).

The TEP program at this university, like many others, is challenged by a lack of racial diversity (U.S. Department of Education, 2002). Due to this limitation, we recruited several participants of color from other departments to which we have access, such as the School of Social Work. However, all of the white participants and one student of color were recruited from the TEP program. The final group consisted of seven students who identified as white, five students who identified as people of color,[1] a facilitator of color (Native American), and a white facilitator.

DATA COLLECTION

Each of the four 2-hour dialogues was videotaped and observed by both authors of this chapter. Robin DiAngelo, a white woman, sat in the back of the room and observed each session, taking field notes. After an initial introduction in session one, she did not participate in the dialogues in any way. David Allen, a white male, videotaped the sessions from a control booth. After an initial introduction in session one, he was not visible to participants, although he could hear and observe the sessions from the control booth. The videotapes permitted revisiting sessions and allowed us to secure reliability via agreement from other researchers in whiteness studies. Although the perspectives of all researchers are situated in and limited by their social locations, as white researchers studying whiteness we faced very specific challenges in our analysis. These challenges ranged from the relative invisibility of whiteness to us as white people, to our positions as white researchers within the context of U.S. culture and our own socialized investment in and enactment of white privilege (Frankenberg, 1997). One way to make more visible (and hopefully reduce) our own role in the reinstatement of whiteness was to also ask for the perspectives of the facilitators, as well as the perspectives of other content experts of different racial locations. Including this range of viewpoints in our analysis served to ensure inter-rater reliability.

Overall, the study documented discourses and practices in racial dialogues that functioned to support white domination and privilege (modes of resistance to decentering whiteness). For this chapter, we are focusing on one dimension of the analysis: the role of experience discourse as performed by white people in the dialogues. The discourse of experience involved a range of signifiers—terms such as "perspective" and "feelings" that are linked to and support the role of experience in shaping these conversations. We analyzed the data (field notes and videotapes) using Gee's (1999) model of discourse analysis, which emphasizes that discourses are not just single terms (e.g., "experience" or "family") but a chain of signifiers that mutually support the practices being analyzed.

Gee (1999) argues that the main functions of language are to scaffold relationships and social structures. Thus, language is a tool that people use to create, maintain, and change relationships and to perform institutional practices that, in turn, create, maintain, reinforce, or challenge social hierarchies (Allen, 2002). We analyzed the data using Gee's (1999) model of discourse analysis. In analyzing whether social processes enhanced, diminished, or were irrelevant to the production of whiteness, we returned to the literature for key definitions and tenets of whiteness. We used these tenets as a kind of template with which to compare and contrast our findings. Gee's (1999) questions linking discourses enacted in social interactions with larger discourses are relevant here:

* What are the relationships among the different discourses being used (institutionally, in society, or historically)?
* How are different discourses aligned or in contention?

We coded conversational patterns by race (based on participant self-identification), by looking at how participants deployed and contested various dominant racial narratives that have been in play over time and across a range of institutions, and by how and when participants and facilitators used these racial narratives. We also coded themes that emerged in the dialogues, such as purpose, unity, and personal experience.

We related these themes and narratives to larger social and historical patterns of whiteness identified in the literature. This coding provided links to the larger discourses and institutions that participants were employing. As Henry Louis Gates (1997) states:

People arrive at an understanding of themselves and the world through narratives—narratives purveyed by school teachers, newscasters, "authorities," and all the other authors of our common sense. Counternarratives are, in turn, the means by which groups contest the dominant reality and the fretwork of assumptions that supports it. (p. 57)

Specific examples of these questions, as applied to this study, include: Do participants take up discourses that position themselves or others as individuals or as group members? If so, who (by race) does so and under what circumstances? Are these discourses (individual vs. group member) contested? If so, by whom? Do individuals switch between discourses—specifically, do they sometimes position themselves as individuals and at other times as group members? What are the institutional consequences of discourses in contention? For example, does a discourse of the individual support or contest larger institutional structures and racialized social arrangements? Does a discourse of group membership support or contest institutional structures and racialized social arrangements?

In linking our analysis of the dialogues to the context in which they were situated—teacher education in the United States—we addressed education as a normative institution whose role within the wider society is to replicate stratified relations of race, class, and gender (Adams et al., 1997; Derman-Sparks & Phillips, 1997). As such, education is a very significant backdrop against which whiteness was being defended or contested.

"THAT'S JUST MY PERSONAL EXPERIENCE"

One significant form of the discourse of personal experience surfaced through the use of ground rules. One of the ground rules stated at the first session was to use personalized knowledge. In other words, participants were asked to speak for themselves rather than make general statements for the entire group. This ground rule was intended to help open the dialogue by allowing alternative interpretations and perspectives to emerge. However, white participants often invoked personalized knowledge in a way that functioned to protect their interpretations rather than broadening them. Several times throughout the dialogues, white participants ended a rebuttal statement with the disclaimer "That's just my personal experience." When used at the end of a statement, this phrase claimed the experience as personal and therefore uncontestable, and thus precluded any question of the statement. These statements are part of a rhetorical or discursive practice that claims an individual position instead of acting as a bridge or interplay (Billig, 2001; Tannen, 2001).

The following excerpt is an example of how a white participant used her experience to block further exploration of her statement. When Tiffany is told by a number of participants of color that Europeans and European Americans are seen as white, she responds with a personal feeling statement:

> *Tiffany (W):* I'm uncomfortable with the label "white" based on what I have learned that people of color perceive "white" to mean and represent. That's what makes me uncomfortable with it. So I'm uncomfortable being associated with what I perceive to be the common perception of what "white" is.
> *Rich (POC):* But European Americans are white.
> *Tiffany (W):* Yeah. I mean, I guess I feel like—
> *Rich (POC):* Well, she said that she felt comfortable identifying herself as a European American. European Americans are white. Columbus, Pizarro, all these guys that came from Italy and Spain and all over, um, they're all white. They're all European American. Um, I don't know. When I—when I look at you, I see a white person.
> *Tiffany (W):* But the term "white" conjures up different feelings, I think, in people who are European American, from my perspective.

When Rich tells Tiffany that he sees her as white, she responds with a feeling statement in order to reclaim her position as an individual outside of a racialized group position. She rejects Rich's interpretation of her as white based on the simple assertion that she doesn't feel white. This lack of feeling is posited as enough to sustain her rebuttal. She finalizes her move by stating that she is speaking "from my perspective."

Rich and others have offered Tiffany an interpretation of herself that is different from her own. From a turn-taking perspective, she could respond with a gesture that would open both her self-interpretation and the dialogue up to further insight and explication, such as asking why they see her the way they do. Instead, she employs a personal psychological reality assertion, making this a classic Cartesian move (Allen & Cloyes, 2005). Tiffany's perspective is conceptualized as internal, private, and individual rather than as social or interrelational. This individual basis provides her claim with validity, and thereby positions her as the only expert on her interpretation. This move depoliticizes experience and says, in effect, "since nobody else has access to my personal experience, it is therefore incontestable."

Tiffany's language employs a constellation of terms linked to personal experience discourse (including her choice of the word "perspective"). For example, she also offers a number of feeling statements. In the above excerpt, she uses the word "uncomfortable" three times. She also repeatedly states that she does not "feel" white. Her discomfort with the label, as well as her not feeling white, are enough for her to sustain a rebuttal in the face of counter statements by participants of color. Although they repeatedly try to engage her in reflecting on herself as white, signaling that it is important to them for her to do so, she holds her position by repeating that she just doesn't feel white and that it is not her experience. These statements, framed in psychological terms, reduce racial privilege to a feeling-state, something that she either feels or does not feel. If she does not feel it, then it is not important and does not count.

The personal experience move is tightly coupled with positioning oneself first and foremost as an individual. Positioning oneself as an individual is a classic signal of whiteness and works to decontextualize and depoliticize race (Ellsworth, 1997; Fine, 1997b; Morrison, 1992; Tatum, 2001). Tiffany's earlier statement occurred in the first dialogue. The following exchange occurred in session two:

Tiffany (W): I was raised in a diverse neighborhood, and I went to diverse schools, and my family is very diverse, and that's my experience. If you have any questions about it, I'm happy to tell you more. I don't know—I don't—this didn't hit a whole bunch of nerves, because I had never been—I never felt terribly white; I felt very un-white, really. I feel very fortunate for that. But my experience may be different from a different white person's experience, so—and I think it was, given what I heard. And I'm really proud to say that I've had a wonderfully diverse, you know, experience growing up, and I think I'm better for it. I think it's really been a gift, so.

Becca (WF): Tiffany, what do you mean, you don't feel white?

Tiffany (W): What I mean by that is that I think the stereotype of— I think that often a label and a stereotype is associated with being white. And because my family is not a hundred percent white, by any stretch, and because my experience in this world has been of exposure to all sorts of different ethnic and racial groups, I feel like that has contributed to my—a broadening of my experience. I mean, I don't know what to say besides that. So, my skin looks this way, but I have Jewish ancestry, so somehow that's—I mean, that qualifies me, right? I mean—anyway.

Malena (FOC): Qualifies you for what?

Tiffany (W): As being a member of a group that has been racially discriminated against. I mean, "qualify" is the wrong word; I'm sorry if that offends anybody, but—I'm done talking for a while.

In the above excerpt, Tiffany attempts three countermoves to the challenge to see herself as white. She begins by conceptualizing racism in terms of feeling and experience. When her feeling statement is challenged by Becca, she tries to discount her whiteness by invoking her Jewish ancestry. When Malena challenges that move, Tiffany abruptly ends the discussion. Although this excerpt is a particularly explicit example of the use of personal experience to protect a white position, Tiffany wasn't the only white participant who employed this move when her self-perception was questioned.

In the following exchange, Courtney, a white participant, responds to challenges by Becca, the white facilitator, and Carolyn, a participant of color. They have challenged some of the white participants who posited that racism is a phenomenon that existed in the past but is not present in the younger generation.

Becca (WF): Uh, there've been a couple of things that people have been talking about that have been really frustrating for me but have been things, I think, that I've felt at—at various times in my consciousness as well. Um, and one of the things that I've noticed is that people keep talking about racism as first of all being a generational thing. The white people continuously have been referring to racism as a generational thing, and I think that, for me when I do that, and when I look at my experience on that—when I do that, that's when I'm keeping that separate from myself, and by doing that I'm not owning my own racism. And the fact is I've been socialized in a society where racism is prevalent, and for me to, as a white person, put it out there that it's a generational thing, I think is very unfair. And I don't know how it affects other people, but—

Caroline (POC): I kind of wanted you to talk about this idea—if white people could really accept that racism exists. I notice with white activists is that sometimes you get to a point where they are just so—"I'm active, I'm active. I'm so active that I could never be racist." But to me it feels like sometimes they are the hardest people to target, because they feel like they're not racist, "because I do not believe in racism, so I am not racist." And so, I think it's really important to really recognize it, because you still have social power, and you are still going to benefit and there is still going to be racism.

Like Tiffany, Courtney draws on both her feelings and her personal experience in her response to these challenges:

Courtney (W): I think, um, speaking for myself, but I think—from my experiences with, you know, older neighbors or people, um—and there aren't many because I do live in . . . and I have all my life—and often you don't hear a lot of white people in . . . openly, you know, speaking in a way that that sounds racist or that's openly talking about stereotypes. There has to be an interplay there and to put it all on—you know, someone coming from the outside and telling a white person, well, "you really—you shouldn't feel that way," you know, it's like "what does that mean?" Because my feelings are not about you.

In Courtney's statement that her feelings "are not about you," she presents her feelings as standing alone or outside social processes, rather than as a function of social processes. Her feelings are thus positioned as independent of the social, political, or historical context in which she is embedded. Here she draws on a deeply individual discourse. By positioning herself as an individual, with a collection of rights, she closes her position off from others—for Courtney, as an individual, has the right to think and feel whatever she wants. Conversationally, this is a blocking move that ends any challenge to her perceptions. Courtney has the opportunity to learn, for example, why the white facilitator, who has experience in dialogues about race, feels frustrated that racism has been relegated to the past. Instead, Courtney defends her position, negates the others, and closes off further exploration.

Through her language, Courtney has also shifted the emphasis from her views or her perceptions to her feelings. Courtney says that she feels that racism is generational; she doesn't say she thinks it is. Had she kept her language in the realm of thinking, she would have been more susceptible to challenge. Thinking, by drawing from the rational realm, is a more public space and thus more open to contestation. Feelings, however, are considered to be in the realm of the personal or private space, and thus are not available for contestation (Allen & Cloyes, 2005). During this exchange, Courtney also states:

> *Courtney (W):* I think it—I think it depends on the individual experience. And since we're all speaking from personal experience, um, I know that I was—I got a little upset to hear people say that they don't think it's fair that someone would say it's generational, because it's a personal thing if we all know our own families and our own communities and we know what we have perceived in our own families and communities. And so I think it's a valid point—if that's what you want to say, then that's what you should be able to say. I just want to put that out there.

Here Courtney invokes the corollary discourse of rights that accompanies personal experience. To attack feelings is to break two rules of the discourse of personal experience: (1) Courtney has the right to feel the way she does, and (2) challenging her feelings risks hurting her (you can hurt someone's feelings, but not their thinking), which makes a challenge to feelings inherently unfair. Cartesianism further protects her by segregating feelings in private minds that are unavailable for public examination. By shifting the discourse from perceptions to feelings, Courtney has protected her interpretations from challenge and simultaneously assumed the higher moral ground in the dialogue.

DISCUSSION

Although encouraging the use of experience was developed as a critical practice designed to undermine elite expertise (Schlegel, 2002), in this study the discourse of personal experience functioned to protect elites—in other words, it privileged white people. This protection was accomplished by positing a white participant's interpretations as the product of a discrete individual, outside the realm of socialization, rather than as the product of multidimensional social interaction. The individual is then responded to as a private mind in the Cartesian sense (Allen & Cloyes, 2005). The discourse of personal experience has particularly significant consequences for dialogues in which the stated goal is to gain understanding of racialized perspectives. Removing these political dimensions mitigates against social change and preserves conventional arrangements (Levine-Rasky, 2000).

In their deconstruction of the use of experience in nursing research, David Allen and Kristin Cloyes (2005) focus on the politics of language. They question the use of experience as evidence in qualitative research, and problematize experience from the framework that language is socially produced. They note that researchers who rely on their subjects' accounts of experience as evidence often do this in two contradictory ways. Sometimes they use experience in terms of the research subject's interpretations of events. This is a sort of witness discourse—we ask someone what happened. In this context, the account is positioned as one perspective on a public event. Consequently, it can be challenged in a number of ways. On the other hand, experience is positioned as internal, private reality, and the account functions as a confessional discourse—reporting what no one else has access to. This lack of access can be practical (no one saw me do it) or ontological (I had impure thoughts). One of the problems with these approaches is that they move back and forth between positing experience as the internal perceptions of an individual and positing experience as interpretations of an external event. This variance in the function of experience as a signifier is usually unmarked, but it is not without political significance. As Allen and Cloyes (2005) state, "So the use of experience as evidence, and the relationship between that evidence and the researcher's conclusions, reproduces the same unmarked shift between individuals and events" (p. 103). In this study, by moving their accounts of racism and white privilege into the "confessional" mode (even if the confession is denial), white participants made their accounts more difficult to challenge.

However, we can and do have ways to challenge self-interpretations. We speak of people fooling themselves or being in denial when we believe we have a better interpretation of their situation than they do. And there are social rules about when and how such a challenge can be raised (Henriques et al., 1984). As it relates to this study, a significant component of Allen and Cloyes's (2005) analysis is their identification of the assumptions underpinning the use of experience. These assumptions are (1) only the individual has access to her own mind, and (2) she cannot be mistaken about what is going on in her own mind (or, at least, there is no way to verify what occurs in someone else's mind). These assumptions function to make experience a kind of sacred text in qualitative analysis and to close claims of experience off from interrogation: How can one possibly question the personal experiences of others?

If we follow Allen and Cloyes's (2005) suggestion to conceptualize experience as a specific discourse with political consequences, we can ask how white participants used experience in the dialogues. Raising questions about claims to experience can illuminate new ways of understanding meaning-making in social interaction. In terms of social co-production, problematizing the concept of experience might shed light on how discourses function in this context and, in particular, how they function to protect whiteness.

If white people use personal experience as the evidence for understanding racism, then they are limited in their ability to validate racism's damaging effects on people of color. Relying on the discourse of experience enables white people to reject claims that racism is real and that it has tangible effects on the lives of people of color, because they do not witness these effects firsthand. If the evidence required is simply whether or not any one particular individual personally experiences racism, the result is likely to be denial. Likewise, if personal experience is the evidence for power and privilege, then this too will be denied. Power and privilege are so normalized for white people that their effects are frequently not noticed or felt (McIntosh, 1988). This situation makes it almost impossible for white people to engage in discussions about how their own lives are also shaped (elevated) by racism. As Jason, the white, heterosexual, able-bodied, upper-class male in this study, states:

> *Jason:* Can I ask a question? Well, you don't have to answer it, but—power versus privilege versus opportunity: I feel like I've had a ton of opportunity, but I don't—but, you know, an often-unemployed, leftist-leaning resident of Bellevue—I've got no power; nobody listens to me where I live.

Jason's personal self-interpretation of not having power is not necessarily aligned with how others perceive or respond to him or his relationship to social and institutional power. Understanding power as power—over someone—rather than, say, as an unearned surplus of resources and opportunities—perpetuates this misunderstanding. Further, as McIntosh (1988) argues, he may not feel much of his power because it is so normalized that it is taken for granted. The discourse of personal experience as performed by white people in this study functioned with the discourse of feeling-states. Given the ways in which dominant society socializes white people not to see, feel, or think about racism, or to perceive loss in the absence of people of color in our lives, depending on experiences to guide one's racial interpretations is highly problematic (McIntosh, 1988; Morrison, 1992; Tatum, 1997; Thandeka, 2000).

Another way in which the discourse of personal experience functions to protect whiteness is in the absolution it offers white people from responsibility for racism. A subtext of this discourse is that we each have the right to our own experience; you cannot question my experience, and I cannot question yours. In this way, we are each responsible for our own experiences and are absolved from any communal responsibility. The subtext says, "If you have a problem with racism, it is your problem. It is not my problem because it is not my experience." The following exchange illustrates how one white participant used this subtext to distance herself from racial responsibility:

> Rich (POC): I just think for any person—for any white person—they can't look me in the eye and then tell me they're not racist—that's crazy. And I think that a lot of what we're talking about here is that . . . you are trying to say that, "no, I'm not racist," but I think when you accept the fact that you are racist, that you're—that, hell, "yeah, I'm racist"—I mean, then that's somewhat of a starting point.
> Courtney (W): I'm not quite sure what you mean, because I don't feel that being the case in the world.

Rich has positioned racism as a collective process, one in which all white people participate. Further, he offers this perspective as a positive—a way out of the racism from which Courtney works so hard to disconnect herself. If Courtney can start from this framework, she is less likely to be perceived as colluding with racism. However, Courtney's response to Rich repositions his collective analysis of racism as merely a matter of difference in opinion. She rejects his analysis, stating flatly that she does not "feel that being the case"—it isn't her experience. This move effectively makes racism Rich's personal problem. Since Courtney doesn't agree with Rich—his experience isn't her experience—she bears no responsibility for the racism he feels.

We want to explore a final problem with the discourse of personal experience: the relationship of this discourse to the social distortions that are necessary to hold the ideology of white dominance in place. White narratives that conceptualize people of color (and African American males in particular) as dangerous are a profound perversion of the historical and current direction of violence between white people and African Americans (Collins, 2000; Lorde, 2001; Morrison, 1992). If we contend that the dominant culture distorts social realities in order to hide and maintain privilege, then using the discourse of personal experience is especially problematic. Through this discourse, white people conflate social and political phenomena such as racial discomfort with questions of safety. Yet without an explication of what personal experience means in this context, there is no way to challenge this conflation. Given these distortions, personal experience is not a particularly solid reference point from which to make sense of racial interpretations.

BUFFERING THE PRIVILEGE OF EXPERIENCE

In thinking about how to anticipate and respond to the effects that personal experience discourses have on conversations like the dialogues in our study, we find the concept of positioning helpful. Positioning refers to the discursive practices through which people place themselves or are placed by others. Positioning is defined as a conversational phenomenon that produces social relations (Davies & Harre, 1990). An individual emerges through the processes of social interaction, not as a fixed personality, but as one who is constituted and reconstituted through the various discursive practices in which they participate. This form of analysis views the subject as open and shifting, depending on the positions made available through their own and others' discursive practices. In a sense, this notion of positioning makes the political impersonal: As students and educators understand their most intimate and biographical narratives to be social and historical products, it becomes easier to shift the conversation from "why did you say that?" to "how did you come to articulate it that way?" The former statement tends to locate both the problem and the solution in the individual, the latter in the social environment.

Bronwyn Davies and Rom Harre (1990) claim that the following processes are involved in generating one's worldview and self-perception:

+ Learning about categories that include some people and exclude others (e.g., Black, white, racist, non-racist)

- ♦ Participating in the discursive practices through which meaning is accorded to those categories (e.g., one must have a concept of non-racist in order to participate in the discursive practices that generate meaning related to the category)
- ♦ Positioning oneself in relation to the categories being generated (e.g., as a non-racist rather than as a racist, or viewing oneself as having the characteristics that locate oneself in one category but not in another)
- ♦ Seeing oneself as belonging to, and viewing the world from the perspective of, one's position

To demonstrate the utility of the approach of positioning, we return to an interaction described earlier: Courtney, a white participant, has made a claim that racism is more of a "generational thing," that older white people are more racist than younger white people such as herself. Along with others, Carolyn, a woman of color, has challenged Courtney's claim. This is Courtney's response to Carolyn's challenge:

> You know, someone coming from the outside and telling a white person, well, "you really—you shouldn't feel that way," you know, it's like what does that mean? Because my feelings are not about you. You know what I mean? They're not about people I associate with you; they're about somebody else. So for you to tell me, it's like—it's almost meaningless in a way.

Courtney is positioning herself in several ways. First, she quite clearly positions Caroline as an outsider, both racially ("They're not about people I associate with you; they're about somebody else") and in terms of Caroline's ability to feel the same things she does ("Because my feelings are not about you"). This positioning of Caroline as a racial outsider (and, conversely, positioning herself as the racial insider) is particularly significant given that Courtney is referring to feelings about race while at the same time placing a woman of color outside of the play—Courtney's feelings about race have nothing to do with the racial realities of people of color ("people I associate with you"). Second, Courtney positions her own knowledge as superior to Caroline's, subordinating Caroline's knowledge to her own ("So for you to tell me"), going so far as to position any racial knowledge that Caroline has as null and void ("it's almost meaningless in a way"). In this way, she claims racial legitimacy as the sole domain of white people.

None of this is likely conscious, and none is idiosyncratic to Courtney's experience. If educators frame these discussions within a theory of positioning, it opens the door to helping students (and ourselves) see white people's reports of experience as part of larger historical and social processes that we inherit, not invent. Thus, it becomes easier to help participants both see these positional moves as performances, and inquire about their historical and social origins. This study may be convincing because it is congruent with a great deal of scholarship, as well as many classroom interactions. But it is far from conclusive. Although the participants in our study exhibit behaviors that are typical of the social practices that produced them and that they perform, more research is needed to establish variations of experience discourse. Further research may illustrate the effects of a discourse of personal experience on conversations about racism and whether—as we suggest—an approach that draws on positioning produces more engaged and productive conversations across differences. By creating a conversational space in which everyone's racialized interpretations are open to political examination, the role of language and memory in preserving social hierarchies will be more apparent and vulnerable to destabilization. In such a setting, marginalized voices may be more easily heard and sustained, and racial perceptions expanded.

NOTE

1. Students of color self-identified as: a Native American female, a Chicano male, an African American female, an African male, and a Chinese American female.

REFERENCES

Adams, M., Bell, L., & Griffin, P. (1997). *Teaching for diversity and social justice: A sourcebook*. Routledge.

Allen, D. G. (1996). Knowledge, politics, culture, and gender: A discourse perspective. *Canadian Journal of Nursing Research, 28*(1), 95–102.

Allen, D. G. (2002). September 11th and the eminent practicality of poststructuralism. *Nursing Inquiry, 9*(1), 1–2.

Allen, D. G., & Cloyes, K. (2005). The language of experience in nursing research. *Nursing Inquiry, 12*(2), 98–105.

Apple, M. (1997). Consuming the other: Whiteness, education, and cheap French fries. In M. Fine, L. Weis, L. C. Powell, & L. M. Wong (Eds.), *Off white: Readings on race, power, and society* (pp. 121–128). Routledge.

Banks, J. A. (1995). Multicultural education: Historical development, dimensions, and practice. In J. A. Banks & C. A. M. Banks (Eds.), *Handbook of research on multicultural education* (pp. 3–24). Macmillan.

Bannerji, H. (1992). But who speaks for us? Experience and agency in conventional feminist paradigms. In H. Bannerji, L. Carty, K. Dehli, S. Heald, & K. McKenna (Eds.), *Unsettling relations: The university as a site of feminist struggles* (pp. 67–107). South End Press.

Bellamy, E. J., & Leontis, A. (1993). A genealogy of experience: From epistemology to politics. *Yale Journal of Criticism, 6*(1), 163–185.

Billig, M. (2001). Discursive, rhetorical and ideological messages. In M. Wetherell, S. Taylor, & S. J. Yates (Eds.), *Discourse theory and practice: A reader* (pp. 210–221). Sage.

Chay, D. G. (1993). Rereading Barbara Smith: Black feminist criticism and the category of experience. *New Literary History, 24*(3), 635–652.

Chor, E. N., Fleck, C., Fan, G., Joseph, J., & Lyter, D. M. (2003). Exploring critical feminist pedagogy: Infusing dialogue, participation and experience in teaching and learning. *Teaching Sociology, 31*(3), 259–275.

Collins, P. H. (2000). *Black feminist thought: Knowledge, consciousness, and the politics of empowerment* (2nd ed.). Routledge.

Davies, B., & Harre, R. (1990). Positioning: The discursive production of selves. *Journal of the Theory of Social Behavior, 20*, 43–65.

Derman-Sparks, L., & Phillips, C. (1997). *Teaching/learning anti-racism: A developmental approach.* Teachers College Press.

DiAngelo, R. (2004). *Whiteness in racial dialogue: A discourse analysis* [Unpublished dissertation]. University of Washington, Seattle.

Dyer, R. (1997). *White.* Routledge.

Editorial Board. (2005, October 10). Breaking the glass ceiling a different way. *The Daily*, p. 6.

Ellsworth, E. (1997). Double binds of whiteness. In M. Fine, L. Weis, C. Powell, & L. Wong (Eds.), *Off white: Readings on race, power, and society* (pp. 259–269). Routledge.

Evans, K. (2002). *Negotiating the self: Identity, sexuality, and emotion in learning to teach*. Routledge.

Fine, M. (1997a). Introduction. In M. Fine, L. Weis, C. Powell, & L. Wong (Eds.), *Off white: Readings on race, power, and society* (pp. vii–xii). Routledge.

Fine, M. (1997b). Witnessing whiteness. In M. Fine, L. Weis, C. Powell, & L. Wong (Eds.), *Off white: Readings on race, power, and society* (pp. 57–65). Routledge.

Fiske, J. (1989). *Reading the popular*. Unwin and Hyman.

Flax, J. (1998). *American dream in Black and white: The Clarence Thomas hearings*. Cornell University Press.

Foss, K. A., & Foss, S. K. (1994). Personal experience as evidence in feminist scholarship. *Western Journal of Communication, 58*(1), 39–43.

Frankenberg, R. (1993). *The social construction of whiteness: White women, race matters*. University of Minnesota Press.

Frankenberg, R. (1997). Introduction: Local whitenesses, localizing whiteness. In R. Frankenberg (Ed.), *Displacing whiteness: Essays in social and cultural criticism* (pp. 1–33). Duke University Press.

Frankenberg, R. (2001). The mirage of an unmarked whiteness. In B. B. Rasmussen, E. Klinenberg, I. J. Nexica, & M. Wray (Eds.), *The making and unmaking of whiteness* (pp. 72–96). Duke University Press.

Gates, H. L. (1997). *Thirteen ways of looking at a Black man*. Random House.

Gee, J. P. (1999). *An introduction to discourse analysis: Theory and method*. Routledge.

Hardin, P. K. (2003). Constructing experience in individual interviews, autobiographies and on-line accounts: A poststructuralist approach. *Journal of Advanced Nursing, 41*(6), 536–544.

Henriques, J., Hollway, W., Urwin, C., Venn, C., & Walkerdine, V. (1984). *Changing the subject: Psychology, social regulation and subjectivity*. Routledge.

Kerdeman, D. (2003). Pulled up short: Challenging self-understanding as a focus of teaching and learning. *Journal of Philosophy of Education, 37*(2), 293–309.

Kruks, S. (2001). *Retrieving experience: Subjectivity and recognition in feminist politics*. Cornell University Press.

Levine-Rasky, C. (2000). Framing whiteness: Working through the tensions in introducing whiteness to educators. *Race, Ethnicity and Education, 3*(3), 271–292.

Lorde, A. (2001). Age, race, class and sex: Women redefining difference. In M. Andersen & P. H. Collins (Eds.), *Race, class and gender: An anthology* (pp. 89–93). Wadsworth.

Macedo, D., & Bartolome, L. (1999). *Dancing with bigotry: Beyond the politics of tolerance*. St. Martin's Press.

Mardorossian, C. M. (2002). Theory, experience and disciplinary contentions: A response to Janice Haaken and Beverly Allen. *Signs, 27*(3), 787–791.

Martin, M. G. F. (2002). The transparency of experience. *Mind & Language, 17*(4), 376–425.

McIntosh, P. (1988). White privilege and male privilege: A personal account of coming to see correspondence through work in women's studies. In M. Anderson & P. Hill Collins (Eds.), *Race, class, and gender: An anthology* (pp. 94–105). Wadsworth.

Mohanty, C. T. (1992). Feminist encounters: Locating the politics of experience. In M. Barrett & A. Phillips (Eds.), *Destabilizing theory: Contemporary feminist debates* (pp. 74–92). Polity Press.

Morrison, T. (1992). *Playing in the dark*. Random House.

Mulinari, D., & Sandell, K. (1999). Exploring the notion of experience in feminist thought. *Acta Sociologica, 42*, 287–297.

Nagda, B., Zúñiga, X., & Sevig, T. (1995). Bridging differences through peer facilitated intergroup dialogues. In S. L. Hatcher (Ed.), *Peer programs on the college campus: Theory, training, and "voice of the peers"* (pp. 25–41). New Resources.

Nieto, S. (2002). School reform and student learning: A multicultural perspective. In J. A. Banks & C. A. M. Banks (Eds.), *Multicultural education: Issues and perspectives* (4th ed., pp. 381–397). Allyn & Bacon.

Richard, N. (1996). Feminism, experience and representation. *Revista Iberoamericana, 62*(176–177), 733–744.

Roediger, D. R. (Ed.). (1998). *Black on white: Black writers on what it means to be white*. Schocken.

Schlegel, J. H. (2002). Flight from fallibility: How theory triumphed over experience in the West. *Journal of Economic History, 62*(2), 632–633.

Scott, J. (1992). Experience. In J. Butler & J. Scott (Eds.), *Feminists theorize the political* (pp. 22–40). Routledge.

Sleeter, C. (1993). How white teachers construct race. In C. McCarthy & W. Crichlow (Eds.), *Race identity and representation in education* (pp. 157–171). Routledge.

Stone-Mediatore, S. (1998). Chandra Mohanty and the revaluing of "experience." *Hypatia, 13*(2), 116–127.

Tannen, D. (2001). The relativity of linguistic strategies: Rethinking power and solidarity in gender and dominance. In M. Wetherell, S. Taylor, & S. J. Yates (Eds.), *Discourse theory and practice: A reader* (pp. 150–166). Sage.

Tatum, B. (1997). *"Why are all the Black kids sitting together in the cafeteria?" And other conversations about race.* Basic Books.

Tatum, B. (2001). Defining racism: Can we talk? In P. Rothenberg (Ed.), *Race, class, and gender in the United States: An integrated study* (5th ed., pp. 100–107). Worth.

Thandeka. (2000). *Learning to be white: Money, race, and God in America.* Continuum.

U.S. Department of Education, National Center for Education Statistics. Race and Ethnicity of Public School Teachers and Their Students (2002).

Van Dijk, T. A. (1993). Analyzing racism through discourse analysis: Some methodological reflections. In J. H. Stanfield II & R. M. Dennis (Eds.), *Race and ethnicity in research methods* (pp. 92–134). Sage.

Weiler, J. (1995). Finding shared meanings: Reflections on dialogue. An interview with Linda Tuerfs. *Seeds Unfolding, 11*(1), 4–10.

Wetherell, M., Taylor, S., & Yates, S. J. (Eds.). (2001). *Discourse theory and practice: A reader.* Sage.

FOUR

Getting Slammed
White Depictions of Race Discussions as Arenas of Violence

ROBIN DIANGELO AND ÖZLEM SENSOY

And so, you know—I'm not talking to this because I feel angry from last week and because I don't want to say a bunch of shit and have it all slammed back in my face.

—Amanda

INTRODUCTION

Imagine a group of 13 university students sitting in a circle, engaged in the second session of a 4-week discussion on race. There are five students of color and eight white students. An interracial team of two facilitators leads the discussion. In session one, several of the students of color challenged the white students' worldviews by pressing them to consider that those worldviews were fundamentally shaped by their race. That session ended with the facilitators giving the group their homework for the next session: asking the participants to pay attention to racial dynamics and patterns during the week.

Originally published as Robin DiAngelo & Özlem Sensoy (2012), "Getting slammed: White depictions of race discussions as arenas of violence," *Race Ethnicity and Education*, doi:10.1080/13613324.2012.674 023. Copyright © 2012, reprinted by permission of Taylor & Francis Ltd, http://www.tandfonline.com.

To begin session two, the facilitators open with a go-around check-in:

Dawn (Facilitator, biracial): What is a racial pattern that you have
noticed that was new since our discussion last week, or if you
are someone who spends a fair amount of time thinking about
race, maybe something that was a pattern or reinforced for you
since our meeting last week?

Laura (Asian American): I was at a reading this weekend, and it was a
white man reading from his novel that he had written, and it was very
striking that, when he described the characters, both before the
reading and during, he only racialized the people of color, and
everyone else he talked about just kind of in these really neutral terms.
And it just stuck out and really reinforced what I've noticed this week.

Caroline (African American): I think the thing that has been
reinforced the past week, and just pretty much every day, is how
much I really think about race and how aware I really am of that
in every single interaction that I have with every single person that
I meet every single day.

Amanda (white): A pattern that I noticed this week is that, every
single day this whole week since this past experience, I felt the
same degree of anger that I had last week from the experience of
being here. And so, you know—I'm not talking to this because I
feel angry from last week and because I don't want to say a bunch
of shit and have it all slammed back in my face.

While Amanda's anger, along with her depiction of a violent outcome if
she expresses herself in the group, may be more explicit than that of many
white students, the sentiment is likely not unfamiliar to those who lead
discussions about race. Her allusion to such a graphic image as "shit" being
"slammed back" in her face is consistent with common white descriptions
of race talk as contexts wherein they will be violated. Indeed, when white
participants negatively evaluate a course or workshop that examines race
and racism, a common complaint is that they were "beaten up" or "attacked," and therefore "didn't feel safe."

There are complicated discursive moves operating in tandem in these
moments that ensure white supremacy is reinforced and protected, especially

in contexts in which the explicit goal is to interrupt that supremacy. We argue that one of these moves is the positioning of cross-racial discussions as "unsafe" for white people. In the exchange that begins this chapter, Amanda is particularly explicit in expressing anger at the violation she feels, but the sentiment is not uncommon for white people engaged in cross-racial discussions. For this reason, many educators and facilitators respond by attending to the perceived lack of safety in the classroom. Guidelines for ensuring safety in cross-racial discussions are typically introduced during the process of establishing group norms. These guidelines are often viewed as fundamental to building the community that is assumed necessary in order for constructive cross-racial discussions to occur. Yet, while there are many problematic dynamics in cross-racial discussions affecting all students in various ways, guidelines for safety are usually driven in anticipation of white responses such as Amanda's.

Examining Safety as a Prerequisite for Race Talk

The concept of safety is so central to these discussions that it is presumed that without a safe climate, the goals of the discussion cannot be achieved. For example, according to Adams et al.'s (1997) well-known sourcebook for teaching social justice education, "Establishing a safe environment in which students can discuss ideas, share feelings and experiences, and challenge themselves and each other to reevaluate opinions and beliefs is one of the primary facilitation responsibilities" (p. 283). Similarly, in Tatum's classic article (1992) "Talking About Race, Learning About Racism," she explains, "Many students are reassured by the climate of safety that is created by these guidelines and find comfort in the nonblaming assumptions I outline for the class" (p. 4). The guidelines that are intended to purportedly establish this safe environment commonly include speaking for oneself ("use 'I' statements") and respecting others ("no shame or blame"). While we are not critiquing dialogue guidelines in general (for we too use guidelines when teaching), what we are critiquing are guidelines intended to ensure safety, and whose safety drives those guidelines.

As a response to the expectation that safety be a prerequisite for social justice talk, some scholars have problematized the very definition of safety and questioned the premise that these spaces can or should be safe to begin with (e.g., see Jones, 1999, 2001; Leonardo & Porter, 2010; Schick, 2000). For this perspective, ensuring a feeling of safety in discussions that ask students to examine their place within relations of inequitable social power is a particularly problematic goal. For example, in the context of cross-racial dialogues that are explicitly about race and racism, what feels safe for white people is presumed to feel safe for people of color. Yet for many students and instructors of color, the classroom is a hostile space virtually all of the time, and especially so when the topic addressed is race (Boler, 2004; Crozier & Davies, 2008; Ellsworth, 1989; Leonardo & Porter, 2010). Many scholars have further argued that "diversity" defined as non-white students studying in classrooms with white people, more often than not benefits the white students at the expense of students of color (Jones, 1999, 2001; Mitchell & Donahue, 2009; Winans, 2005). In practice, the expectation that safety can be created in racial discussions through universalized procedural guidelines can block students of color from naming the racial violence they experience on a daily basis, as well as the racial violence they may experience in the discussion itself. In other words, the discourse of safety in the context of race talk is always about white safety (Leonardo & Porter, 2010).

In addition to critiques of concepts of safety in general, specific guidelines, such as speaking for oneself and/or from one's own personal experience, have also been problematized. For example, in our own work examining the dynamics of cross-racial discussions, we have shown how the guideline of "personal experience" can in fact be co-opted by white students (DiAngelo & Allen, 2006). This co-option functions to protect and inoculate white students' claims from further exploration. Our research illustrates that the "speak from personal experience" guideline rests on two problematic assumptions: first, that only the individual herself has access to her own mind; and second, because she is presumed to have sole access, her experiences cannot be challenged. In this way, claims of experience are closed off from interrogation, for how can one question the "personal" experience of others? Thus, the discourse of personal experience, while commonplace, runs counter to a dialogic and discursive understanding of identity construction and therefore functions to make experience itself a kind of "sacred text." While the guideline to speak for oneself may be intended to prevent white participants from negating the perspectives of students of color, in effect, it often protects white perspectives from critical analysis.

Building on the idea of personal experience as sacred text, we have also examined how students privilege "opinion" over informed knowledge in ways that invalidate informed study of social inequality (DiAngelo & Sensoy, 2009). The "right to my opinion" discourse (e.g., "I have the right to think and say what I want, and you don't have the right to challenge what I think and say") is another strategy that closes off one's "personal" experiences and perspectives. Yet not all people have been granted the right to speak, or had their perspectives heard equally in a society that is racially stratified (Applebaum, 2008; Boler, 2004; Matsuda et al., 1993). Thus, when the request to situate oneself as knower in order to examine positionality in relation to knowledge is reinterpreted as "the right to my opinion," positionality and its relation to the production and legitimization of knowledge is denied. In this way, historically marginalized experiences and perspectives are dismissed or trumped via "just as valid" dominant perspectives, in effect recentering whiteness.

Similarly, we and others have examined the dynamics of challenging white students in racial discussions (Applebaum, 2008; Picower, 2009). DiAngelo (2011) has described one of these dynamics as "white fragility," in which even a minimum amount of challenge to white positionality is intolerable and triggers a range of defensive moves and displays of emotions such as anger, fear, and guilt, and behaviors such as argumentation, silence, and leaving the stress-inducing situation (DiAngelo, 2011). In defending the validity of these emotions and resultant behaviors, many white people use the speech of self-defense (McIntyre, 1997; Van Dijk, 1992). Focusing on restoring their moral standing, white people avoid addressing white privilege (Levine-Rasky, 2000; Marty, 1999; Van Dijk, 1992). This speech enables defenders to protect their moral character against what they perceive as accusation and attack while deflecting any culpability or need of accountability. In turn, these responses pressure facilitators to lessen the challenge to white students, often by implementing guidelines intended to make white students feel safer.

Thus, critiques of safety have focused on the meaning of safety from various racial positions, as well as the effects of attempts to establish safety in cross-racial discussions on race. Building on this body of scholarship examining the various dynamics of cross-racial discussions, we are interested in the discursive effects of responses such as Amanda's, in which she claims she is being slammed. Her response starkly illustrates both the graphic and subtle allusions to violence embedded in claims that cross-racial discussions are unsafe for white people. We want to shift the spotlight regarding race talk from safety to violence. It is important to acknowledge that many rich theoretical discussions of violence exist, among them those examining symbolic violence (Pierre Bourdieu), epistemic violence (Gayatri Spivak), colonial violence (Frantz Fanon), and political power and violence (Hannah Arendt). We draw from these discussions the idea that violence is much more complicated than the imposition of physical force. When we refer to the discourse of violence, we include normative social discourses, as well as assaultive speech (Matsuda et al., 1993), and violent imagery—all of which our participants utilized in the dialogue. In this context, we argue that the discourse of violence manifests through the expectation of safe discussion spaces as defined by white people. The demand for safety harnesses violent imagery as a means by which white students project racist ideologies onto racialized people, and in so doing, re-inscribe white supremacy.

We want to acknowledge the dilemma in documenting white students' discourses of violence. To be transparent, our goal in offering this analysis is to support other educators in our collective work with white people who may use these discourses. Thus, it is not lost on us that the violence against people of color that is reproduced by putting the words in print will be primarily for the benefit of those working with white people. We have not found a way out of this dilemma other than that of purpose: Rather than stabilize it, our goal is to reveal, interrogate, and ultimately interrupt white supremacy.

In what follows, we explicate five powerful ways in which the discourse of violence in race talk re-inscribes white supremacy. In focusing on the effects of the discourse, we want to move beyond the interpretation of the "mood" of a given space as safe or unsafe for white people, and instead examine and destabilize white depictions of racial discussions as dangerous and violent exchanges.

BACKGROUND TO THE DATA

The data we draw on are taken from a larger study with university students involving a focused discussion on race and racism. What follows is not a presentation of the study findings. Rather, we have strategically selected excerpts from key moments in the dialogues that demonstrate the effects of the discourse of violence. These discussions were observed by one of the authors (DiAngelo), video- and audiotaped, and transcribed. The study took place at a large research institution in the United States. The study protocols and procedures were reviewed and approved by the researchers' university ethnics review board. Thirteen university students in total (eight white and five of color) responded to a third-party recruitment email call for participation. An interracial team of two facilitators (not including the authors) with extensive training in facilitation of cross-racial discussions led the group through a series of 2-hour sessions meeting once a week for 4 weeks.

At the start of session one, the facilitators Dawn (Biracial: Native American and white) and Emily (white) explain the goals of the four sessions:

> *Emily:* Some of the goals that we came up with, the first one was to provide an opportunity for people to talk in a mixed group about race, which is an opportunity that for a lot of people doesn't come up very often, where you have an environment that is set up for you to talk about race.
>
> *Dawn:* Another one was to have an opportunity to deepen our understanding about how different groups have different experiences. So I guess a simpler way of saying that is, how do our different racial identities play into how we have the conversation . . . does that make sense to most people?
>
> *Emily:* We wanted to provide people an opportunity to practice talking about sensitive issues.
>
> *Dawn:* And then just to notice some patterns that come up when we talk about these issues.

Following the description of the goals, the facilitators overviewed the following two ground rules: to speak for yourself and to seek dialogue rather than debate.

Drawing on the following exchanges, we examine how the discourse of violence accomplishes these effects: positions white people as racially innocent, positions people of color as perpetrators of violence, maintains white solidarity, stabilizes the ideologies of individualism and universalism, and re-inscribes the ideal imagined community. While we map these out as distinct effects, they often work simultaneously and are interlocking.

1. Positions White People as Racially Innocent

One of the central effects of the discourse of violence is its capacity to stabilize historical and current discourses of white racial innocence. For example, white students often position themselves as racially open, unknowing, and willing to learn. These students embody what Dion (2009) has described as a stance of "perfect stranger"; that is, when confronted with the history of colonialism and racism and its effects on racialized people, white people tend to claim racial innocence and take up the role of admirer or moral helper. Dion explains this move in the following way:

> I often begin my work with teachers and teacher candidates asking them to write about and reflect on their relationship with Aboriginal people. Teachers respond with comments that go something like "Oh I know nothing, I have no friends who are Aboriginal, I didn't grow up near a reserve, I didn't learn anything in school, I know very little or I know nothing at all about Native people." One way or another, teachers, like many Canadians, claim the position of "perfect stranger" to Aboriginal people. (p. 330)

The positioning of white people as racially innocent was prominent in the discussions, as illustrated in the following comments. At the opening to session two, participants were asked to share a new awareness of a pattern related to racism. Two of the white students' responses, in particular, illustrate the racial innocence discourse:

> Apparently I'm just pretty darned clueless here, because I haven't—I mean, racism; I don't know. I guess I'm just still out of touch. (Mike)

> How could I possibly know? I don't know; right—or know what the world would look like from another perspective. (Amy)

Mike and Amy's comments are examples of Dion's concept of "perfect stranger." When white people "don't know anything about racism," how could they be held accountable for their investments in and enactments of it? Yet, in reality, rather than "knowing nothing," these students have learned a great deal from dominant narratives that position racialized people in a range of problematic ways. In effect, this stance closes off any examination of their own implication and attachment to racism and colonialism (Dion, 2009).

Challenging white innocence often ignites anger, as illustrated in Amanda's response to Caroline's closing remarks later in that same session, calling for participants to consider how their racial identities inform their responses:

> I'm a little upset. I feel like some people aren't really thinking as deep as they really should and could about some of the comments that they're making and where those comments are coming from when we're talking about social identity. And they're not really thinking about what social identity your comments are coming out of. And so, I'm thinking that maybe that will come out some more as the sessions go on. (Caroline, African American)

> A pattern that I noticed this week is that, every single day this whole week since this past experience, I felt the same degree of anger that I had last week from the experience of being here. (Amanda, white)

hooks (1992) has noted that white people who conceptualize themselves as the least racist often become the most angry when confronted with people of color viewing them as white. She states:

> Often their rage erupts because they believe that all ways of looking that highlight difference subvert the liberal belief in a universal subjectivity that

they think will make racism disappear. They have a deep emotional investment in the myth of "sameness," even as their actions reflect the primacy of
whiteness as a sign informing who they are and how they think. (p. 167)

Perhaps hooks's analysis can help frame the anger and defensiveness that
surfaced when white participants were pressed to racialize their perspectives. In the following statement, Courtney implicitly conveys this anger
through her dismissal of the discussion as a "waste of her time":

> I guess this week I thought about why I didn't really feel like last week was at
> all useful to me and that if anything it was—a waste of my time, just because
> I didn't feel like I gained anything from it, and I just was thinking about why.
> And I realized I've never engaged in conversations about race with a group of
> people for that purpose. (Courtney, white)

Here, Courtney moves between contempt and innocence, claiming that
the discussion was useless to her because it was new to her. Rather than
viewing this new experience as an opportunity to learn, she views it as a
waste of time. She repeats this sentiment in a subsequent session:

> And—but it's [the discussion's]—you know, usefulness—it doesn't matter if
> I think it's useful; I mean, that's not the purpose of this study. But it matters
> to me, because I'm here, and this is my precious time. So, that's where I'm
> coming from. I came in here thinking this would be a useful experience for
> me. (Courtney)

Consider the discursive violence of these claims for the participants of
color, who have shared their experiences with racism—experiences that
presumably Courtney has never heard before. Their voices and perspectives, and the risks they took in offering them, are summarily dismissed;
not only were they useless, but they actually infringed on "precious time."

Similarly, in the following exchange, Amanda (white student) moves
between anger and innocence. During session one, Caroline (African
American student) presses Amanda to view her comments from the lens
of race. However, by session two, a week later, Amanda is still upset.
Amanda begins session two by claiming that the environment is not safe,

and thus she is "pissed off." When challenged by the facilitator, she claims she is being silenced. Finally, she moves into a discourse of "perfect stranger" by offering to "listen with her whole heart" to the experiences of a person of color:

Amanda: It's not fair that—I feel like I have to be on the defense because I feel like, whenever I start speaking, someone cuts me off—mainly the facilitators. . . . So, I've been pissed off ever since last week. And I feel like I can't be honest in this group. I feel like only with one-on-one do I have some sense of safety, like I'm not going to be cut off or I'm not going to be told that I'm a white girl with no sense of anybody else's experience. And so, I'm not going to sit here and defend my race; I can only defend myself. And I'm sorry; I'm—not sorry for being white; that's not something I'm sorry about. But I'm—I don't want to feel so—so shut up in this group. I feel like I cannot say what I feel.

Caroline: That's something I've felt my whole life.

Amanda: I feel completely silenced in here and talking, so—

Emily (white facilitator): Amanda, did you hear Caroline's comment?

Amanda: I did hear her comment, and I'm responding to her comment.

Emily: No. Did you hear the comment that she just made?

Amanda: Yeah; that she felt—has felt that way her whole life. I did hear that.

Dawn (facilitator of color): What does that mean to you?

Amanda: I'm listening.

Dawn: Well, I would just like your opinion on her comment. Like, what do you—what do you think about the fact that maybe you're experiencing something for this period and this conversation that she's been feeling her whole life, and how frustrating it feels for you, obviously, and maybe carry that over to what it feels like for her—it's more difficult when she wants to finally talk about something, other people are shutting down and finding reasons not to say anything and aren't meeting her at the table.

Amanda: Oh, wow. I'd love for you to be able to share from your heart with me for hours and days. And I don't care how long you want to talk; I want to hear. I would love to hear your experience. But in this group I have been feeling tremendously defensive, because I feel like I've been critiqued and not understood. So, I honor your experience, whatever your experience has been. I would love to hear more about it. And I can't take away my race, but I can take away, you know, my defensiveness, potentially. And so, I—I'm sorry that you feel upset. And I'd like to hear more. That's all I have to say.

For Amanda and many of the other white participants, talking about race and racism was an unfamiliar experience. Not only were they pressed to racialize their perspectives, but the facilitators worked to shift the amount of airtime white students took in the discussion space. Even though Amanda's needs and concerns directed much of the agenda and she was the most vocal participant (evidenced by the transcripts), she still felt silenced when her interpretations were contested through counter-narratives.

Whiteness can in part be characterized by a contradictory consciousness in which an insistent innocence is contingent upon involvement in racial oppression (Schick, 2000). The concept of innocence that is embedded in the discourse of violence is not benign; it has material consequences as it allows white people to ignore the impact of racism on people of color while enjoying its benefits at their expense. For Mike, Amy, Courtney, and Amanda, this could be a profound opportunity for self-reflection, and there are many questions that could potentially provide them with greater awareness about their racial socialization. Yet their various claims work to protect and maintain their narrative of racial innocence. For participants such as Amanda, the inability to expand their racial knowledge rests on a claim that the context is not safe enough. Thus, their attention must go to continually monitoring and protecting what they perceive as their racial safety.

2. Positions People of Color as Perpetrators of Violence

The second and corollary effect of the discourse of violence is that while positioning white people as innocent, it simultaneously positions people of color who attempt to insert antiracist discourses into race discussions as perpetrators of violence. For example, Amanda consistently positions the students of color in the discussions as violating her in a range of ways:

> It seems like this has been a study in my development, and I don't like that. And I feel like everything I've said, especially the past session and a half, has been kind of strategically pulled apart, syllable by syllable. I would love to explore all of this more if you have more questions. I don't know how else to—I feel like everything I say is thrown at me as, "Well, you're saying that because you're white," and—Okay. I accept that. And I'm willing to learn and look at it. But in this group it feels like white people are being slammed and blamed and that we have—I as a white person feel like I have to defend myself or just be a punching bag or something. And so, it's totally a repressive environment for me. I don't want to speak more about it, because I already feel upset enough in being here and talking. It's already hard enough. So, I don't want to keep going. (Amanda)

Amanda positions herself as a victim of abuse through the use of provocative terms of physical aggression. When she is challenged by people of color and the facilitators to consider that her responses are informed by a white frame of reference, she counters, "I feel like everything I say is thrown at me as, 'Well, you're saying that because you're white.'" While she claims to be willing to examine her whiteness, she depicts the environment in which she is asked to examine it as "repressive." This repressive environment makes it impossible—even dangerous—for her to carry out this examination. She claims that if she does not defend herself against these challenges, the only possible outcome is to submit to further abuse via serving as a "punching bag." The challenge to consider her white location has become so unbearable that she feels unable to continue in this direction. This language of victimization also enables Amanda to demand that more social resources (such as time and attention) be channeled in her direction to help her cope with this mistreatment (Amanda does not attempt to rise to the challenge and explore the question).

By employing terms that connote physical abuse, Amanda taps into the classic discourse that people of color are inherently dangerous and violent towards white people. This discourse distorts reality and perverts the actual direction of danger that has historically existed between white people and people of color. Mills (1999) argues that the racial state employs two traditional "weapons" of coercion: physical violence and ideological conditioning. Racist images necessary for ideological conditioning and resultant fears can be found at all levels of society, and myriad studies demonstrate that white people believe that people of color (and Blacks in particular) are dangerous (Dyer, 1997; Feagin, 2000; Johnson & Shapiro, 2003; Myers, 2003). These beliefs are fueled by the mass media via relentless representations of people of color associated with criminality. Indeed, much of white flight and the resulting segregation in housing and schooling can be attributed to this representation (Johnson & Shapiro, 2003). Feagin (2000), addressing anti-Black discourse specifically, states that

> For whites, specific antiblack images, prejudices, and stereotypes are part of a broader ideological structure. . . . The persistence of antiblack attitudes, images and emotions over several centuries is much more than a matter of scattered bigots acting on prejudiced notions and feelings; they are the legacy of the material and ideological frameworks of slavery and segregation . . . they are present in many situations of inter-group contact and often get translated into alienated racist relations. (pp. 105–106).

The history of extensive, brutal, and explicit physical violence perpetrated by white people against people of color as well as its ideological rationalizations, are trivialized through white claims of a lack of safety when in the rare situation of merely talking about race with people of color.

3. Maintains White Solidarity

The discourse of violence also has the effect of shoring up white solidarity in and beyond cross-racial discussions. White solidarity can be conceptualized as the tacit agreement of white people to support one another's engagement in the processes that maintain white supremacy. Sleeter (1996) describes this solidarity as white "racial bonding," referring to "interactions in which whites engage that have the purpose of affirming a common stance on race-related issues, legitimating particular interpretations of groups of color, and drawing conspiratorial we–they boundaries" (p. 249). In the discussions, white solidarity manifested through explicit support of other white people's claims of victimization, as well as the implicit consent conveyed through white silence and the absence of social censure.

In the following statement, Courtney explicitly aligns with a fellow white student in negating the request by participants of color and facilitators for white participants to racialize their perspectives by asking them questions such as

> So, can you think about or can you speak to how you feel your social identity as a white person might play into your preference to have a group that's not facilitated by two people or to have a group where you feel like it could kind of go where you want it to go? (Emily, white facilitator)

and

> What would it mean to you, though, if we could set aside the question of usefulness? What would it mean if everything, regardless of temperament, was about race, and you are still uncomfortable with what this group is doing? (Dawn, facilitator of color)

When Amanda's racial position has been challenged, Courtney comes to her defense:

> I don't know; I just feel—yeah, the same thing—you're trying to say something, and . . . it's hard to really explain yourself and really get an understanding between individuals in the group. And I think personally Amanda has really put herself out there. And there were comments made a couple weeks ago about how the white people weren't really saying things and they were holding back. And number one, I think that was a

really stupid comment, because how are you going to know
who's holding back? (Courtney)

Here, Courtney positions herself as having understood Amanda, invoking
white solidarity by supporting the assertion that the problem lies not with
Amanda but with the people of color and those who align with them (such
as Emily). In her explicit support, Courtney positions Amanda as both
brave and vulnerable, having "really put herself out there." Simultaneously,
while Amanda is praised for taking risks, the risks the students of color
take in naming racism and describing its effects in their lives are dismissed.
When a student of color comments on the white withdrawal at various
points in the dialogue, Courtney describes this comment as "stupid."

Further, the transcripts do not capture the affective dimensions of the
dialogue; Courtney's statement is uttered with hostility and sarcasm. The
criticism leveled by these white participants towards the facilitators and
participants of color is high, yet these same participants consistently position themselves as being victimized by the facilitators and participants of
color. Courtney's unabashedly critical evaluation and dismissal indicate a
deeply internalized sense of racial entitlement to indulge in her immediate
reactions without fear of censure or reprisal. White solidarity protects
white people from public penalties resulting from their racial attitudes and
behaviors.

White solidarity also emerged in response to the definition of racism
that the facilitators introduced and posted in the room:

racial prejudice + social power = racism

Dawn explained that this definition is the most widely used by
organizations doing antiracism work and that it is a definition with con-
sensus among academics and community organizers. Following, there is
an exchange that lasts approximately 20 minutes, in which every white
participant in the group raises at least one question. Despite the facilitators' repeated attempts to move the discussion forward, the white participants continue. In the following excerpt, we have removed the facilitators'
detailed responses in order to highlight the range of questions asked by
the white participants:

Jack: Does "prejudice" imply like distaste for, versus just difference from?

Barb: So, how does discrimination fit into that? Does it?

Courtney: I just wondered if what—what was your thinking when you decided to use this definition versus—I mean, what was the purpose of using this definition of racism as opposed to another within the context of this conversation?

Amanda: What does the "plus" mean in this case? In other words, can racism be just racial prejudice or just social power, or does it have to be the combination? And if so, someone with less social power can't be racist then?

Amy: I'm just wondering how we're—what we're saying about social power, then. Like—because you can be—are we saying all white people have social power?

Jessica: Is it the same as—I had heard the whole "race plus power equals racism"? Is that the same thing? Because the racial prejudice threw me off. Is that the same thing?

Mike: I was going to ask about the idea of a racial hierarchy. Does that enter into it? Can a person who's—I mean, let's assume that everybody has power over somebody. Is only the bottom free of that tag of racism, or any—and then every step above that could be racist towards them?

Courtney: Okay. I was just curious how I am supposed to interpret this definition, because many people here are in the elementary [teacher education] program. And when I think about racism in the context of children under the age of 10, no child under the age of 10 has power outside the power of their parents. And because they don't have social power, because they are children, it's—I can look at racism exists in a classroom within a greater social context, but I can't—you know, the active racial prejudice exists among all the kids in my class, and none of them have social power.

Several things stand out about this interrogation. First, it is the only time over the four sessions in which every white student voluntarily participates. The exchange is very rapid and there are no pauses, indicating heightened interest. Although the definition is fairly short and simple, every aspect of it is questioned, including the plus sign. A fair amount of time is spent on the definition, in the face of repeated attempts by the facilitators to move on and explore the implications the definition has for the exercise they have just completed. The main issues appear to be power and the implication that all white people, by virtue of their social position, hold social, historical, and institutional power in relation to all peoples of color; and whose racial knowledge is legitimate. In their questioning, the white participants hold the discussion at the intellectual level, control the intellectual space, enact their positions as the legitimizers of knowledge, and avoid the self-reflection the facilitators want to guide them in. In striking contrast, not one student of color questioned the definition.

While there were exchanges of explicit alignment, white solidarity more often manifested implicitly through the power of silence. Although less visible in the transcripts, these roles were critical to protecting whiteness, for white dominance depends, in part, on the silence of other whites (DiAngelo, 2012; Mura, 1999). White silence served to embolden the actively resistant participants because it implied agreement. Even if white people who were silent found the behavior of their cohorts problematic, their silence allowed these vocal participants to dictate the agenda of virtually every discussion. At the minimum, the resistant participants received no social penalty from other white people, and the silence of their cohorts effectively maintained white solidarity.

4. Stabilizes the Ideologies of Individualism and Universalism

A fourth effect of the discourse of violence is the way it works complicitly with other ideologies that uphold white supremacy. Two of these ideologies are individualism and universalism. In explaining the ideology of individualism, Flax (1998) notes that there is an irreconcilable tension in society. The legitimacy of so-called Western institutions depends upon the idea that all citizens are equal. At the same time, we each occupy distinct raced (and gendered, and classed) positions that profoundly shape our lives in ways that are not random, nor equal. In order to manage this tension, the ideology of individualism posits that we all act independently from one another, that we all have the same possibility of achievement, and that those possibilities are unmarked by social positions such as race, class, and gender (Bonilla-Silva, 2006; DiAngelo, 2010).

White people depend on the ideology of individualism to inscribe their racial innocence and to position themselves as standing outside of hierarchical social relations (Razack, 1998). Amanda demonstrates this in the following claim:

> I feel like, uh, what started out being an interesting introspection and kind of exposition of our feelings and everyone expressing their thoughts has turned into something where I'm feeling judged and misunderstood and, um, angry that everything I say somehow gets twisted around. Um, and maybe that's institutional racism coming up right there, but I just feel like much of what I said has been misunderstood. And I want to—maybe to echo Courtney [white student], who has understood a lot of what I said, because I'm feeling pretty bad right now, just pretty—pretty, um, misunderstood, and I think I just need to go cry about this and think about, you know, my own racism in all this, but, I'm upset. (Amanda)

Amanda begins by restating her expectation that a discussion on race would be an opportunity to share her thoughts. Here she draws on an individualistic rather than an institutional or group framework. Although Amanda makes cursory reference to both her own racism and institutional racism, each time she follows these with a "but," in essence negating the previous point and shifting emphasis to what follows. What follows in both cases is a declaration of personal upset and hurt feelings, which serves to keep the conversation on the individual level and pull the focus and the resources of the group towards her and her needs. By insisting that the problem is that she has been misunderstood, Amanda depoliticizes race and places the responsibility for the "miscommunication" onto those who have misunderstood her—the participants of color. When Amanda is pressed, Courtney comes to her rescue:

> I think it—I think it depends on the individual experience. And since we're all speaking from personal experience, um, I

know that I was—I got a little upset to hear people say that they don't think it's fair that someone would say it's generational, because it's a personal thing if we all know our own families and our own communities and we know what we have perceived in our own families and communities. And so I think it's a valid point—if that's what you want to say, then that's what you should be able to say. I just want to put that out there. (Courtney)

Courtney presents her feelings as "a personal thing," standing alone or outside social processes, rather than as the function of social processes. Her feelings are thus independent of the social, political, or historical context in which she is embedded.

A parallel ideology upheld by the discourse of violence is the ideology of universalism. Dyer (1997) explains universalism as the power to represent the human norm, which is positioned as belonging to white people. As with the ideology of individualism, universalism places white people outside of racialization, a subject position only available to them. Within this ideology, people of color can only represent their own raced perspectives, while white people can speak for all. Mike demonstrated the ideology of universalism in the following exchange with Dawn:

> Mike (white): There's another level, though, that's below that, below the level of groups too, that's human, I think. And I think that it goes beyond that too. I'm sort of a spiritual person, and I—in looking at that—(pauses briefly)—I don't—I've had the realization before that I wasn't an individual. But I guess I don't identify with being part of a group, you know. So, that's probably something I need to look at. But I also think that there are ways to transcend that—or [I don't know if] it's above or below—but to be more in tune with what's human instead of what's only white.
>
> Dawn (facilitator of color): I think that there are a lot of different things that play into how white people encounter and deal with racism. As a person of color, I don't have the luxury of considering how racism works or my race plays into like a spiritual level,

because it's sort of like a survival obstacle course every day. And I don't really have the option to be quiet, you know, and sit back and not speak up or share. And so, I am wondering how you see race playing into the ways that you have just responded to us, in terms of wanting to transcend that and go to a spiritual level and then just thinking about it for the first time. And I'm wondering if you see your race playing into that at all.

Mike: [No audible response]

Dawn: And if not, why not?

Mike: Do I—you're asking do I think the fact that I'm white allows me the luxury of seeing the world in that way?

Emily (white facilitator): [Nods head]

Mike: How could I possibly know? I don't know; right—or know what the world would look like from another perspective.

Emily: What about when she just told you that every day for her is a survival obstacle course?

Mike: Well, I know that that's what it looks like to her, but how can I know what that would look like?

Dawn: Would you have to know what that looked like, though?

Mike: (Pauses) I would have to know more. I would have to know more what you were talking about. I would have to have more information. I—for you to say that without any sort of, I guess, tie to anything that is any more substantial, doesn't give me a whole lot of information.

Caroline (African American): [Nods head] You were talking about how you were a spiritual person, and like, I guess I definitely want to know, in keeping spiritual how does that . . . in terms of how you . . . understand this idea of racism or—I guess it's not clear— so I just wanted to ask you to clarify if you can.

Mike: No. I think I was more referring to how it affects my status as an individual.

Caroline: All right. I guess you said it affects your status as an individual person.

Mike: Because I don't think of myself as separate from everyone else in the world.

Dawn: How is that helpful in terms of dealing with racism right
    now?
Mike: (Long pause) It's not.
Dawn: That's what I was thinking.

Mike's resort to the more abstract discourse of spirituality occurs when
pressed to acknowledge his racial status. With this move he invokes the
discourse of a universal humanity outside of racialized effects, which he
extends to the participants of color, even in the face of hours of discussion
in which they have said that they do not share his experience. Mike's insistence that he does not see the group in raced or powered terms re-inscribes
his racial innocence, while simultaneously positioning people of color as
the ones who perpetrate racial divisions.

5. Re-inscribes the Ideal Imagined Community

Standing behind the effects of individualism (wherein we all have equal
opportunity as citizens devoid of any raced, gendered, or classed group
position) and universalism (wherein we all have equal value as human beings devoid of any raced, gendered, or classed group position) is the ideology of an ideal imagined community.

Anderson (1983/2006) argues that nation, nationality, and national-
ism are notoriously difficult to define despite the fact that they are concepts that organize so much of the modern world. This difficulty of
defining what a nation is and is not (and by extension who does and does
not belong) occurs for at least two reasons: first, nations are inherently
limited in that there are clear boundaries constructed between what constitutes "us" and what we know to be "not-us" as there is a border and
boundary between ours and a different nation; and second, nations are
inherently unlimited in terms of their constituencies (i.e., nations are not
limited to a single "dynastic" or racial group).

Anderson (1983/2006) argues that understanding nations is thus
most centrally a project of understanding how they are imagined into being. This imagined community manifests in all aspects of that nation's narration of itself. Anderson writes:

the nation's biography snatches, against the going mortality rate, exemplary suicides, poignant martyrdoms, assassinations, executions, wars, and holocausts. But, to serve the narrative purpose, these violent deaths must be remembered/forgotten as "our own." (p. 210)

In this way, the narratives of the nation and their capacity to help us remember and forget certain violent events and their sanctioned interpretations are important aspects of building a nation's biography. In the United States, where this dialogue occurred—a white settler colonialist state—we see this narration in official accounts of national events that paradoxically present and then dilute and absorb the stories of non-white, non-settler others. As Anderson argues, the deaths that are revered and that structure the nation's biography (e.g., Harriet Tubman, Crazy Horse, Martin Luther King, Jr.) are of a special kind. The deaths that matter are those that are constructed as creating a biography that erases the very real violence done to millions of anonymous non-white bodies.

In the race discussions, this narration of the ideal imagined community was re-inscribed through the story elements that white participants drew on to describe their communities, neighborhoods, and society: America as the great "melting pot" wherein differences are subsumed; a past of inequality (genocide, slavery, racism) that is long over and should now unite rather than divide "us"; and an Enlightenment view of history as an inevitable march toward ever greater progress and freedom. For example, Courtney, Ruth, and Jessica all talked about the "progress" that had occurred between what was the past (and the "generational" racist ideologies that may have existed then) and the present (in which we have moved beyond, learned more, and come together to "become more inclusive"):

> *Courtney:* But I think—from my experiences with you know, older
> neighbors or people, and there aren't many because I do live in
> [my city] and I have all my life—and often you don't hear a lot of
> white people in [my city], openly, you know, speaking in a way
> that sounds racist or that's openly talking about stereotypes. I've
> been in situations like that, you know, that are usually older, and
> it's generational, if—it's a matter of not being around anyone who

isn't white. White people in [my city] don't hear other white people saying racist things.

Ruth: I see it personally in my family as being a generational thing, but I think it is also exposure to a multicultural atmosphere that changes the generations. So although I see it changing in my family as my family is exposed to more multiculturalism around the community, um, it's also—it's generational for each family in a different format. But I think it is—there is generational change, but it's also about community and exposure to those things.

Jessica: I do. I think it's generational. I think every generation isn't as educated, but if they can have this open dialogue that we can have right now—I think this is a foreign discussion to them. I think there is hope, and I think you just have to help educate them little by little. I mean, you don't want to attack them. I think they'll probably see it as confrontational and not want to listen to you. But I think that they would be curious. I think that they feel kind of left out when it comes to pop culture and current issues that are going on with becoming more, you know, inclusive.

In fact, whenever the facilitators attempted to move the discussion away from discourses that align with the national story, and press participants to conceptualize group relations from a framework of unequal structural power, the white participants argued that the facilitators were dividing this imagined community. Thus, the counter-narratives of facilitators and the participants of color were challenging not only the group's work but also critical elements in the fabric of "America's" story.

Jessica's worry that the older [racist white] generation be educated "little by little" and her caution not to "attack them" are also noteworthy. In her narrative, she imbues this older and allegedly more racist generation with a childlike innocence. Their presumed lack of awareness of progressive new racial ideas results in a corresponding need to go slowly when speaking with them about race. Granting their receptivity the benefit of the doubt, she assumes that they will be curious—provided that they are treated kindly and not confronted. In these ways, white racial innocence, the potential dangers of race discussions, and the nation's narrative of ever-forward marching racial progress are simultaneously re-inscribed.

In the following exchange, when Mike is pressed to consider the effect of his spirituality narrative, we can see how Mike organizes this imagined community in line with mainstream national narratives about America as racially united:

Dawn (facilitator of color): Emily and I, in reflecting on the group last week and what we talked about, something we noticed was that there was a lot of energy that was kind of expended when we introduced the idea or definition of racism. And so, we wanted to bring this back to the group and ask people if they had noticed anything about which group it was that seemed to be spending all of its energy around the definition of racism. So, when we put the definition up there last week, people were like—oh, whoa, what's going on? And it seemed to be—the people that responded were . . .

Barb (white): Were white.

Dawn: Exactly. And so, we were wondering if you guys had picked up on that. And what does the group make of that, or what do people think about that? And why do you think maybe people of color weren't responding? Or people of color can speak for themselves.

Mike (white): I think I responded to it because I found it—I found the idea of it to be divisive to us as a group, and I—I preferred . . .

Dawn: "Divisive" meaning like . . .

Mike: That it was dividing us. That it would divide us into those with power and those without. And I would prefer not to go—you know, I would prefer to remain as a whole group.

Dawn: What would it mean, though, that, if that definition is true and if it did do that? What would that mean to you?

Mike: Well, if it comes down—well, if it comes down—it would mean that half the group were racist, and half were not, by definition. Well, the people with power would be racist, and the people without power would not. I didn't want that line to be drawn, I guess.

Laura (Asian American): So, what—I'm just not—I'm not understanding how we could have a conversation about racism that wouldn't be—I . . .

Mike: That wouldn't be divisive?

Laura: Yeah. I mean, because—I guess I'm not quite clear on . . . [trails off]

Dawn: Well, one question I would have is: Do you think that that line was there before the definition went up, or the definition created that line?

Mike: There were—the definition created that line in the discussion.

Dawn: For you it did?

Mike: Yeah.

Emily (white facilitator): Are there other people that want to respond to that, that already you are seen as someone who has power?

Mike: But—okay; I can accept that. But I guess my expectation of the group is that it sort of operated as a—as a whole, not as two parts; that it was sort of working towards a similar end, instead of at cross purposes. I don't not accept it. And I have heard it before. But I don't know; I guess I was less—I don't want to say "comfortable," but less happy hearing—having that be the discussion.

Dawn: Why?

Mike: I guess because of—because of, like I say, because it's a divisive nature; it creates an "us" and a "them."

The problem for Mike is not the existence of power itself, but its recognition. His main concern is that naming power breaks a unity that he assumes is shared—even though this assumption is contrary to the repeated claims of participants of color. He thus erases (and denies) alternate racial experiences and locations. These alternative perspectives put them at "cross purposes"; presumably his purpose is to maintain an imagined unity while theirs is to divide it. Although Dawn tells him that she sees the power difference and that, in fact, for her and the people of color present, it is not naming power that divides the group, Mike continues to maintain his claim.

A final way that the story of nation circulated was in narratives about a "shared purpose." At multiple points in the discussion, the facilitators were explicit about the purpose of the discussion, and had also articulated it at the start of the study. However, a number of white participants continually raised questions about purpose. In response, at the start of session three the facilitators rearticulated the goals by reading directly from the consent form, which stated, "This research will provide valuable information about how white student teachers engage in racial dialogue. This information is intended to help design multicultural education courses that are more effective in preparing white teachers to teach students from racial groups different from their own. You may benefit from taking part in this study by gaining increased understanding of a range of viewpoints on race."

Yet during session three some white participants were still raising questions about the discussion's purpose with claims that it ought to "bring people together" and "work towards a similar end":

> *Matthew:* But—okay; I can accept that. But I guess my expectation of the group is that it sort of operated as a—as a whole, not as two parts; that it was sort of working towards a similar end, instead of at cross purposes.
>
> *Amanda:* What is the purpose of the racial dialogue? You know, ultimately, what are we trying to reveal or prove or pursue? And what is my role as a white person in this world? I would like for anyone to give me some clarity about how to proceed—people of color—how white people—I want to know what the purpose of this group is, because I feel like it's really evolved from what I understood to be the purpose, of how to teach and bring people together and understanding more about race issues or whatever. But it feels like it's becoming a strange debate that isn't productive, instead, it's a divisive forum; it's not unifying. So, I want to know what as a collective is our purpose here?

While several white students expressed confusion over the purpose of the discussion, to participants of color the purpose was clear. Later in the same session, Marie attempted to connect white concerns about the group's purpose to group-level racial location. She did so by positioning herself specifically as a person of color in her response:

> Clearly somebody gets to choose who gets to be on what scale on the hierarchy. And it's those who get to choose that are

teaching our kids. Those that get to choose are going to teach my kids. There really are very, very few teachers that are minorities. They're not teaching our kids. And I think that's what the whole purpose of this is, is white people teach our kids, and what are they teaching them? What do they recognize about themselves before they go into the classroom and try and teach these kids that they don't know anything about. They've never lived in their shoes; they have no idea what they think about every day, you know. That's the point of this. (Marie, Native American)

Laura also addresses the question of purpose, from her position as a person of color. She refers to white assertions that the group isn't talking about anything "real" or "useful," and that the dialogue is not a positive experience for them:

I'm kind of just struck by a couple things. One is the whole idea of like what—for some of the white people, what would be a positive experience that would come out of this or what—since I've heard the phrases like "what's real and tangible"; "what's really useful." Because I feel like this is real and tangible. I mean, the dynamics are real and tangible, and this is a microcosm of everything that goes on out there. So, it's not like we're looking at it in a vacuum. It's everything about this conversation. I'm curious about something that Courtney said about a negative versus a positive experience. And I'm curious to know for a white person what would be a positive experience of talking about racism, what would that look like? I do think we're getting diverted into talking about all this stuff when—when the conversation itself is what's real. (Laura, Asian American)

When Laura asks the white participants how they might define a "positive experience" in a dialogue about different racial perspectives, the white participants are not able to articulate a response to her question. The more nuanced and complex analysis offered by participants of color was characterized by white people at various times in the discussion as both "academic" and "hypersensitive." This analysis placed the white participants in the rare situation of being on unfamiliar racial ground. This ground is "dangerous" as it violates the imagined story of an America in which "we are all united." Further, white students' claims of division are somewhat ironic, given that they all acknowledged that they have grown up, gone to school, and currently live in contexts of racial separation. It appears that it is the naming of racial separation that is problematic, not the actual lived separation itself. Thus, the ideal imagined community can (and does) exclude people of color, as long as that exclusion remains unnamed.

Notably, the participants of color never questioned the group's purpose. They saw value in the difficult process and articulated a deep investment in the task, despite inevitable discomfort. In fact, the participants of color stated that they view racial comfort, particularly white racial comfort, as problematic, for it indicates maintenance of the status quo. Because they are expecting discomfort, and perhaps even hoping for it as a sign of movement, they do not express dissonance between their previous expectations and what is happening in the sessions.

CONCLUSION

> Anger, hostility, frustration, and pain are characteristics that are not to be avoided under the banner of safety. . . . They are attributes that are to be recognized on the part of both whites and people of color in order to engage in a process that is creative enough to establish new forms of social existence, where both parties are transformed.
>
> —Leonardo & Porter, 2010, p. 149

The white participants in this study have positioned themselves as victimized, slammed, blamed, having their words "strategically pulled apart" and their "precious time wasted," misunderstood, silenced, repressed, and under threat for use as a "punching bag." They are responding to the mere articulation of counter-narratives; nothing physically out of the ordinary occurs in the sessions. These self-defense claims work to position the speakers as both vulnerable and superior, while obscuring the true power of their racial locations. The discourse of violence simultaneously obscures micro and macro levels of racism and positions members of social groups who name racism as irrational, scary, and dangerous.

While the comments shared here express anger, hostility, frustration, and pain, these are not the forms of expression that Leonardo and Porter (2010) describe as transformative in race discussions. Rather, the expressions documented here functioned to prevent the transformative forms of hostility, frustration, or pain that might have unsettled the white supremacy circulating in these discussions. The exchanges reproduced in this chapter indicate that it is personal and ideological comfort that is at stake, not safety.

If it is the case that safety and guidelines for establishing safe classroom space for discussions about race and racism are false (or at least ineffective) strategies, then what might more productive contexts for these discussions look like? The analysis we offer in this chapter lends support to the questions raised by some scholars about whether antiracism education that does not perpetuate discursive violence towards students of color can occur in cross-racial settings (cf. Chinnery, 2008; Crozier & Davies, 2008; Jones, 1999, 2001; Leonardo & Porter, 2010). Their argument is that such spaces ultimately foreground the needs of white students and position students of color as "native informants and unpaid sherpas" (Thompson, 2004), guiding white students into a racial awakening. Leonardo and Porter go further and argue that the conditions of "safety" are meant to maintain white comfort and thus are a symbolic form of violence experienced by people of color. That is, it is students of color who are metaphorically "slammed" in these conversations, intensifying the real violence—physical, as well as structural and discursive—that they already bear in society at large.

Ironically, Amanda's description of this temporary and exceptional experience for her in this discussion fairly well describes daily dimensions of this violence for students of color (Crozier & Davies, 2008). We return to an earlier quote from Amanda and replace the term "white" with "person of color" to capture very familiar dynamics often described by students of color:

> I feel like everything I've said, has been strategically pulled apart, syllable by syllable. I feel like everything I say is thrown at me as, "Well, you're saying that because you're [a person of color]" . . . in this group it feels like [people of color] are being slammed and blamed and that . . . I have to defend myself or just be a punching bag or something . . . it's totally a repressive environment for me. I already feel upset enough in being here and talking. It's already hard enough. So, I don't want to keep going.

The historical and socio-political context these participants are situated in, both inside and outside the discussion, is not neutral; it consistently does violence to people of color, discursively, physically, and structurally. For participants of color, this is likely one of the few environments in which they can feel somewhat protected, given their numbers and the support of the facilitators. Still, in surfacing white umbrage and defensiveness, cross-racial discussions actually increase the degree of discursive violence meted out to them. In her work, antiracist educator Darlene Flynn regularly encounters the demand that discussions on race be made safe for white people. She exposes this discourse as a manifestation of white privilege when she replies, "You mean you usually feel safe racially? That must be a great feeling. It's not something people of color can take for granted or expect, much less demand."

While the *feelings* may be real for white people struggling with a sense of safety, it may be useful to consider what safety means from a position of social, cultural, historical, and institutional power. If one does not fear actual physical harm, then some reflection on what one does fear can be a rich avenue of self-knowledge and social insight.

REFERENCES

Adams, M., Bell, L., & Griffin, P. (1997). *Teaching for diversity and social justice. A sourcebook*. Routledge.

Anderson, B. (2006). *Imagined communities*. Verso. (Original work published 1983)

Applebaum, B. (2008). "Doesn't my experience count?" White students, the authority of experience and social justice pedagogy. *Race Ethnicity and Education, 11*(4), 405–414.

Boler, M. (Ed.). (2004). *Democratic dialogue in education: Troubling speech, disturbing silence.* Peter Lang.

Bonilla-Silva, E. (2006). *Racism without racist: Color-blind racism and the persistence of racial inequality in the United States* (2nd ed.). Rowman & Littlefield.

Chinnery, A. (2008). Revisiting "The Master's Tools": Challenging common sense in cross-cultural teacher education. *Equity & Excellence in Education, 41*(4), 395–404.

Crozier, G., & Davies, J. (2008). "The trouble is they don't mix": Self-segregation or enforced exclusion? *Race Ethnicity and Education, 11*(3), 285–301.

DiAngelo, R. (2010). Why can't we all just be individuals? The discourse of individualism in anti-racist education. *InterActions: UCLA Journal of Education and Information Studies, 6*(1), article 4.

DiAngelo, R. (2011). White fragility. *International Journal of Critical Pedagogy, 3*(3), 54–70.

DiAngelo, R. (2012). Nothing to add: The role of white silence in racial discussions. *Journal of Understanding and Dismantling Privilege, 2*(2), 1–17.

DiAngelo, R., & Allen, D. (2006). "My feelings are not about you": Personal experience as a move of whiteness. *InterActions: UCLA Journal of Education and Information Studies, 2*(2). http://escholarship.org/uc/search?keyword =DiAngelo,1/5/12

DiAngelo, R., & Sensoy, Ö. (2009). "We don't want your opinion": Knowledge construction and the discourse of opinion in the equity classroom. *Equity & Excellence in Education, 42*(4), 443–455.

Dion, S. (2009). *Braiding histories: Learning from Aboriginal peoples' experiences and perspectives.* UBC Press.

Dyer, R. (1997). *White.* Routledge.

Ellsworth, E. (1989). Why doesn't this feel empowering? Working through the repressive myths of critical pedagogy. *Harvard Educational Review, 59*(3), 297–325.

Feagin, J. (2000). *Racist America: Roots, current realities, and future reparations.* Routledge.

Flax, J. (1998). *American dream in Black and white: The Clarence Thomas hearings.* Cornell University Press.

hooks, b. (1992). *Black looks: Race and representation.* South End Press.

Johnson, H. B., & Shapiro, T. M. (2003). Good neighborhoods, good schools: Race and the "good choices" of white families. In A. Doane & E. Bonilla-Silva (Eds.), *White out: The continuing significance of racism* (pp. 173–187). Routledge.

Jones, A. (1999). The limits of cross-cultural dialogue: Pedagogy, desire, and absolution in the classroom. *Educational Theory, 49*(3), 299–316.

Jones, A. (2001). Cross-cultural pedagogy and the passion for ignorance. *Feminism & Psychology, 11*(3), 279–292.

Leonardo, Z., & Porter, R. (2010). Pedagogy of fear: Toward a Fanonian theory of 'safety' in race dialogue. *Race Ethnicity and Education, 13*(2), 139–157.

Levine-Rasky, C. (2000). The practice of whiteness among teacher candidates. *International Studies in Sociology of Education, 10*, 263–284.

Marty, D. (1999). White antiracist rhetoric as apologia: Wendell Berry's *The Hidden Wound*. In T. Nakayama & J. Martin (Eds.), *Whiteness: The communication of social identity* (pp. 51–68). Sage.

Matsuda, M., Lawrence, C., Delgado, R., & Crenshaw, K. (1993). *Words that wound: Critical race theory, assaultive speech, and the First Amendment*. Westview Press.

McIntyre, A. (1997). Constructing the image of a white teacher. *Teachers College Record, 98*(4), 653–681.

Mills, C. (1999). *The racial contract*. Cornell University Press.

Mitchell, T., & Donahue, D. (2009). "I do more service in this class than I ever do at my site": Paying attention to the reflections of students of color in service-learning. In J. R. Strait & M. Lima (Eds.), *The future of service-learning: New solutions for sustaining and improving practice* (pp. 174–192). Stylus.

Mura, D. (1999). Racism explained to my daughter. In B. Jelloun Tahur (Ed.), *Racism explained to my daughter* (pp. 90–137). New Press.

Myers, K. (2003). White fright: Reproducing white supremacy through casual discourse. In A. W. Doane & E. Bonilla-Silva (Eds.), *White out: The continuing significance of racism* (pp. 129–144). Routledge.

Picower, B. (2009). The unexamined whiteness of teaching: How white teachers maintain and enact dominant racial ideologies. *Race Ethnicity and Education, 12*(2), 197–215.

Razack, S. (1998). *Looking white people in the eye: Gender, race, and culture in courtrooms and classrooms*. University of Toronto Press.

Schick, C. (2000). "By virtue of being white": Resistance in anti-racist pedagogy. *Race Ethnicity and Education, 3*(1), 83–102.

Sleeter, C. E. (1996). White silence, white solidarity. In N. Ignatiev & J. Garvey (Eds.), *Race traitors* (pp. 257–265). Routledge.

Tatum, B. D. (1992). Talking about race, learning about racism: The application of racial identity development theory in the classroom. *Harvard Educational Review*, 62(1), 1–25.

Thompson, A. (2004). Anti-racist work zones. In K. Alston (Ed.), *Philosophy of education yearbook 2003* (pp. 387–395). Philosophy of Education Society.

Van Dijk, T. A. (1992). Discourse and the denial of racism. *Discourse and Society*, 3(1), 87–118.

Winans, A. E. (2005). Local pedagogics and race. Interrogating white safety in the rural college classroom. *College English*, 67(3), 253–273.

FIVE

Nothing to Add

A Challenge to White Silence in Racial Discussions

> As unconscious, habits of white privilege do not merely go unnoticed. They actively thwart the process of conscious reflection on them, which allows them to seem non-existent even as they continue to function.
>
> —Sullivan, 2006, pp. 5–6

As a white person involved in national antiracist education in the United States for the last 15 years, I have had the unique opportunity to observe, across time and place, consistent patterns of white engagement in discussions about race. Although, like most white people, I have been socialized to avoid explicit racial discussions, years of intentional commitment and practice have enabled me to continually challenge this socialization. On a daily basis, I lead or participate in racial discussions, working with both primarily white groups and cross-race groups—sometimes alone and sometimes with a co-facilitator of color. My position leading these discussions allows me a kind of concentrated exposure to the discourses and practices taken up in racial dialogues that function to support white domination and privilege ("whiteness"). Although these discourses and practices have been well documented by others (see Bonilla-Silva, 2006; Picca & Feagin, 2007; Pollock, 2004; Trepagnier, 2006), I focus on the

Originally published as "Nothing to Add: A Challenge to White Silence in Racial Discussions." *Journal of Understanding and Dismantling Privilege*, 2(1). Retrieved from https://www.wpcjournal.com/article/view /10100. Reprinted with permission.

group dynamics involved in the production of whiteness in "real time": the unspoken, unmarked norms and behavioral patterns that bolster the advantageous social position of white people at the expense of people of color.

In cross-racial discussions it is easy to be distracted by white participants who dominate; indeed, facilitators spend a lot of energy strategizing about how to rein in these participants. For example, in the educational film *The Color of Fear*, in which a racially diverse group of men discuss racism, the white man who continually dominates the discussion and invalidates the men of color receives the greatest amount of attention in every discussion of the film I have attended. Yet there is another white man in the film who is at the other end of the participation spectrum, one who rarely speaks and has to be asked directly to join in. This participant receives little if any attention following the film, but his role in the discussion is no less racially salient. In this chapter, I want to direct our attention to this often-neglected end of the participation continuum—white silence—and provide an analysis of and challenge to that silence. Using whiteness theory as the frame, I will explicate the various ways that white silence functions in discussions of race to maintain white privilege, and challenge common white rationales for this silence. These rationales include "It's just my personality—I rarely talk in groups"; "Everyone has already said what I was thinking"; "I don't know much about race so I will just listen"; "I don't feel safe / don't want to be attacked so I am staying quiet"; "I am trying to be careful not to dominate the discussion"; "I don't want to be misunderstood / say the wrong thing / offend anybody"; and "I don't have anything to add." In so doing, I hope to provide an accessible challenge to silence for white participants in these discussions, regardless of the context in which it may occur—in the classroom, workplace, workshops, or professional developments. My goal is to unsettle the complacency that often surrounds this silence and motivate silent white people to break their silence.

Within the current racial construct, white racial comfort and sense of racial equilibrium are rooted in norms and traditions that uphold relations of inequality; one of these norms is to avoid talking openly about race, especially in mixed-race groups. When white normative taboos against talking directly about race are broken, especially within the context of deliberately challenging the norms that hold racial inequality in place, it is uncomfortable and destabilizing for many white people, and they will seek to regain their comfort and sense of racial stability (DiAngelo, 2006a). Therefore, whatever moves white people make in a racial discussion that are intended to regain or maintain racial comfort or the racial equilibrium that has been interrupted by the discussion itself, necessarily work to maintain traditional racial relations. In this context, when white people employ silence to maintain some degree of comfort, that silence functions (albeit seldom explicitly) as a means to regain white dominance.

Race is a dynamic and ongoing production; there is no race-neutral space. As Dyer (1997) states, race is "never not a factor, never not in play" (p. 1). Focusing on specific incidences of racism rather than on racism as an all-encompassing system makes a personal, interpersonal, cultural, historical, and structural analysis difficult (Macedo & Bartolome, 1999). Using a relational and systematic definition of whiteness and racism allows white people to explore their own relationship to racism and move beyond isolated incidences and/or intentions.

In the following section, I focus on one key way that whiteness is reproduced within the context of antiracist education: white silence. I discuss common white rationales for white silence in discussions of race, and challenge these rationales from an antiracist framework. I acknowledge that silence can, of course, be a constructive mode of white engagement in racial discussions, by differentiating between the temporary and contextual silence that results from active listening, and silence as the primary or only mode of engagement.

OVERALL EFFECTS OF WHITE SILENCE

In racial dialogue, white silence functions overall to shelter white participants by keeping their racial perspectives hidden and thus protected from exploration or challenge. Not contributing one's perspectives serves to ensure that those perspectives cannot be expanded. While one can of course gain deeper understanding through listening, there are several problems with this being one's primary mode of engagement. Listening alone leaves everyone else to carry the weight of the discussion. And, of course, if everyone chose this mode, no discussion (and hence no learning) would occur at all. On the other hand, one may have something to say that is insightful and contributes to everyone's learning, but if a lack of confidence can't be overcome, everyone loses.

The role of silent white people is critical to protecting whiteness, for white dominance depends, in part, on the silence of other white people (Mura, 1999; Picca & Feagin, 2007). In the context of particularly difficult discussions, white silence serves to embolden explicitly resistant participants because it establishes that no challenge will be forthcoming, and can even imply agreement. Even if white people who are silent find the behavior of their peers problematic, their silence allows vocally resistant participants to continually dictate the agenda of the discussion and rally resources around themselves, as facilitators (and others) work to move them forward. At the minimum, the resistant participants receive no social penalty from other white people, and the silence effectively maintains white solidarity. Although silent white people might recognize and be troubled by the behavior of some of their white cohorts, they ultimately maintain their white privilege by not contesting this behavior. An internal awareness of whiteness is a necessary start, but if it isn't accompanied by a change in behavior, alliance with whiteness remains intact.

Silence has different effects depending on what move it follows. For example, if white silence follows a story shared by a person of color about the impact of racism on their lives, that silence serves to invalidate the story. People of color who take the social risk of revealing the impact of racism only to be met by white silence are left with their vulnerability unreciprocated. White people could offer validation, for example, by sharing how the story impacted them, what insight they gained from hearing it, or what questions it raised for them. Conversely, when white silence follows a particularly problematic move made by a white participant, that silence supports the move by offering no interruption; in essence, white silence operates as a normative mechanism for these tactics. When white silence follows a white antiracist stand (such as challenging one's fellow whites to racialize their perspectives), it serves to isolate the person who took that stand. This isolation is a powerful social penalty and an enticement to return to the comfort of white solidarity. In this context, white silence denies the support that is critical to other white people working to develop antiracist practice.

WHEN IS WHITE SILENCE A CONSTRUCTIVE MOVE IN RACIAL DIALOGUE?

White silence, when used strategically from an antiracist framework, can be a constructive move in racial discussions. Indeed, too much white participation simply reinscribes the white dominance and centrality embedded in the larger society. I am arguing that white silence based on the rationale I will discuss in this chapter is not a constructive move. I am also arguing against white silence as one's default mode of engagement. What differentiates constructive use of white silence from a reinforcement of white racism is that the person is using their best judgment, based in an antiracist framework and at each phase of the discussion, of how to engage with the goal of deepening racial self-knowledge, building antiracist community, and interrupting traditional racist power relations. No one way for white people to engage is likely to be effective in all contexts, but antiracist white engagement asks that one continually grapple with the question of how best to interrupt white power and privilege. The following are generally good times for white people to just listen when in interracial groups:

- When people of color are discussing the sensitive issue of internalized racial oppression
- When one tends to take up a lot of airspace and, in recognition of the history of white dominance, is trying to pull back and have a less dominant voice
- When other white people have already spoken first and most to an issue in the discussion
- When intentionally trying not to speak first and most in the discussion
- When a person of color has spoken and we feel drawn to re-explain, clarify, or "add to" their point (and thereby "say it better" and have the last word on the matter)
- When a facilitator asks for white people to just listen, hold back, or not go first

The above list addresses silence in the context of racially mixed groups. In all-white settings, the dynamics are different because white people are not navigating their relationships to people of color in the group. In the context of all-white groups, white silence functions to pass up the opportunity to explore one's racial perspectives, feelings, blind spots, and assumptions without fear of causing microaggressions to people of color. To not take advantage of a structured discussion in an all-white group prevents community building and antiracist alignment among white people, and fails to support those who are actively taking risks and being vulnerable in the pursuit of antiracist growth. In this context, the main reason for white silence should be for periods of personal reflection, to provide time and space for other more reticent white people who need a slower pacing to speak up, and because the person is someone who tends to speak often. These forms of silence can more authentically be seen as active listening.

RATIONALES FOR WHITE SILENCE AND AN ANTI-RACIST CHALLENGE

"It's just my personality; I rarely talk in groups."

Our personalities are not separate from the society in which we were raised. All white people are socialized in a white-dominant society. Seeing one's patterns of engagement as merely a function of a unique personality rather than as sociopolitical and co-produced in relation with social others is a privilege only afforded to white people (McIntosh, 1988). By focusing on ourselves as individuals, white people are able to conceptualize the patterns in our behavior that have a racist impact as "just our personality" and not connected to intergroup dynamics. For example, I might be an extrovert and talk over people when I am engaged in a discussion. I can say, "That is just my personality, I do that to everyone. That is how we talked at the dinner table in my family. And because I do it to everyone, it can't be racism." However, when I talk over a person of color, the impact of that behavior is different because we bring the racial history of our groups with us (DiAngelo, 2006b). While white people tend to see themselves as individuals, people of color tend to see us as white individuals, thus the meaning of cutting off or talking over a person of color is very different. Conversely, remaining silent in an interracial dialogue also has a cross-racial impact. Antiracist action requires us to challenge our patterns and respond differently than we normally would (Thompson, 2001). The freedom to remain oblivious to that fact, with no sense that this oblivious-ness has any consequences of importance, is a form of white privilege. In effect, we are saying, "I will not adapt to you or this context, I will continue to act the way I always act and you will have to adapt to me." Participants of color seldom see themselves as having the option to disengage or with-draw from the discussion based solely on their personal preferences for engagement (DiAngelo, 2010). They understand that dominant culture does not position them as individuals and has a different set of stereotypical expectations for them. If they hold back, they reinforce these expectations, a concern that puts constant pressure on them. Two people of color in a recent cross-racial discussion express these expectations:

> *Rich (POC):* Well, in terms of putting ourselves out there, I think I put myself out there too. But if I was to come into this group and not put myself out there, everybody would look at me kind of strange, because I'm a person of color. So, oh, my god, this person of color is not putting himself out there. What's up with that? This is a dialogue about race; you're supposed to put yourself out there. So, I mean, Tiffany has put herself out there, but I don't know how much Tiffany should be commended—well, I guess she should be commended in the sense that she is like probably the only white person that put herself out there. But I think every-body should be putting themselves out there.
>
> *Laura (POC):* I feel frustrated by the fact that white people can just choose to disengage, where I'm supposed to say something, and like if I don't say something, then I'm the quiet Asian one or something like that. And so, I feel like I need to put myself out there even more just to contradict that. And that gets really tiring to me . . . to constantly feel like I have to display something, when—even if I don't feel like saying anything; I might want to step back, but I'm conscious all the time of what that looks like to people.

As these two participants make clear, the pressure of being seen as people of color compels them to speak up, even when they don't want to. Not speaking up because one doesn't want to—without penalty—is a privilege they are not afforded; if they remain silent they don't challenge the racism that constricts their lives. Their comments also illustrate the difference in the way white people and people of color often conceptualize themselves. White people tend to see themselves as unique individuals and not members of a racial group whose actions represent that group. People of color, who don't have that luxury, want white people to meet them halfway—to understand white patterns at the group level and push through the temporary discomfort of not engaging in their "preferred" mode in order to challenge those patterns. Challenging whiteness requires, as Rich expresses above, "putting ourselves out there" and engaging differently in order to break problematic racial dynamics.

"Everyone has already said what I was thinking" or "I don't have much to add."

Perhaps others have expressed our sentiments, but no one will express them the way that we will. It's essential to the discussion to hear everyone's voice, and even vocalizing one or two sentences makes a difference. Further, it is important to support those who have voiced our perspective—to validate it and give people of color a read of the room; they cannot assume everyone has already said what we are thinking. In fact, given the history of harm between white people and people of color, people of color may assume white people haven't spoken because they are not aligned with what has been said and don't want to reveal that misalignment. It is important for us to contribute our thoughts in order to demonstrate to people of color that what they have shared has made a difference in terms of helping increase our understanding. If we are moved or gained insight from what someone shared, we should say so, even if others have also said it.

Sometimes the reticence to speak is based on a perception that those who have expressed similar thoughts are far more articulate, and that we won't be as eloquent. In my experience, openness, humility, and vulnerability are the most important aspects of participation, not perfection. Positioning ourselves as having less of value to contribute than others in the group may be rooted in dominant culture's expectation that knowledge should be a form of "correct" information. Yet sharing what we are thinking, whether "right" or "wrong," articulate or clumsy, is important in terms of building trust, conveying empathy, or validating a story or perspective.

"I am trying to be careful not to dominate the discussion."

While it is important not to dominate discussions in general and, as a white person, not to dominate an interracial discussion in particular, the problem with this strategy is that it is inflexible. Antiracist practice asks us to think strategically—to be racially attentive to who is talking, when, how much, and for how long. As a white person in the discussion, we need to ask ourselves when it is a constructive time to speak up, and when is it most constructive to just listen. The more practiced we become in racial discussions, the more easily we will be able to make sound strategic judgments about where and when to enter. When we remain silent we leave the weight of the dialogue on either people of color or other, more dominant white people. If these dominant whites are expressing hostility, we aren't challenging them; if they are taking risks, we aren't supporting them. When one is trying not to dominate the discussion and so never joins in, one errs on the opposite side of domination—ineffective passivity.

"I feel intimidated by people in this group who have power over me."

Complex socio-political power relations circulate in all groups, and there are other identities besides race at play in any discussion. While one is in a power position as a white person, there are other identities that may obscure that sense of that power because they position us in a subordinated (or "target") position—that is, gender or class. Because we "swim against the current" in our target identities, they are generally more salient to us. However, not being salient does not mean inoperative; indeed, much of the power we derive from our dominant identities is in its unremarkable, taken-for-granted status. In a setting in which I feel intimidated because my target identities are more salient to me, this feeling of intimidation may indeed be coming from a place of internalized inferiority, but in practice my silence colludes with racism and ultimately benefits me by protecting my white privilege and maintaining racial solidarity with other white people. This solidarity connects and realigns me with white people across other lines of difference that separate us, such as gender or class. When I work to keep my race privilege salient and speak up in this context, I not only break white solidarity, I simultaneously interrupt (and thus work to heal the "lie" of) my internalized inferiority where I am also in a target position.

In situations in which we may share key identities such as race and gender with someone but fear there may be repercussions because they hold more power in the specific context than we do—that is, I am a staff worker and my supervisor is in the room, or the professor who is grading me is in the group—a different kind of courage is needed. This is the courage to put our integrity to do the right thing above the possibility of repercussions. Ultimately, we have to make a decision. Do I protect myself and maintain white solidarity and power, or do I authentically engage in antiracist practice?

"I don't know much about race so I will just listen."

Dyer (1997) states that "There is a specificity to white representations, but it does not reside in a set of stereotypes so much as in narrative structural positions, rhetorical tropes and habits of perception" (p. 12). One of these narrative structural positions is that of racial innocence. This position functions as a kind of blindness: an inability to think about whiteness as an identity or as a "state" of being that would or could have an impact on one's life and thus be a source of meaning. Because white people are socially positioned as individuals, or "just people" (the writer, the man, the friend), while people of color are always positioned as members of a racial group (the Latino writer, the Asian man, the Black friend), we have the privilege of seeing ourselves as outside of race and thus unfamiliar with it (DiAngelo, 2004).

The white claim that one does not know much about race is particularly problematic because, while it positions whiteness as "innocence," it simultaneously reinforces the projection of race onto people of color— they have race, not us, and thus are the holders of racial knowledge. In so doing, we position ourselves as standing outside of hierarchical social relations—as if the oppression of people of color occurs in a vacuum. White obliviousness is not benign; it has material consequences because it allows us to ignore the impact of racism on people of color while enjoying its benefits at their expense.

Many white people have not thought about race in the way that antiracist education conceptualizes it, but once we are introduced, it's important to share our thoughts. If I have never thought about these issues before, what am I thinking about them now as a result of the discussion? What specifically is new to me? What questions do I have? What insights am I having? What emotions am I feeling? Why might I have never thought about these things before, and what role might this play in keeping racism in place? In other words, how might racism depend on white people not thinking about these issues? Being new to the concepts is not an end point or a pass to only listen and not speak; it is a key entry point into the discussion and into furthering self-knowledge.

While as white people we may have not thought explicitly about race from an antiracist perspective, we do have knowledge of how we are socialized into denial of ourselves as racialized. We can speak to why we believe we don't know anything about race—for example, if we don't know much about it, who do we believe does and why do they have this knowledge when we do not? Further, why have we not sought out this knowledge prior to this conversation? Many white people who grew up in segregated neighborhoods and attended segregated schools with primarily white teachers often believe that they were completely unaware of race until later in childhood. I have found a series of reflection questions helpful in unpacking this belief: At what age was I aware that people of color existed, and Black people in particular (most white people acknowledge that they knew by age 5, if not earlier)? What was I told about them? Where did they live? Why did they live there and not in my neighborhood? What was it like where they lived? Was it considered nice, and was I encouraged to go to the places where they lived? Was I taught that I had lost anything by their absence? If I was not taught I had lost anything by not knowing people of color, what has that meant for my relationships with them? While these questions were not likely explicitly addressed in childhood, somehow we had to make sense of our racially segregated worlds. Explorations such as these have the potential to reveal our racial paradigms, an essential precursor to antiracist action; they are a great place to start engaging in the discussion without depending on people of color to teach us.

"I already know all this."

While the previous rationale positions the listener as racially innocent and thus only able to absorb the discussion, this rationale positions the listener as so sophisticated as to be beyond the discussion. This claim gives the message to the people of color in the group that there is nothing to be gained from what they might share—their stories, experiences, perspectives, or feelings. This claim is particularly problematic because it conveys superiority: reinscribing the historical invalidation of people of color as not having any knowledge of value to white people, elevating oneself above other white people in the group and the potential to work together with them against racism, and accomplishing all of this by presenting oneself as so advanced as to be beyond the discussion.

The antiracist framework undergirding these discussions holds that racism is a deeply embedded, complex system that will not end in our lifetimes, and certainly will not end through our complacency. If one sincerely believes their understanding of racism is more advanced than the discussion allows for (which can happen when the majority of the white participants are very new to the concepts and the facilitators assess that they must move at a slower pace), then the antiracist way to engage is to make strategic points that will help guide the other white people. White people who have more knowledge than the majority of the group are in an excellent position to "mentor from the sidelines." They can share their process and how they came to their current understanding, validate the struggle while reinforcing its worthiness, take the discussion deeper, and back up the facilitators and participants of color.

We may have an intellectual grasp of the dynamics, but awareness of racial inequity alone is not enough to trump our participation. White people, while served well by the dynamics of whiteness, are simultaneously in a prime position to interrupt it, yet to do so we must take unambiguous action. Claiming that we already know is meaningless without demonstration of that knowledge, and remaining silent is not a demonstration of antiracist action or understanding. People of color involved in antiracist endeavors generally assume that all white people have a racist perspective unless demonstrated otherwise (hooks, 1995; Sue, 2003). To not explicitly take up an antiracist stance in such a context can only reinforce the perception that we are actively choosing to align with whiteness. Being "advanced" is not a reason for us to disengage; the disengagement itself makes the claim unconvincing.

"I need time to process."

In my experience, participants who use this rationale seldom return after processing and share the results, suggesting that this may be a deflection against "putting ourselves out there," rather than an expression of a sincere difference in how people process information. We may indeed need time to process, but taking the time we need is still a privilege not everyone can afford. At the minimum, we can try articulating what we are hearing that we need to process, and then let the group know that these are new ideas, that we are feeling overwhelmed, and that we want to let things settle in. At the minimum, we can let the group know why we need the time to process and what we will be processing, rather than remain silent and leave others to wonder. When we have had time to process, we can share the results with the group.

It's also helpful to distinguish between the need to process and the need to sound controlled, correct, and coherent. If composure is what we are waiting for, we are working at cross-purposes to the discussion. Emotions, confusion, inner conflict, and inarticulation are all usually welcome in racial discussions. Vulnerability and openness build trust, and while thoughtfulness and respect are critical, control and composure are not necessary and can be counterproductive.

"I don't want to be misunderstood."

To not speak up in case we are misunderstood is to protect our perspective from deepening or expanding. It is not possible, given the embeddedness of racism in the culture, for white people not to have problematic racial assumptions and blind spots. Of course, it is uncomfortable and even embarrassing to see that we lack certain forms of knowledge, but we can't gain the knowledge we lack if we don't take risks. It is imperative that we enter the discussion with a willingness (even enthusiasm) to have our assumptions uncovered so we can increase our knowledge and cross-racial skills, for how will we realize that we have misconceptions and only a partial view if we don't share our views and open them up to exploration?

When white people do feel misunderstood in a racial discussion, it is usually because we were given feedback on an assumption we made or a blind spot we have in our racial awareness. Sadly, pointing out gaps in a white person's understanding is often experienced as being attacked or judged. When we insist that the issue is that we were misunderstood, rather than engage with the possibility that we are the ones who don't understand the feedback we have received, we close ourselves off to further learning. By insisting that the problem is that we have been misunderstood, we place the responsibility for the "misunderstanding" onto those who we believe have misunderstood us—usually the participants of color. There is no opening in this position for the possibility that the lack of understanding could be ours. If we are unable or unwilling to consider this possibility, or the corollary possibility that people of color might have information that we do not, we cannot gain new insight into how racism functions. If the only way one will engage in cross-racial discussion is to never be challenged, there is minimal point to the discussion.

"I don't feel safe." Subdiscourses: "I don't want to be attacked." "I don't want to be judged."

The safety discourse, while one of the most familiar and understandable, is also one of the most problematic. On the surface it conveys a kind of vulnerability and desire for protection. Unfortunately, it rests on a lack of understanding of historical and ongoing institutional, cultural, and interpersonal power relations between white people and people of color. While the feelings may be real for white people struggling with a sense of safety, some clarification may help clarify the difference between actual safety and what is more realistically a concern about comfort. To help differentiate safety from comfort, one might ask what safety means from a position of social, cultural, historical, and institutional power? If one does not fear that they are in actual physical harm, then some reflection on what one fears is actually at risk can offer much insight. Often, it is our self-image; because we have been taught that only bad people participate in racism, we often fear that if it is somehow revealed that we participate in racism, we will lose face and be judged. Indeed, many white people feel very uncomfortable in racial discussions, but this discomfort is actually a positive sign, for it indicates that the status quo (unnamed and unexamined racism) is being challenged. It is therefore critical that we feel uncomfortable, and not confuse discomfort with danger. As for being judged, there is no human objectivity—all people judge and we cannot protect ourselves from judgments in any context. But feeling judged, while dismaying, should not be confused with safety.

Further, the language of safety is not without significance in this context. By employing terms that connote physical threat, we tap into the classic discourse of people of color (particularly African Americans) as dangerous and violent. This discourse twists the actual direction of danger that exists between white people and people of color. People of color seldom have the luxury of withdrawing because they don't feel safe. It doesn't benefit people of color to remain silent, as it does us. To not put themselves "out there" makes them complicit in their own oppression, as Rich and Laura express above. If people of color are not self-advocating and pushing back against whiteness, they can't depend on white people to do it for them, as has been amply demonstrated time and again in racial discussions—often via white silence. While the pushing back we might get from people of color can be very uncomfortable, that discomfort is a key way to unsettle our worldviews and create the stretching and growing that is necessary for authentic change.

"I don't want to offend anybody."

Similar to "I don't want to be misunderstood," this rationale allows one to protect themself against alternative perspectives, responses, constructive conflict, or taking the risks that could potentially expand one's awareness. This rationale is unfair to people of color because, if we fear offending, it can only be assumed that is because we are having offensive thoughts or are hostile toward what is being said. If this is the case, to not put our disagreement into the room is to deny the group knowledge of where we are coming from and the ability for others to make any adjustments they might need in response to our hostility. If we are not hostile to what is being said but just worried that we may inadvertently offend someone, how will we learn that what we think or say is offensive if we don't share it and open ourselves up to feedback? In effect, by not taking this intentional opportunity to discover which ideas we hold are offensive, we protect these ideas and enable them to surface at a later date and offend someone else. In the unique and often rare learning environment of racial discussions, to remain silent so as not to offend is to offend twice—once through our silence and again in our unwillingness to discover and change racially problematic dimensions in our thinking. If unsure, we can simply offer our thoughts with openness and humility rather than as declarations of certainty or truth—that is, "Please let me know if something is off in my thinking, but here is how I am responding to this.... Can you help me understand why ...?" "I have often heard.... What are your thoughts on that?"

"Anything I say won't be listened to because I am white."

At the point that this discourse emerges, we have usually been challenged in the way we conceptualize race—either directly or via the content of the dialogue, and we are unable to rise to that challenge. Clearly we have not understood the objectives of the discussion or the theoretical framework that it rests on: There is a relationship of unequal power between white people and people of color that all of us have been taught to collude in, but that only white people benefit from. One way that antiracist education tries to interrupt this relationship is by acknowledging the power differential and affirming the perspectives of those whose voices dominant society seldom hears or validates (Schiele, 2000). In turn, challenging white perspectives is necessary because the way that dominant culture understands race actually functions to hold racism in place. The issue is not that we won't be listened to because we are white; the issue is that—counter to what we are accustomed to—our perspectives will be challenged at times and are not going to be affirmed just because we are white.

A NOTE ON THE SILENCE OF PEOPLE OF COLOR IN RACIAL DISCUSSIONS

Although this analysis is limited to a white person addressing white silence in racial discussions, I would be remiss if I did not at least raise the issue of the silence of people of color and offer some preliminary thoughts. First, as should be clear via my argument thus far, the silence of white people has a very different foundation and impact than the silence of people of color, based on the unequal positioning of the two groups in society; these silences are not equivalent. For Laura and Rich, quoted above, silence is generally not an option. However, there are several key reasons why people of color, including Laura and Rich, may at times choose silence in a racial discussion, including: in response to resistance or hostility expressed (consciously or not) by white participants (this unconscious expression of hostility could include silence based on many of the reasons discussed above); a lack of trust based on well-founded experience that one will be penalized for challenging white perspectives; a sense of hopelessness in the face of white denial; taking risks and being vulnerable about one's racial experiences and perspectives and being met with silence, argumentation, explanation, or guilt, all of which function as forms of invalidation; being outnumbered in ratio to white people and assessing that there are no allies present for support were one to challenge white privilege; and being acutely aware of the power differentials and choosing to protect oneself in the face of inevitable hurt.

It is important to keep in mind that so much of how white racism operates is invisible to and/or denied by white people. A room that seems perfectly comfortable to white people may not feel that way to people of color; in fact, given white racism as the status quo, the more comfortable a space is for white people, the more likely it is to be harmful to people of color. Further (and especially for well-intended white people), because we are deeply invested materially, psychically, socially, and politically as the producers and beneficiaries of white privilege, the very behaviors we think are benign or even supportive (as I have argued above) may be the very behaviors that are so toxic to people of color. Adding to these roots of our denial, our very identities as good people rests on our not seeing our racism. As Sullivan (2006) states, "As unconscious habit, white privilege operates as non-existent and actively works to disrupt attempts to reveal its existence" (pp. 1–2). In other words, white people work hard not to see white privilege, which is a key way we keep it protected and intact. In this context, it should be apparent why people of color might choose silence.

IN CONCLUSION

It may be clear at this point that much of the rationale for white silence is based on a racial paradigm that posits racism as isolated to individual acts of meanness (McIntosh, 1988) that only some people do. This dominant paradigm of racism as discrete, individual, intentional, and malicious acts makes it unlikely that white people will see our silence as a function of, and support to, racism and white privilege. Yet to challenge one's most comfortable patterns of engagement in a racial dialogue, while it may be counterintuitive, is necessarily to interrupt one's racial socialization. From an antiracist perspective, we can assume that our racial socialization has not prepared us to be competent in cross-racial relationship building. Although consistent silence in racial discussions often feels benign to those who practice it, in this chapter I have argued that no form of white engagement that is not informed by an antiracist perspective is benign. Going against one's "grain" for engagement, while difficult, is necessary and will result in the least harmful and most authentic and rewarding engagement. A white student expresses this powerfully in a class-assigned journal entry. In response to a person of color in the class sharing the impact of a recent racist incident, she writes:

> As Jane finished speaking, and I raised my hand, I became completely overwhelmed by the enormity of what she had said. . . . I was terrified that anything that I said would seem trivial or, even more frightening, would make things worse. I felt paralyzed by the moment, feeling in my stomach how utterly raw and open Jane seemed—but my need to speak, to address what

she had said, despite the probability that I would mess it up, was greater than my guilt or my shame or my desire to remain quiet. I realized that the notion that I can make it worse—that I do have that power—requires that I speak. I realized that, in our silence, we are complicit. In my silence for the past four weeks of this course—and for a lifetime before it—I have been complicit. I no longer feel comfortable letting my silence speak for me—it is inarticulate and offensive. I would rather blunder along than stay silent. I hope the people around me, who witness my blundering, can see beyond the errors... because remaining silent—maintaining my complicity—is no longer conscionable. (Student Journal, July 5, 2009)

REFERENCES

Akintunde, O. (1999). White racism, white supremacy, white privilege, and the social construction of race: Moving from modernist to postmodernist multiculturalism. *Multicultural Education, 7*(2), 2–8.

Bonilla-Silva, E. (2006). *Racism without racists: Color-blind racism and the persistence of racial inequality in the United States* (2nd ed.). Rowman & Littlefield.

DiAngelo, R. (2004). *Whiteness in racial dialogue: A discourse analysis* [Unpublished dissertation]. University of Washington, Seattle.

DiAngelo, R. (2006a). "I'm leaving!": White fragility in racial dialogue. In B. McMahon & D. Armstrong (Eds.), *Inclusion in urban educational environments: Addressing issues of diversity, equity, and social justice* (pp. 213–240). Centre for Leadership and Diversity. Ontario Institute for Studies in Education of the University of Toronto.

DiAngelo, R. (2006b). My race didn't trump my class: Using oppression to face privilege. *Multicultural Perspectives, 8*(1), 51–56.

DiAngelo, R. (2006c). The production of whiteness in education: Asian international students in a college classroom. *Teachers College Record, 108*(10), 1960–1982.

DiAngelo, R. (2010). Why can't we all just be individuals? The discourse of individualism in anti-racist education. *InterActions: UCLA Journal of Education and Information Studies, 6*(1).

Dyer, R. (1997). *White.* Routledge.

Feagin, J. (2000). *Racist America: Roots, current realities, and future reparations.* Routledge.

Frankenberg, R. (1997). Introduction: Local whitenesses, localizing whiteness. In R. Frankenberg (Ed.), *Displacing whiteness: Essays in social and cultural criticism* (pp. 1–33.). Duke University Press.

Frankenberg, R. (2001). The mirage of an unmarked whiteness. In B. B. Rasmussen, E. Klinenberg, I. J. Nexica, & M. Wray (Eds.), *The making and unmaking of whiteness* (pp. 72–96). Duke University Press.

Hilliard, A. (1992). *Racism: Its origins and how it works* [Paper presentation]. Mid-West Association for the Education of Young Children, Madison, WI.

hooks, b. (1995). *Killing rage.* Henry Holt.

Lipsitz, G. (1999). *The possessive investment in whiteness: How white people profit from identity politics.* Temple University Press.

Macedo, D., & Bartolome, L. (1999). *Dancing with bigotry: Beyond the politics of tolerance.* St. Martin's Press.

McIntosh, P. (1988). White privilege and male privilege: A personal account of coming to see correspondence through work in women's studies. In M. Anderson & P. Hill Collins (Eds.), *Race, class, and gender: An anthology* (pp. 94–105). Wadsworth.

Mills, C. (1999). *The racial contract.* Cornell University Press.

Morrison, T. (1992). *Playing in the dark: Whiteness in the literary imagination.* Harvard University Press.

Mura, D. (1999). Explaining racism to my daughter. In T. B. Jelloun, C. Volk, & P. Williams (Eds.), *Racism explained to my daughter* (pp. 93–137). The New Press.

Picca, L., & Feagin, J. (2007). *Two-faced racism: Whites in the backstage and frontstage.* Routledge.

Pollock, M. (2004). *Colormute: Race talk dilemmas in an American school.* Princeton University Press.

Roediger, D. (2007). *The wages of whiteness: Race and the making of the American working class* (2nd ed.). Verso.

Schiele, J. H. (2000). *Human service and the Afro-centric paradigm.* Haworth.

Sue, D. W. (2003). *Overcoming our racism: The journey to liberation.* Jossey-Bass.

Sullivan, S. (2006). *Revealing whiteness: The unconscious habits of racial privilege.* Indiana University Press.

Tatum, B. (1997). *"Why are all the Black kids sitting together in the cafeteria?" And other conversations about race.* Basic Books.

Thandeka. (2000). *Learning to be white: Money, race, and God in America.* Continuum.

Thompson, B. (2001). *A promise and a way of life: white antiracist activism.* University of Minnesota Press.

Trepagnier, B. (2006). *Silent racism: How well-meaning white people perpetuate the racial divide.* Paradigm.

Van Ausdale, D., & Feagin, J. (2002). *The first R: How children learn racism.* Rowman & Littlefield.

SIX

White Fragility

I am a white woman. I am standing beside a Black woman. We are facing a group of white people who are seated in front of us. We are in their workplace, and have been hired by their employer to lead them in a dialogue about race. The room is filled with tension and charged with hostility. I have just presented a definition of racism that includes the acknowledgment that white people hold social and institutional power over people of color. A white man is pounding his fist on the table. His face is red and he is furious. As he pounds he yells, "White people have been discriminated against for 25 years! A white person can't get a job anymore!" I look around the room and see 40 employed people, all white. There are no people of color in this workplace. Something is happening here, and it isn't based in the racial reality of the workplace. I am feeling unnerved by this man's disconnection with that reality, and his lack of sensitivity to the impact this is having on my co-facilitator, the only person of color in the room. Why is this white man so angry? Why is he being so careless about the impact of his anger? Why are all the other white people either sitting in silent agreement with him or tuning out? We have, after all, only articulated a definition of racism.

◇   ◇   ◇

White people in North America live in a social environment that protects and insulates them from race-based stress.[1] Fine (1997b) identifies

Originally published as "White Fragility," *The International Journal of Critical Pedagogy, 3*(3). Copyright 2011. https://libjournal.uncg.edu/ijcp/article/view/249

this insulation when she observes "how whiteness accrues privilege and status; gets itself surrounded by protective pillows of resources and/or benefits of the doubt; how whiteness repels gossip and voyeurism and instead demands dignity" (p. 57). White people are rarely without these "protective pillows," and when they are, it is usually temporary and by choice. This insulated environment of racial privilege builds white expectations for racial comfort while at the same time lowering the ability to tolerate racial stress.

For many white people, a single required multicultural education course taken in college, or required "cultural competency training" in their workplace, is the only time they may encounter a direct and sustained challenge to their racial understandings. But even in this arena, not all multicultural courses or training programs talk directly about racism, much less address white privilege. It is far more the norm for these courses and programs to use racially coded language such as "urban," "inner city," and "disadvantaged" but to rarely use "white" or "overadvantaged" or "privileged." This racially coded language reproduces racist images and perspectives while it simultaneously reproduces the comfortable illusion that race and its problems are what "they" have, not us. Reasons why the facilitators of these courses and trainings may not directly name the dynamics and beneficiaries of racism range from the lack of a valid analysis of racism by white facilitators, personal and economic survival strategies for facilitators of color, and the overall pressure from management to keep the content comfortable and palatable for white people. However, if and when an educational program does directly address racism and the privileging of white people, common white responses include anger, withdrawal, emotional incapacitation, guilt, argumentation, and cognitive dissonance (all of which reinforce the pressure on facilitators to avoid directly addressing racism). So-called progressive white people may not respond with anger, but they may still insulate themselves via claims that they are beyond the need for engaging with the content because they "already had a class on this" or "already know this." These reactions are often seen in antiracist education endeavors as forms of resistance to the challenge of internalized dominance (Horton & Scott, 2004; McGowan, 2000; O'Donnell, 1998; Whitehead & Wittig, 2005). These reactions do indeed function as resistance, but it may be useful to also conceptualize them as the result of the reduced psychosocial stamina that racial insulation inculcates. I call this lack of racial stamina "white fragility."

Although mainstream definitions of racism are typically some variation of individual "race prejudice," which anyone of any race can have, whiteness scholars define racism as encompassing economic, political, social, and cultural structures, actions, and beliefs that systematize and perpetuate an unequal distribution of privileges, resources, and power between white people and people of color (Hilliard, 1992). This unequal distribution benefits white people and disadvantages people of color overall and as a group. Racism is not fluid in the United States; it does not flow back and forth, one day benefiting white people and another day (or even era) benefiting people of color. The direction of power between white people and people of color is historic, traditional, normalized, and deeply embedded in the fabric of U.S. society (Feagin, 2006; Mills, 1999). Whiteness itself refers to the specific dimensions of racism that serve to elevate white people over people of color. This definition counters the dominant representation of racism in mainstream education as isolated in discrete behaviors that some individuals may or may not demonstrate, and it goes beyond naming specific privileges (McIntosh, 1988). White people are theorized as actively shaped, affected, defined, and elevated through their racialization and the individual and collective consciousness formed within it (Frankenberg, 2001; Morrison, 1992; Tatum, 1997). Recognizing that the terms I am using are not "theory neutral 'descriptors'" but theory-laden constructs inseparable from systems of injustice" (Allen, 1996, p. 95), I use the terms "white" and "whiteness" to describe a social process. Frankenberg (1993) defines whiteness as multidimensional:

> Whiteness is a location of structural advantage, of race privilege. Second, it is a "standpoint," a place from which white people look at ourselves, at others, and at society. Third, "whiteness" refers to a set of cultural practices that are usually unmarked and unnamed. (p. 1)

Frankenberg (1993) and other theorists (Dyer, 1997; Fine, 1997a; Sleeter, 1993; Van Dijk, 1993a) use whiteness to signify a set of locations that are historically, socially, politically, and culturally produced, and which are intrinsically linked to dynamic relations of domination. Whiteness is thus conceptualized as a constellation of processes and practices rather than as a discrete entity (i.e., skin color alone). Whiteness is dynamic, relational, and operating at all times and on myriad levels. These processes and practices include basic rights, values, beliefs, perspectives, and experiences purported to be commonly shared by all but which are actually only consistently afforded to white people. Whiteness studies begin with the premise that racism and white privilege exist in both traditional and modern forms, and rather than work to prove its existence, work to reveal it.

TRIGGERS

White fragility is a state in which even a minimum amount of racial stress becomes intolerable, triggering a range of defensive moves. These moves include the outward display of emotions such as anger, fear, and guilt, and behaviors such as argumentation, silence, and leaving the stress-inducing situation. These behaviors, in turn, function to reinstate white racial equilibrium. Racial stress results from an interruption to what is racially familiar. These interruptions can take a variety of forms and come from a range of sources, including

+ Suggesting that a white person's viewpoint comes from a racialized frame of reference (challenge to objectivity)
+ People of color talking directly about their racial perspectives (challenge to white racial taboos)
+ People of color choosing not to protect the racial feelings of white people in regards to race (challenge to white racial expectations and need/entitlement to racial comfort)
+ People of color not being willing to tell their stories, answer questions, or teach white people about racism (challenge to colonialist relations)
+ A fellow white person not providing agreement with one's interpretations (challenge to white solidarity)
+ Receiving feedback that one's behavior had a racist impact (challenge to white liberalism)

+ Suggesting that group membership is significant (challenge to individualism)
+ An acknowledgment that access is unequal between racial groups (challenge to meritocracy)
+ Being presented with a person of color in a position of leadership (challenge to white authority)
+ Being presented with information about other racial groups through, for example, movies in which people of color drive the action but are not in stereotypical roles, or multicultural education (challenge to white centrality)

In a white-dominant environment, each of these challenges becomes exceptional. In turn, white people are often at a loss for how to respond in useful ways, not having had to build the cognitive or affective skills or develop the stamina that would allow for constructive engagement across racial divides. Bourdieu's (1993) concept of habitus may be useful here.

According to Bourdieu (1993), habitus is a socialized subjectivity—a set of dispositions that generate practices and perceptions. As such, habitus only exists in, through, and because of the practices of actors and their interaction with each other and with the rest of their environment. Based on the previous conditions and experiences that produce it, habitus produces and reproduces thoughts, perceptions, expressions, and actions. Strategies of response to "disequilibrium" in the habitus are not based on conscious intentionality but rather result from unconscious dispositions towards practice, and depend on the power position the agent occupies in the social structure. White fragility may be conceptualized as a product of the habitus, a response or "condition" produced and reproduced by the continual social and material advantages of the white structural position.

Omi and Winant (1986) posit the U.S. racial order as an "unstable equilibrium," kept equilibrated by the state, but still unstable due to continual conflicts of interests and challenges to the racial order (pp. 78–79). Using Omi and Winant's concept of unstable racial equilibrium, white privilege can be thought of as unstable racial equilibrium at the level of habitus. When any of the above triggers (challenges in the habitus) occur, the resulting disequilibrium becomes intolerable. Because white fragility finds its support in and is a function of white privilege, fragility and privilege result in responses that function to restore equilibrium and return the resources "lost" via the challenge—resistance toward the trigger, shutting down and/or tuning out, indulge in emotional incapacitation such as guilt or "hurt feelings," exiting, or a combination of these responses.

FACTORS THAT INCULCATE WHITE FRAGILITY

Segregation

The first factor leading to white fragility is the segregated lives that most white people live (Frankenberg et al., 2003). Even if white people live in physical proximity to people of color (and this would be exceptional outside of an urban or temporarily mixed-class neighborhood), segregation occurs on multiple levels, including representational and informational. Because white people live primarily segregated lives in a white-dominated society, they receive little or no authentic information about racism and are thus unprepared to think about it critically or with complexity. Growing up in segregated environments (schools, workplaces, neighborhoods, media images, and historical perspectives), white interests and perspectives are almost always central. An inability to see or consider significance in the perspectives of people of color results (Collins, 2000).

Further, white people are taught not to feel any loss over the absence of people of color in their lives and, in fact, this absence is what defines their schools and neighborhoods as "good"; white people come to understand that a "good school" or "good neighborhood" is coded language for "white" (Johnson & Shapiro, 2003). The quality of white space being in large part measured via the absence of people of color (and Blacks in particular) is a profound message indeed, one that is deeply internalized and reinforced daily through normalized discourses about good schools and neighborhoods. This dynamic of gain rather than loss via racial segregation may be the most profound aspect of white racial socialization of all. Yet, while discourses about what makes a space good are tacitly understood as racially coded, this coding is explicitly denied by white people.

Universalism and Individualism

White people are taught to see their perspectives as objective and representative of reality (McIntosh, 1988). The belief in objectivity, coupled with positioning white people as outside of culture (and thus the norm for humanity), allows white people to view themselves as universal humans who can represent all of human experience. This is evidenced through an unracialized identity or location, which functions as a kind of blindness; an inability to think about whiteness as an identity or as a "state" of being that would or could have an impact on one's life. In this position, whiteness is not recognized or named by white people, and a universal reference point is assumed. White people are just people. Within this construction, they can represent humanity, while people of color, who are never just people but always most particularly Black people, Asian people, and so forth, can only represent their own racialized experiences (Dyer, 1997).

The discourse of universalism functions similarly to the discourse of individualism but instead of declaring that we all need to see each other as individuals (everyone is different), the person declares that we all need to see each other as human beings (everyone is the same). Of course we are all humans, and I do not critique universalism in general, but when applied to racism, universalism functions to deny the significance of race and the advantages of being white. Further, universalism assumes that white people and people of color have the same realities, the same experiences in the same contexts (i.e., I feel comfortable in this majority white classroom, so you must too), and the same responses from others, and it assumes that the same doors are open to all. Acknowledging racism as a system of privilege conferred on the white collective challenges claims to universalism.

At the same time that white people are taught to see their interests and perspectives as universal, they are also taught to value the individual and to see themselves as individuals rather than as part of a racially socialized group. Individualism erases history and hides the ways in which wealth has been distributed and accumulated over generations to benefit white people today. It allows white people to view themselves as unique and original, outside of socialization and unaffected by the relentless racial messages in the culture. Individualism also allows white people to distance themselves from the actions of their racial group and demand to be granted the benefit of the doubt, as individuals, in all cases. A corollary to this unracialized identity is the ability to recognize whiteness as something that is significant and that operates in society, but to not see how it relates to one's own life. In this form, a white person recognizes whiteness as real, but as the individual problem of other "bad" white people (DiAngelo, 2010).

Given the ideology of individualism, white people often respond defensively when linked to other whites as a group or "accused" of collectively benefiting from racism, because as individuals, each white person is "different" from any other white person and expects to be seen as such. This narcissism is not necessarily the result of a consciously held belief that white people are superior to others (although that may play a role), but is a result of the white racial insulation ubiquitous in dominant culture (Dawkins, 2004; Frankenberg et al., 2003); it is a general white inability to see non-white perspectives as significant, except in sporadic and impotent reflexes, which have little or no long-term momentum or political usefulness.

White people invoke these seemingly contradictory discourses—we are either all unique or we are all the same—interchangeably. Both discourses work to deny white privilege and the significance of race. Further, on the cultural level, being an individual or being a human outside of a racial group is a privilege only afforded to white people. In other words, people of color are almost always seen as "having a race" and described in racial terms ("the Black man"), but white people rarely are ("the man"), allowing white people to see themselves as objective and nonracialized. In turn, being seen (and seeing ourselves) as individuals outside of race frees white people from the psychic burden of race in a wholly racialized society. Race and racism become their problems, not ours. Challenging these frameworks becomes a kind of unwelcome shock to the system.

The disavowal of race as an organizing factor, both of individual white consciousness and the institutions of society at large, is necessary to support current structures of capitalism and domination, for without it, the correlation between the distribution of social resources and unearned white privilege would be evident (Flax, 1998). The existence of structural inequality undermines the claim that privilege is simply a reflection of hard work and virtue. Therefore, inequality must be hidden or justified as resulting from lack of effort (Mills, 1999; Ryan, 2001). Individualism accomplishes both of these tasks. At the same time, the individual presented as outside these relations cannot exist without its disavowed other. Thus, an essential dichotomy is formed between specifically raced others and the unracialized individual. White people have deep investments in race, for the abstract depends on the particular (Flax, 1998); they need raced others as the backdrop against which they may rise (Morrison, 1992). Exposing this dichotomy destabilizes white identity.

Entitlement to Racial Comfort

In the dominant position, white people are almost always racially comfortable and thus have developed unchallenged expectations to remain so (DiAngelo, 2006b). White people have not had to build tolerance for racial discomfort and thus when racial discomfort arises, white people typically respond as if something is "wrong" and blame the person or event that triggered the discomfort (usually a person of color).

This blame results in a socially sanctioned array of countermoves against the perceived source of the discomfort, including penalization, retaliation, isolation, ostracization, and refusal to continue engagement. White insistence on racial comfort ensures that racism will not be faced. This insistence also functions to punish those who break white codes of comfort. White people often confuse comfort with safety and state that we don't feel safe when what we really mean is that we don't feel comfortable. This trivializes our history of brutality towards people of color and perverts the reality of that history. Because we don't think complexly about racism, we don't ask ourselves what safety means from a position of societal dominance, or the impact on people of color, given our history, for white people to complain about our safety when we are merely talking about racism.

Racial Arrogance

Ideological racism includes strongly positive images of the white self as well as strongly negative images of racial "others" (Feagin, 2000, p. 33). This self-image engenders a self-perpetuating sense of entitlement because many white people believe their financial and professional successes are solely the result of their own efforts while ignoring the fact of white advantage. Because most white people have not been trained to think complexly about racism in schools (Derman-Sparks & Ramsey, 2006; Sleeter, 1993) or mainstream discourse, and because it benefits white dominance not to do so, we have a very limited understanding of racism. Yet dominance leads to racial arrogance, and in this racial arrogance, white people have no compunction about debating the knowledge of people who have thought complexly about race. White people generally feel free to dismiss these informed perspectives rather than have the humility to acknowledge that they are unfamiliar, reflect on them further, or seek more information. This intelligence and expertise are often trivialized and countered with simplistic platitudes (i.e., "People just need to . . .").

Because of white social, economic, and political power within a white dominant culture, white people are positioned to legitimize people of color's assertions of racism. Yet white people are the least likely to see, understand, or be invested in validating those assertions and being honest about their consequences, which leads to claims that they disagree with perspectives that challenge their worldview, when in fact they don't understand the perspective. Thus, they confuse not understanding with not agreeing. This racial arrogance, coupled with the need for racial comfort, also has white people insisting that people of color explain racism in the "right" way. The right way is generally politely and rationally, without any show of emotional upset. When explained in a way that white people can see and understand, racism's validity may be granted (references to dynamics of racism that white people do not understand are usually rejected out of hand). However, white people are usually more receptive to validating white racism if that racism is constructed as residing in individual white people other than themselves.

Racial Belonging

White people enjoy a deeply internalized, largely unconscious sense of racial belonging in U.S. society (DiAngelo, 2006b; McIntosh, 1988). This racial belonging is instilled via the whiteness embedded in the culture at large. Everywhere we look, we see our own racial image reflected back to us—in our heroes and heroines, in standards of beauty, in our role-models and teachers, in our textbooks and historical memory, in the media, in religious iconography including the image of God "himself," and so forth. In virtually any situation or image deemed valuable in dominant society, white people belong. Indeed, it is exceptional for most white people to experience a sense of not belonging, and such experiences are usually very temporary, easily avoidable situations. Racial belonging becomes deeply internalized and taken for granted. In dominant society, interruption of racial belonging is rare and thus destabilizing and frightening to white people.

White people consistently choose and enjoy racial segregation. Living, working, and playing in racial segregation is unremarkable as long as it is not named or made explicitly intentional. For example, in many antiracist endeavors, a common exercise is to separate into caucus groups by race in order to discuss issues specific to your racial group, and without the pressure or stress of other groups' presence. Generally, people of color appreciate this opportunity for racial fellowship, but white people typically become very uncomfortable, agitated, and upset—even though this temporary separation is in the service of addressing racism. Responses include a disorienting sense of themselves as not just people, but most particularly white people; a curious sense of loss about this contrived and temporary separation that they don't feel with respect to the real and ongoing segregation in their daily lives; and anxiety about not knowing what is going on in the groups of color. The irony, again, is that most white people live in racial segregation every day, and in fact are the group most likely to intentionally choose that segregation (albeit obscured in racially coded language such as seeking "good schools" and "good neighborhoods"). This segregation is unremarkable until it is named as deliberate—that is, "We are now going to separate by race for a short exercise." I posit that it is the intentionality that is so disquieting—as long as we don't mean to separate, as long as it "just happens" that we live segregated lives, we can maintain a (fragile) identity of racial innocence.

Psychic Freedom

Because race is constructed as residing in people of color, white people don't bear the social burden of race. We move easily through our society without a sense of ourselves as racialized subjects (Dyer, 1997). We see race as operating when people of color are present, but all-white spaces as "pure" spaces—untainted by race vis-á-vis the absence of the carriers of race (and thereby the racial polluters)—people of color. This perspective is perfectly captured in a familiar white statement, "I was lucky. I grew up in an all-white neighborhood so I didn't learn anything about racism." In this discursive move, whiteness gains its meaning through its purported lack of encounter with non-whiteness (Nakayama & Martin, 1999).

Because racial segregation is deemed socially valuable while simultaneously unracial and unremarkable, we rarely, if ever, have to think about race and racism, and we receive no penalty for not thinking about it. In fact, white people are more likely to be penalized (primarily by other white people) for bringing race up in a social justice context than for ignoring it (however, it is acceptable to bring race up indirectly and in ways that reinforce racist attitudes, i.e., warning other white people to stay away from certain neighborhoods, etc.). This frees white people from carrying the psychic burden of race. Race is for people of color to think about—it is what happens to "them"—they can bring it up if it is an issue for them (although if they do, we can dismiss it as a personal problem, the "race card," or the reason for their problems). This allows white people to devote much more psychological energy to other issues, and it prevents us from developing the stamina to sustain attention on an issue as charged and uncomfortable as race.

CONSTANT MESSAGES THAT WE ARE MORE VALUABLE— THROUGH REPRESENTATION IN EVERYTHING

Living in a white-dominant context, we receive constant messages that we are better and more important than people of color. These messages operate on multiple levels and are conveyed in a range of ways. For example: our centrality in history textbooks, and historical representations and perspectives; our centrality in media and advertising (e.g., a recent *Vogue* magazine cover boldly stated "The World's Next Top Models," and every woman on the front cover was white); our teachers, role-models, heroes, and heroines; everyday discourse on "good" neighborhoods and schools and who is in them; popular TV shows centered on friendship circles that are all white (often taking place in New York City, e.g., *Friends, Seinfeld, Girls*); religious iconography that depicts God, Adam and Eve, and other key figures as white; commentary on new stories about how shocking any crime is that occurs in white suburbs; and the lack of a sense of loss about the absence of people of color in most white people's lives. While one may explicitly reject the notion that one is inherently better than another, one cannot avoid internalizing the message of white superiority, as it is ubiquitous in mainstream culture (Doane, 1997; Tatum, 1997).

What Does White Fragility Look Like?

A large body of research about children and race demonstrates that children start to construct ideas about race very early; a sense of white superiority and knowledge of racial power codes appears to develop as early as preschool (Clark, 1963; Derman-Sparks & Ramsey, 2006). Marty (1999) states,

> As in other Western nations, white children born in the United States inherit the moral predicament of living in a white supremacist society. Raised to experience their racially based advantages as fair and normal, white children receive little if any instruction regarding the predicament they face, let alone any guidance in how to resolve it. Therefore, they experience or learn about racial tension without understanding Euro-Americans' historical responsibility for it and knowing virtually nothing about their contemporary roles in perpetuating it. (p. 51)

At the same time that it is ubiquitous, white superiority also remains unnamed and explicitly denied by most white people. If white children become adults who explicitly oppose racism, as do many, they often organize their identity around a denial of the racially based privileges they hold that reinforce racist disadvantage for others. What is particularly problematic about this contradiction is that white moral objection to racism increases white resistance to acknowledging complicity with it. In a white supremacist context, white identity in large part rests upon a foundation of (superficial) racial toleration and acceptance. White people who position themselves as liberal often opt to protect what they perceive as their moral reputations, rather than recognize or change their participation in systems of inequity and domination. In so responding, white people invoke the power to choose when, how, and how much to address or challenge racism. Thus, pointing out white advantage will often trigger patterns of confusion, defensiveness, and righteous indignation. When confronted with a challenge to white racial speech taboos, many white liberals use the speech of self-defense (Van Dijk, 1993b). This discourse enables defenders to protect their moral character against what they perceive as accusation and attack while deflecting any recognition of culpability or need of accountability. Focusing on restoring their moral standing through these tactics, white people are able to avoid the question of white advantage (Marty, 1999; Van Dijk, 1993b).

Those who lead white people in discussions of race may find the discourse of self-defense familiar. Via this discourse, white people position themselves as victimized, slammed, blamed, attacked, and being used as "punching bag[s]" (DiAngelo, 2006a). White people who describe interactions in this way are responding to the articulation of counter-narratives; nothing physically out of the ordinary has ever occurred in any interracial discussion that I am aware of. These self-defense claims work on multiple levels to position the speakers as morally superior while obscuring the true power of their social locations; blame others with less social power for their discomfort; falsely position that discomfort as dangerous; and reinscribe racist imagery. This discourse of victimization also enables white people to avoid responsibility for the racial power and privilege they wield. By positioning themselves as victims of antiracist efforts, they cannot be the beneficiaries of white privilege. Claiming that they have been treated unfairly via a challenge to their position or an expectation that they listen to the perspectives and experiences of people of color, they are able to demand that more social resources (such as time and attention) be channeled in their direction to help them cope with this mistreatment.

A cogent example of white fragility occurred recently during a workplace antiracism training I co-facilitated with an interracial team. One of the white participants left the session and went back to her desk, upset at receiving (what appeared to the training team as) sensitive and diplomatic feedback on how some of her statements had impacted several people of color in the room. At break, several other white participants approached us (the facilitators) and reported that they had talked to the woman at her desk, and she was very upset that her statements had been challenged. They wanted to alert us to the fact that she "might be having a heart-attack." Upon questioning from us, they clarified that they meant this literally. These co-workers were sincere in their fear that the young woman might actually physically die as a result of the feedback. Of course, when news of the woman's potentially fatal condition reached the rest of the participant group, all attention was immediately focused back onto her and away from the impact she had had on the people of color. As Vodde (2001) states, "If privilege is defined as a legitimization of one's entitlement to resources, it can also be defined as permission to escape or avoid any challenges to this entitlement" (p. 143).

The language of violence that many white people use to describe anti-racist endeavors is not without significance, as it is another example of the way that white fragility distorts and perverts reality. By employing terms that connote physical abuse, white people tap into the classic discourse of people of color (particularly African Americans) as dangerous and violent. This discourse perverts the actual direction of danger that exists between white people and others. The history of brutal, extensive, institutional-ized, and ongoing violence perpetrated by white people against people of color—slavery, genocide, lynching, whipping, forced sterilization, and medical experimentation, to mention a few—becomes profoundly trivial-ized. The use of this discourse illustrates how fragile and ill-equipped most white people are to confront racial tensions, and their subsequent projection of this tension onto people of color (Morrison, 1992). Goldberg (1993) argues that the questions surrounding racial discourse should not focus so much on how true stereotypes are, but on how the truth claims they offer are a part of a larger worldview that authorizes and normalizes forms of domination and control. Further, it is relevant to ask, Under what conditions are those truth-claims clung to most tenaciously?

Bonilla-Silva (2006) documents a manifestation of white fragility in his study of color-blind white racism. He states, "Because the new racial climate in America forbids the open expression of racially based feelings, views, and positions, when white people discuss issues that make them uncomfortable, they become almost incomprehensible—I, I, I, I don't mean, you know, but . . ." (p. 68). Probing forbidden racial issues results in verbal incoherence—digressions, long pauses, repetition, and self-corrections. He suggests that this incoherent talk is a function of talking about race in a world that insists race does not matter. This incoherence is one demonstration that many white people are unprepared to engage, even on a preliminary level, in an exploration of their racial perspectives that could lead to a shift in their understanding of racism. This lack of preparedness results in the maintenance of white power because the ability to determine which narratives are authorized and which are suppressed is the foundation of cultural domination (Banks, 1996; Said, 1994; Spivak, 1990). Further, this lack of preparedness has further implications, for if white people cannot engage with an exploration of alternate racial perspectives, they can only reinscribe white perspectives as universal.

However, an assertion that white people do not engage with dynamics of racial discourse is somewhat misleading. White people do notice the racial locations of racial others and discuss this freely among themselves, albeit often in coded ways. Their refusal to directly acknowledge this race talk results in a kind of split consciousness that leads to the incoherence Bonilla-Silva (2006) documents above (Feagin, 2000; Flax, 1998; hooks, 1992; Morrison, 1992). This denial also guarantees that the racial misinformation that circulates in the culture and frames their perspectives will be left unexamined. The continual retreat from the discomfort of authentic racial engagement in a culture infused with racial disparity limits the ability to form authentic connections across racial lines and results in a perpetual cycle that works to hold racism in place.

CONCLUSION

White people often believe that multicultural/antiracist education is only necessary for those who interact with "minorities" or in "diverse" environments. However, the dynamics discussed here suggest that it is critical that all white people build the stamina to sustain conscious and explicit engagement with race. When white people posit race as nonoperative because there are few, if any, people of color in their immediate environments, whiteness is re-inscribed ever more deeply. When white people only notice "raced others," we re-inscribe whiteness by continuing to posit whiteness as universal and non-whiteness as other. Further, if we can't listen to or comprehend the perspectives of people of color, we cannot bridge cross-racial divides. A continual retreat from the discomfort of authentic racial engagement results in a perpetual cycle that works to hold racism in place.

While antiracist efforts ultimately seek to transform institutionalized racism, antiracist education may be most effective by starting at the micro level. The goal is to generate the development of perspectives and skills that enable all people, regardless of racial location, to be active initiators of change. Since all individuals who live within a racist system are enmeshed in its relations, this means that all are responsible for either perpetuating or transforming that system. However, although all individuals play a role in keeping the system active, the responsibility for change is not equally shared. White racism is ultimately a white problem, and the burden for interrupting it belongs to white people. Conversations about whiteness might best happen within the context of a larger conversation about racism. It is useful to start at the micro level of analysis, and move to the macro, from the individual out to the interpersonal, societal, and institutional. Starting with the individual and moving outward to the ultimate framework for racism—whiteness—allows for the pacing that is necessary for many white people engaged in the challenging study of race. In this way, a discourse on whiteness becomes part of a process rather than an event (Zúñiga et al., 2002).

Many white people have never been given direct or complex information about racism before, and often cannot explicitly see, feel, or understand it (Trepagnier, 2006; Weber, 2001). People of color are generally much more aware of racism on a personal level, but due to the wider society's silence and denial of it, often do not have a macro-level framework from which to analyze their experiences (Bonilla-Silva, 2006; Sue, 2003). Further, dominant society "assigns" different roles to different groups of color (Smith, 2005), and a critical consciousness about racism varies not only between individuals within groups, but also between groups. For example, many African Americans relate having been "prepared" by parents to live in a racist society, while many Asian-heritage people say that racism was never directly discussed in their homes (hooks, 1992; Lee, 1996). A

macro-level analysis may offer a framework to understand different interpretations and performances across and between racial groups. In this way,
all parties benefit and efforts are not solely focused on white people (which
can work to recenter whiteness).

Talking directly about white power and privilege, in addition to providing much-needed information and shared definitions, is also in itself a
powerful interruption of common (and oppressive) discursive patterns
around race. At the same time, white people often need to reflect upon
racial information and be allowed to make connections between the information and their own lives. Educators can encourage and support white
participants in making their engagement a point of analysis. White fragility doesn't always manifest in overt ways; silence and withdrawal are also
functions of fragility. Who speaks, who doesn't speak, when, for how long,
and with what emotional valence are all keys to understanding the relational patterns that hold oppression in place (Gee, 1999; Powell, 1997).
Viewing white anger, defensiveness, silence, and withdrawal in response to
issues of race through the framework of white fragility may help frame the
problem as an issue of stamina-building, and thereby guide our interventions accordingly.

NOTE

1. Although white racial insulation is somewhat mediated by social class
(with poor and working class urban whites being generally less racially insulated
than suburban or rural whites), the larger social environment insulates and protects whites as a group through institutions, cultural representations, media,
school textbooks, movies, advertising, dominant discourses, etc.

REFERENCES

Allen, D. (1996). Knowledge, politics, culture, and gender: A discourse perspective. *Canadian Journal of Nursing Research, 28*(1), 95–102.
Banks, J. A. (Ed.). (1996). *Multicultural education, transformative knowledge, and
action: Historical and contemporary perspectives.* Teachers College Press.

Bonilla-Silva, E. (2006). *Racism without racists: Color-blind racism and the persistence of racial inequality in the United States* (2nd ed.). Rowman & Littlefield.

Bourdieu, P. (1993). *The field of cultural production.* Columbia University Press.

Clark, K. B. (1963). *Prejudice and your child.* Beacon Press.

Collins, P. H. (2000). *Black feminist thought: Knowledge, consciousness, and the politics of empowerment* (2nd ed.). Routledge.

Dawkins, C. J. (2004). Recent evidence on the continuing causes of Black–white residential segregation. *Journal of Urban Affairs, 26*(3), 379–400.

Derman-Sparks, L., & Ramsey, P. (2006). *What if all the kids are white? Anti-bias multicultural education with young children and families.* Teachers College Press.

DiAngelo, R. (2006a). "I'm leaving!" White fragility in racial dialogue. In B. McMahon & D. Armstrong (Eds.), *Inclusion in urban educational environments: Addressing issues of diversity, equity, and social justice* (pp. 213–240). Centre for Leadership and Diversity, Ontario Institute for Studies in Education of the University of Toronto.

DiAngelo, R. (2006b). My race didn't trump my class: Using oppression to face privilege. *Multicultural Perspectives, 8*(1), 51–56.

DiAngelo, R. J. (2010). Why can't we all just be individuals? Countering the discourse of individualism in anti-racist education. *InterActions: UCLA Journal of Education and Information Studies, 6*(1). Retrieved from http://escholarship.org/uc/item/5fm4h8wm

Doane, A. W. (1997). White identity and race relations in the 1990s. In G. L. Carter (Ed.), *Perspectives on current social problems* (pp. 151–159). Allyn and Bacon.

Dyer, R. (1997). *White.* Routledge.

Feagin, J. (2000). *Racist America: Roots, current realities, and future reparations.* Routledge.

Feagin, J. (2006). *Systematic racism: A theory of oppression.* Routledge.

Fine, M. (1997a). Introduction. In M. Fine, L. Weis, C. Powell, & L. Wong (Eds.), *Off white: Readings on race, power, and society* (pp. vii–xii). Routledge.

Fine, M. (1997b). Witnessing whiteness. In M. Fine, L. Weis, C. Powell, & L. Wong (Eds.), *Off white: Readings on race, power, and society* (pp. 57–65). Routledge.

Flax, J. (1998). *American dream in Black and white: The Clarence Thomas hearings.* Cornell University Press.

Frankenberg, E., Lee, C., & Orfield, G. (2003). *A multiracial society with segregated schools: Are we losing the dream? The Civil Rights Project.* Retrieved from http://www.civilrightsproject.ucla.edu/research/reseg03/reseg03_full.php

Frankenberg, R. (1993). *The social construction of whiteness: White women, race matters*. University of Minnesota Press.

Frankenberg, R. (1997). Introduction: Local whitenesses, localizing whiteness. In R. Frankenberg (Ed.), *Displacing whiteness: Essays in social and cultural criticism* (pp. 1–33.). Duke University Press.

Frankenberg, R. (2001). The mirage of an unmarked whiteness. In B. B. Rasmussen, E. Klinenberg, I. J. Nexica, & M. Wray (Eds.), *The making and unmaking of whiteness* (pp. 72–96). Duke University Press.

Gee, J. P. (1999). *An introduction to discourse analysis: Theory and method*. Routledge.

Goldberg, D. T. (1993). *Racist culture*. Blackwell.

Hilliard, A. (1992). *Racism: Its origins and how it works* [Paper presentation]. Mid-West Association for the Education of Young Children, Madison, WI.

hooks, b. (1992). *Black looks: Race and representation*. South End Press.

Horton, J., & Scott, D. (2004). White students' voices in multicultural teacher education preparation. *Multicultural Education, 11*(4). Retrieved from http://findarticles.com/p/articles/mi_qa3935/is_200407/ai_n9414143/

Johnson, H. B., & Shapiro, T. M. (2003). Good neighborhoods, good schools: Race and the "good choices" of white families. In A. W. Doane & E. Bonilla-Silva (Eds.), *White out: The continuing significance of racism* (pp. 173–187). Routledge.

Lee, T. (1996). *Unraveling the "model-minority" stereotype: Listening to Asian-American youth*. Teachers College Press.

Marty, D. (1999). White antiracist rhetoric as apologia: Wendell Berry's *The Hidden Wound*. In T. Nakayama & J. Martin (Eds.), *Whiteness: The communication of social identity* (pp. 51–68). Sage.

McGowan, J. (2000). Multicultural teaching: African-American faculty classroom teaching experiences in predominantly white colleges and universities. *Multicultural Education, 8*(2), 19–22.

McIntosh, P. (1988). White privilege and male privilege: A personal account of coming to see correspondence through work in women's studies. In M. Anderson & P. Hill Collins (Eds.), *Race, class, and gender: An anthology* (pp. 94–105). Wadsworth.

Mills, C. (1999). *The racial contract*. Cornell University Press.

Morrison, T. (1992). *Playing in the dark*. Random House.

Nakayama, T., & Martin, J. (1999). *Whiteness: The communication of social identity*. Sage.

O'Donnell, J. (1998). Engaging students' recognition of racial identity. In R. C. Chavez & J. O'Donnell (Eds.), *Speaking the unpleasant: The politics of (non) engagement in the multicultural education terrain* (pp. 56–68). State University of New York Press.

Omi, M., & Winant, H. (1986). *Racial formation in the United States.* Routledge.

Powell, L. (1997). The achievement (k)not: Whiteness and 'Black underachievement.' In M. Fine, L. Powell, C. Weis, & L. Wong (Eds.), *Off white: Readings on race, power and society* (pp. 3–12). Routledge.

Ryan, W. (2001). Blaming the victim. In P. Rothenberg (Ed.), *Race, class, and gender in the United States: An integrated study* (pp. 572 582). Worth.

Sleeter, C. (1993). How white teachers construct race. In C. McCarthy & W. Crichlow (Eds.), *Race identity and representation in education* (pp. 157–171). Routledge.

Smith, A. (2005). *Conquest: Sexual violence and American Indian genocide.* Southend Press.

Sue, D. W. (2003). *Overcoming our racism: The journey to liberation.* Jossey-Bass.

Tatum, B. (1997). *"Why are all the Black kids sitting together in the cafeteria?" And other conversations about race.* New York: Basic Books.

Trepagnier, B. (2006). *Silent racism: How well-meaning white people perpetuate the racial divide.* Paradigm.

Van Dijk, T. A. (1993a). Analyzing racism through discourse analysis: Some methodological reflections. In J. H. Stanfield II & R. M. Dennis (Eds.), *Race and ethnicity in research methods* (pp. 92–134). Sage.

Van Dijk, T. A. (1993b). Principles of critical discourse analysis. *Discourse and Society*, 4(2), 249–283.

Vodde, R. (2001). De-centering privilege in social work education: Whose job is it anyway? *Journal of Race, Gender and Class*, 7(4), 139–160.

Weber, L. (2001). *Understanding race, class, gender, and sexuality: A conceptual framework.* McGraw-Hill.

Whitehead, K. A., & Wittig, M. A. (2005). Discursive management of resistance to a multi-cultural education programme. *Qualitative Research in Psychology*, 1(3), 267–284.

Zúñiga, X., Nagda, B., & Sevig, T. (2002). Intergroup dialogues: An educational model for cultivating engagement across differences. *Equity & Excellence in Education*, 6(1), 115–132.

SEVEN

White Fragility
An Abbreviated Version for Non-Academic Readers

I am white. I have spent years studying what it means to be white in a society that proclaims race meaningless, yet is deeply divided by race. This is what I have learned: Any white person living in the United States will develop opinions about race simply by swimming in the water of our culture. But mainstream sources—schools, textbooks, media—don't provide us with the multiple perspectives we need.

Yes, we will develop strong emotionally laden opinions, but they will not be informed opinions. Our socialization renders us racially illiterate. When you add a lack of humility to that illiteracy (because we don't know what we don't know), you get the breakdown we so often see when trying to engage white people in meaningful conversations about race.

Mainstream dictionary definitions reduce racism to individual racial prejudice and the intentional actions that result. The people who commit these intentional acts are deemed bad, and those that don't are good.

If we are against racism and unaware of committing racist acts, we can't be racist; racism and being a good person are mutually exclusive. But this definition does little to explain how racial hierarchies are consistently reproduced.

Social scientists understand racism as a multidimensional and highly adaptive *system*—a system that ensures an unequal distribution of resources between racial groups. Because white people built and dominate all significant institutions (often at the expense of and on the uncompensated

Originally published as "White Fragility and the Rules of Engagement," June 2015, https://goodmenproject.com/featured-content/white-fragility-and-the-rules-of-engagement-twlm/

labor of other groups), their interests are embedded in the foundation of U.S. society.

While individual white people may be against racism, they still benefit from the distribution of resources controlled by their group. Yes, an individual person of color can sit at the tables of power, but the overwhelming majority of decision makers will be white.

Yes, white people can have problems and face barriers, but systematic racism won't be one of them. This distinction—between individual prejudice and a system of unequal institutionalized racial power—is fundamental. One cannot understand how racism functions in the United States today if one ignores group power relations.

This systemic and institutional control allows those of us who are white in North America to live in a social environment that protects and insulates us from *race-based stress*.

We have organized society to reproduce and reinforce our racial interests and perspectives. Further, we are centered in all matters deemed normal, universal, benign, neutral, and good.

Thus, we move through a wholly racialized world with an unracialized identity (e.g., white people can represent all of humanity, people of color can only represent their racial selves).

Challenges to this identity become highly stressful and even intolerable. The following are examples of the kinds of challenges that trigger racial stress for white people:

- Suggesting that a white person's viewpoint comes from a racialized frame of reference (challenge to objectivity)
- People of color talking directly about their own racial perspectives (challenge to white taboos on talking openly about race)
- People of color choosing not to protect the racial feelings of white people in regard to race (challenge to white racial expectations and need/entitlement to racial comfort)
- People of color not being willing to tell their stories or answer questions about their racial experiences (challenge to the expectation that people of color will serve us)
- A fellow white not providing agreement with one's racial perspective (challenge to white solidarity)

+ Receiving feedback that one's behavior had a racist impact (challenge to white racial innocence)
+ Suggesting that group membership is significant (challenge to individualism)
+ An acknowledgment that access is unequal between racial groups (challenge to meritocracy)
+ Being presented with a person of color in a position of leadership (challenge to white authority)
+ Being presented with information about other racial groups through, for example, movies in which people of color drive the action but are not in stereotypical roles, or multicultural education (challenge to white centrality)

Not often encountering these challenges, we withdraw, defend, cry, argue, minimize, ignore, and in other ways push back to regain our racial position and equilibrium. I term that pushback "white fragility."

This concept came out of my ongoing experience leading discussions on race, racism, white advantage, and white supremacy with primarily white audiences. It became clear over time that white people have extremely low thresholds for enduring any discomfort associated with challenges to our racial worldviews.

We can manage the first round of challenge by ending the discussion through platitudes—usually something that starts with "People just need to," or "Race doesn't really have any meaning to me," or "Everybody's racist." Scratch any further on that surface, however, and we fall apart.

Socialized into a deeply internalized sense of superiority and entitlement that we are either not consciously aware of or can never admit to ourselves, we become highly fragile in conversations about race.

We experience a challenge to our racial worldview as a challenge to our very identities as good, moral people. It also challenges our sense of rightful place in the hierarchy. Thus, we perceive any attempt to connect us to the system of racism as a very unsettling and unfair moral offense.

The following patterns make it difficult for white people to understand racism as a *system* and lead to the dynamics of white fragility. While they do not apply to every white person, they are well documented overall.

Segregation: Most white people live, grow, play, learn, love, work, and die primarily in social and geographic racial segregation. Yet, our society does not teach us to see this as a loss. Pause for a moment and consider the magnitude of this message: We lose nothing of value by having no cross-racial relationships.

In fact, the whiter our schools and neighborhoods are, the more likely they are to be seen as "good." The implicit message is that there is no inherent value in the presence or perspectives of people of color. This is an example of the relentless messages of white superiority that circulate all around us, shaping our identities and worldviews.

The Good/Bad Binary: The most effective adaptation of racism over time is the idea that racism is conscious bias held by mean people. If we are not aware of having negative thoughts about people of color, don't tell racist jokes, are nice people, and even have friends of color, then we cannot be racist.

Thus, a person is either racist or not racist; if a person is racist, that person is bad; if a person is not racist, that person is good. Although racism does of course occur in individual acts, these acts are part of a larger system that we all participate in. The focus on individual incidences prevents the analysis that is necessary in order to challenge this larger system. The good/bad binary is the fundamental misunderstanding driving white defensiveness about being connected to racism. This defensiveness indicates that we simply do not understand how socialization and implicit bias work.

Individualism: White people are taught to see themselves as individuals, rather than as part of a racial group. Individualism enables us to deny that racism is structured into the fabric of society. This erases our history and hides the way in which wealth has accumulated over generations and benefits us, *as a group*, today.

It also allows us to distance ourselves from the history and actions of our group. Thus, we get very irate when we are "accused" of racism, because as individuals, we are "different" from other white people and expect to be seen as such; we find intolerable any suggestion that our behavior or perspectives are typical of our group as a whole.

Entitlement to Racial Comfort: In the dominant position, white people are almost always racially comfortable and thus have developed unchallenged expectations to remain so. We have not had to build tolerance for racial discomfort and thus when racial discomfort arises, we typically respond as if something is "wrong" and blame the person or event that triggered the discomfort (usually a person of color).

This blame results in a socially sanctioned array of responses towards the perceived source of the discomfort, including penalization, retaliation, isolation, and refusal to continue engagement. Since racism is necessarily uncomfortable in that it is oppressive, white insistence on racial comfort guarantees racism will not be faced except in the most superficial of ways.

Racial Arrogance: Most white people have a very limited understanding of racism because we have not been trained to think in complex ways about it and because it benefits white dominance not to do so. Yet, we have no compunction about debating the knowledge of people who have thought complexly about race. White people generally feel free to dismiss these informed perspectives rather than have the humility to acknowledge that they are unfamiliar, reflect on them further, or seek more information.

Racial Belonging: White people enjoy a deeply internalized, largely unconscious sense of racial belonging in U.S. society. In virtually any situation or image deemed valuable in dominant society, white people belong. The interruption of racial belonging is rare and thus destabilizing and frightening to white people and usually avoided.

Psychic Freedom: Because race is constructed as residing in people of color, white people don't bear the social burden of race. We move easily through our society without a sense of ourselves as racialized. Race is for people of color to think about—it is what happens to "them"—they can bring it up if it is an issue for them (although if they do, we can dismiss it as a personal problem, the race card, or the reason for their problems). This allows white people much more psychological energy to devote to other issues and prevents us from developing the stamina to sustain attention on an issue as charged and uncomfortable as race.

Constant Messages That We Are More Valuable: Living in a white-dominant context, we receive constant messages that we are better and more important than people of color. For example: our centrality in history textbooks, and historical representations and perspectives; our centrality in media and advertising; our teachers, role-models, heroes, and heroines; everyday discourse on "good" neighborhoods and schools and who is in them; popular TV shows centered on friendship circles that are all white; religious iconography that depicts God, Adam and Eve, and other key figures as white.

While one may explicitly reject the notion that one is inherently better than another, one cannot avoid internalizing the message of white superiority, as it is ubiquitous in mainstream culture.

These dynamics and the white fragility that results prevent us from listening to or comprehending the perspectives of people of color and bridging cross-racial divides. The antidote to white fragility is ongoing and lifelong, and includes sustained engagement, humility, and education. We can begin by

- Being willing to tolerate the discomfort associated with an honest appraisal and discussion of our internalized superiority and racial advantage
- Challenging our own racial reality by acknowledging ourselves as racial beings with a particular and *necessarily limited* perspective on race; we need to have some racial humility
- Attempting to understand the racial realities of people of color through authentic interaction rather than through the media or unequal relationships
- Taking action to address our own racism, the racism of other white people, and the racism embedded in our institutions—that is, get educated and act

"Getting it" when it comes to race and racism challenges our very identities as good white people. It's an ongoing and often painful process of seeking to uncover our socialization at its very roots.

It asks us to rebuild this identity in new and often uncomfortable ways. But I can testify that it is also the most exciting, powerful, intellectually stimulating, and emotionally fulfilling journey I have ever undertaken. It has impacted every aspect of my life—personal and professional.

I have a much deeper and more complex understanding of how society works. I can challenge much more racism in my daily life, and I have developed cherished and fulfilling cross-racial friendships I did not have before.

I do not expect racism to end in my lifetime, and I know that I continue to have problematic racist patterns and perspectives. Yet, I am also confident that I do less harm to people of color than I used to. This is not a minor point of growth, for it impacts my lived experience and that of the people of color who interact with me. If you are white, I urge you to take the first step—let go of your racial certitude and reach for humility.

EIGHT

"We Put It in Terms of Not-Nice"
White Antiracists and Parenting

SARAH A. MATLOCK AND ROBIN DIANGELO

INTRODUCTION

A foundational principle in the antiracist literature is that white antiracism requires an ongoing process of understanding white privilege and supremacy; challenging color-blindness; countering internalized white superiority; being an ally to people of color; being accountable to people of color; and engaging in meaningful action against racism at a personal, interpersonal, and community level (Derman-Sparks & Ramsey, 2006; Raible, 2009). This process entails a critical analysis of the forces of racial socialization and their manifestation in one's own life. There are various sites of entry into this analysis, including schooling, media, economics, family, and geography. This study focuses on the family as one primary site of racial socialization and thus a primary site for interrupting racism.

There has been little written about antiracist childrearing in general, and white antiracist parenting in particular. Our aim was to explore how white people who identify as antiracists and who are also parents of white children apply antiracism principles to their parenting. Specifically, how do white parents who identify themselves as antiracist socialize their children with these values and practices? Our findings indicate significant

Originally published as Sarah A. Matlock & Robin DiAngelo (2015), "We Put It in Terms of Not-Nice": White Antiracists and Parenting, *Journal of Progressive Human Services*, 26(1), 67–92, DOI: 10.1080 /10428232.2015.977836. Copyright © 2015, reprinted by permission of Taylor & Francis Ltd, http://www.tandfonline.com.

inconsistencies between the values of white parents who identify as antiracist and their parenting practices. These inconsistencies manifested most clearly through patterns in neighborhood and school choice and in denial of their child's racial knowledge. We found that the main difference between antiracist white parents and non-antiracist-identified white parents was one of *awareness*. While antiracist white parents overall were aware of racism as a system of oppression that conferred unearned privileges, and they conveyed this awareness to their children, there was minimal modeling of antiracist *action*.

White Parenting and Color-Blindness

Much of the contemporary writing about racism includes discussion of the phenomenon of color-blindness—the assertion that one doesn't see color or that "we are all human" and thus race has no significance. While there is no biological race as we understand it, race as a *social idea* has profound significance and impacts every aspect of our lives. This impact includes where we are most likely to live, which schools we will attend, who our friends and partners will be, what careers we will have, how much money we will earn, how much education we will have, how healthy we will be, and even how long we can expect to live (Adelman, 2003). Yet color-blind ideology is prominent among white Americans, many of whom consider themselves to be politically progressive (Bonilla-Silva, 2006; Wise, 2010). Bonilla-Silva (2006) describes color-blind racism as a modern version of the Jim Crow era of the 1960s and 1970s, and "the main force behind contemporary inequality . . . it is as effective as slavery and Jim Crow in maintaining the racial status quo" (p. 272). This is one of the most inherently racist consequences of color-blindness; if institutional racism does not account for disparity, personal shortcomings become the de facto cause. Color-blindness—as a discourse that is ubiquitous in mainstream culture—is also highly evident among white parents (Johnson & Shapiro, 2003; Park, 2010; Van Ausdale & Feagin, 2001). For example, Tatum (1997) discusses how color-blindness is evoked when she addresses parent groups, wherein white parents often contend with pride that their children are color-blind, and offer as evidence a story of friendship with a child of color whose race has never been mentioned. Yet Tatum identifies the legacy of silencing children around race and notes that white people often refer to someone as *Black* in hushed tones that imply there is something wrong with such an identification.

Johnson and Shapiro (2003) explicate color-blindness in a research study in which they interviewed approximately 200 white families in Boston, St. Louis, and Los Angeles about their school and neighborhood choices. While the parents consistently opened their discussions with the claim that race does not matter, as the interviews continued it became clear that race powerfully informed their decisions. Some of the content was overtly racist while some was coded by terms such as "good" (white) schools or neighborhoods versus "bad" ones. Johnson and Shapiro conclude that despite the widespread popularity of color-blindness, race was a primary factor, if not *the* primary factor, in determining white decisions on community and school choice.

Child Development and Racial Attitudes

While there is some disagreement in the literature about the *degree* of complexity in children's racial understandings, it is well established that children do notice racial distinctions and recognize that it is taboo (at least among white people) to talk about them (Tatum, 1997; Van Ausdale & Feagin, 2001). Further, there are a small number of compelling studies that indicate children's racial knowledge is much more sophisticated than commonly thought.

Monteiro et al. (2009) examined white children's expressions of racial prejudice under different conditions. They hypothesized that those children older than 7 would express less prejudice if an antiracism norm was present. The antiracism norm was created by the presence of a white researcher, whom they hypothesized would create—just by virtue of their presence in the room—the expectation that racial bias or discrimination should not be shown. They tested 283 white children aged 6 to 7 and 9 to 10 years old who performed a task of money allocation to white and Black target children. They were tested with and without the presence of a white researcher to create more or less salience of the antiracism norm. They found that the 6- to 7-year-old children discriminated against the Black targets in both conditions, and the 9- to 10-year-old children discriminated against the Black children only when the antiracism norm was not salient (Monteiro et al., 2009). This is significant because it indicates the older children clearly had racial prejudice but repressed blatant expressions of it under certain social conditions; bias does not decline with the age of the children, but rather their ability to self-regulate to social cues increases.

Earlier studies conducted by Kenneth and Mamie Clark illustrate that children internalize society's racial hierarchy very early (Clark & Clark, 1939, 1950). They found that by age 3, Black children had begun to internalize a sense that they were inferior to white people; by age 7, this sense was firmly in place. They conducted their studies by asking the children to choose which doll they preferred, a white doll or a Black doll. Their questions included "Give me the doll that you like to play with," "Give me the doll that looks bad," and "Give me the doll that is a nice color." The majority of the children preferred the white doll to the Black, and this preference was stable regardless of whether they lived in the northern or southern United States, although northern children had a more definite preference for white skin. Similar studies have been informally conducted on both Black and white children in recent years with the same results. When asked why the Black doll looks bad, both white and Black children consistently attributed it to the doll's Blackness.

In conclusion, the research indicates that children are aware of race and that they internalize both implicit and explicit messages about race from their environment. Thus, children are more aware that racial difference has social meaning than they are often given credit for. Children's early awareness of racial difference lends itself well to providing them with guidance about racism and other forms of oppression. However, this opportunity is lost through the tendency for white parents and teachers to identify children as racially naïve or color-blind, framing the discussion in terms of interpersonal difference rather than an unequal power structure that benefits white people. This study assumed that white parents who self-identify as antiracist are more likely to understand this distinction, and that they provide guidance in antiracist principles and practices to their children. Thus, this study sought to identify *how* they provide this guidance.

METHODOLOGY

This research was conducted as an exploratory qualitative study of the experiences, practices, and values of white people who identify as antiracist, and how these influence their parenting of white children. This study attempts to shed light on what antiracism means to white people in the United States who claim to identify with it, and how they attempt to incorporate antiracism into their parenting. Of particular interest was how these parents' childrearing practices compared to current antiracism theory and literature. As a qualitative study with 20 participants, this research does not represent white antiracist parents as a whole. However, it will offer insight into families within the white antiracism movement and hopefully encourage future directions for research.

Sample

The data was collected by way of individual interview and consists of the narrative responses of 20 white Americans who identified as antiracist and were the parents of white children. The interviews spanned 30–105 minutes each, with 1,222 minutes of audio data collected in total on a digital recorder. The inclusion criteria for this study were that the individual identified their primary racial identity as white, they identified as antiracist, they were over the age of 18 and English speaking, and they had at least one child over the age of 3 whose primary racial identity was also white. The sample included 18 people who identified as female and 2 who identified as male, with an age range of 30–58. The majority of participants had a middle-class upbringing and currently identified as middle class, and they reported a variety of sexual orientations, religious backgrounds, and current religions.

Data Collection

Participants were recruited through organizations in the Seattle area where we anticipated white people with antiracism values would likely be. This included a local university, community colleges, and organizing collectives involved in racial equity or social justice work. We made contacts within these organizations and advertised the study via poster and email listserv. Recruitment was snowball and ongoing. As participants were interviewed, they were encouraged to forward the recruitment email to others who might qualify for the study.

Once a participant responded to recruitment efforts by email or phone, inclusion criteria was verified, and for those who met criteria, in-person interview sessions were scheduled. No one who met the criteria and responded before the deadline was excluded. This served to strengthen the validity of this small sample and include as many perspectives as possible. Informed consent was obtained and participants were informed participation was voluntary and they could refuse to answer any questions. The researcher used a structured interview guide starting with demographic questions, then open-ended questions related to the research objectives.

These open-ended questions included asking participants to define what antiracism means to them, as well as questions about their childhood experiences regarding race and racism, and the racial makeup of their friendship circles, neighborhoods, and schools. These were followed up by questions on how participants attempt to incorporate antiracism values into their parenting, how they conceptualize the racial awareness of their children, and how they feel race and racism impact their children. Participants were also asked about the racial makeup of their children's friendship circles, neighborhoods, and schools. Audio data was transcribed by the researcher with identifying information such as names or places was removed. Participants were provided a $30 gift card to a local bookstore as an honorarium.

Data Analysis

Data was analyzed by grouping responses and identifying major themes. Responses to each question by an individual participant were coded into categories based on what was mentioned or discussed, such as white privilege, institutional racism, "reverse racism," color-blindness, tracking within schools, slavery, and talking about skin color. Coding was initiated with the first transcript and was refined to accommodate subsequent data as it was collected. The variety and prevalence of coded categories across participants were reviewed and reported, including patterns and anomalies.

Many themes surfaced across multiple interviews, including color-blindness, school program choices, gentrification, economic privilege, valuing diversity, activism, degree of awareness of whiteness, and underestimating the sophistication of children's racial understanding. Due to the limits of this chapter, we selected for discussion the themes that arose most frequently, directly addressed the research question, and/or were discussed in antiracism literature. Quotations were used to illustrate salient themes.

FINDINGS

How does being an antiracist white person influence your parenting?
All participants stated that their antiracism values influenced their parenting; however, how they influenced it varied greatly. The themes cited most frequently were choice of school and neighborhood. Also mentioned were choice of books, toys, and media; exposure to parent's antiracism; and discussions about various aspects of race and racism.

Six participants (30%) discussed living in a primarily white neighborhood either before they had children or early in their child's life, and then moving to a racially diverse neighborhood so their child would have exposure to people of color. Many parents spoke with pride about the diversity of their neighborhood. However, these participants also spontaneously discussed gentrification. Several who had lived in their neighborhoods for many years acknowledged their neighborhood had once been primarily people of color, but now families of color were moving out and more white people were moving in.

Of the 20 participants, only 4 (20%) indicated they had lived in their diverse neighborhood when it was primarily people of color. The 13 who cited racial diversity as a reason for moving to their neighborhood did so once the wave of gentrification had already begun; these parents were aware that the neighborhood they bought into would continue to become whiter. This was framed as an unfortunate occurrence, and none indicated whether or not they were motivated by this knowledge when they bought their homes.

School Choice and Racial Makeup of School and Program

As illustrated in Figure 8.1, 13 out of 21 parents (65%) interviewed mentioned school choice as being directly influenced by their antiracism values, and several important themes emerged in the parents' discussions about schools. Participants were not asked about the type of school their child attended; however, all participants spontaneously discussed it. Of the 21 parents, 15 (75%) reported their child or children were in a public school, and 5 reported their child or children were in a private school, including Waldorf, private elementary, home, or Montessori. Of the 9 parents who reported that their child/children went to a diverse school, their definition of diverse is unknown in terms of the actual racial makeup of the schools. Additionally, of the participants who reported that their children attended a diverse school, the children tended to be in the whiter honors, alternative, or Montessori programs.

Five of the 21 parents (25%) reported their child or children were in a school program that was almost all children of color (see Figure 8.2). Of the 5 with children in programs that were predominately children of color, 4 (80%) of them had their child enrolled in schools that were majority Asian, including two Asian language immersion programs. It is noteworthy that 4 participants (20%) of the sample felt comfortable with their child in programs with majority Asian children, but only 1 (5%) of 21

Figure 8.1. Racial Makeup of Children's Schools

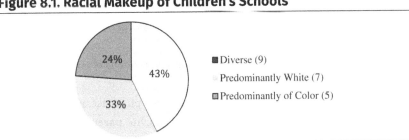

Figure 8.2. Racial Makeup of Children's Programs Within Diverse Schools

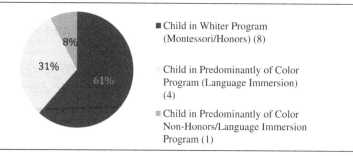

■ Child in Whiter Program (Montessori/Honors) (8)

Child in Predominantly of Color Program (Language Immersion) (4)

▥ Child in Predominantly of Color Non-Honors/Language Immersion Program (1)

parents stated they sent their child to a school program that was majority Black or Latino.

The Use of Books, Media, Toys, and Music

Eleven of 21 participants (55%) mentioned the use of books when trying to instill antiracism values. Two parents (10%) also described going to the public library in their neighborhood with their child and expressed that they valued the diversity of the staff and patrons of the library. Five of the participants (25%) mentioned media as one way antiracism and parenting intersect, selecting specific shows for their child to watch because they had characters of color or of various cultural backgrounds.

Two parents talked about the subliminal racial messaging their sons receive from toys. For example:

> Leanne: It's sort of like the playmobile version of history . . . it's mostly about Western Europeans' interactions with other cultures . . . we won't let him get some of the themes, like ancient *Rome* where people were quite horrible to one another. . . . And so he learns about slavery, in a context like that, it's not fun, it's real, and it's the legacy of millions and millions of Americans.

Both of these parents reported they still purchase playmobiles for their children, in spite of their reservations. One parent stated that she limited the television and movies her children were exposed to because of the racist content in the mainstream media, and one stated that she allowed her teenage child to watch television but asks her to analyze what she watches and points out images of white supremacy and racism.

Talking About Skin Color

Seven of 21 of participants (35%) named talking about skin color as a way they implemented antiracism in their child's lives. This was one of the top four themes brought up by the parents in this study. Many used books or mentioned activities in their child's school in which they talked about skin color and diversity, especially for elementary school age children. For example, Willa describes conversations about skin color with her 3- and 5-year-old children:

> My kids would comment on ... that brown guy. ... I've never shushed them, because I remember being shushed for saying Black, like that's a bad word or something ... we would talk about ... their skin, and I would never say it's white or Black, but I would say it's kind of pinkish, whitish, yellowish, brownish. ... We're Christians, so we talk a lot about how God made people all different colors ... And when they started noticing differences, I would point them out as just you know, my purse is black ... just a fact, not carrying any weight other than what it is.

Wendy also discussed skin color with her 3-year-old:

> Well we've already had a discussion about skin. She's the one that brought it up, at 3 she's just very tuned in. And she said, "What is that Black woman doing?" ... so we just started talking about, "You noticed she has brown skin," you know, "What color is your skin? What color is my skin, what color is teacher's?" ... I've been trying to do that pretty regularly, and then I've been really trying to have books that have brown children, so that it's not just, you know, white characters in her books. ...

Wendy and Willa are examples of a more color-blind approach. Wendy repeatedly stated that her daughter was "only 3-years-old" during the interview, implying there was not much antiracism work to do with her yet.

Stephanie approached skin color differently, stressing whiteness and privilege instead of difference:

> We had the *mala* on our wrists with white beads and I was able to teach her, when she was in middle childhood that when she looked at it was a reminder that she was white, because it was the only thing to remind her, everyday . . . she has this language and she understands white privilege. . . . I think the most important thing for my daughters to know is . . . to say something as a white person in all white situations, just speak up, whenever there is racism.

Unlike most of the parents, Stephanie names racism often and directly, encourages her daughter to speak up, and mentions the importance of allyship.

Exposure to Antiracism Activism Through Their School and Parent's Work

Six of the 20 participants (30%) mentioned engaging in antiracism within their child's school. Examples of the type of antiracist work they did was organizing parents' groups to address issues of racism/unexamined privilege and promote diversity within the school, working against under-resourced school closure, and collaborating with teachers to address incidents of racism. Here Maria describes what she did in her children's school:

> In the grade-school they went to I was co-facilitator of an antiracist group of parents and teachers. . . . Their mission statement said something about racial justice or diversity or something, but in reality . . . the disproportionality in outcomes for kids of color at that school were still the same, so now playing a leadership role, co-facilitating with a woman of color, and really trying to get to a point where it's not just "Blah blah blah" but *really* trying to turn that . . . into a different reality.

Five of the 20 parents (25%) mentioned that their children were exposed to their antiracism work, either because antiracism was part of their job, or because they engaged in antiracism work voluntarily in their community, or both.

Talking About Racism

When asked how they incorporate antiracism into their childrearing, many of the participants described talking to their kids about racism. Five of 21 parents (25%) described teaching their child an anti-oppression framework, or explaining to them how to analyze systems of power and privilege in order to understand the racialized world around them. Six of 21 (30%) stated that they discussed incidents of racism in their children's lives. Several of the parents with young children mentioned struggling to find the right words or to discuss racism in an age-appropriate way. The quote used in the study's title "We put it in terms of 'not-nice'" was one father's approach to discussing racism with his child. Willa's comments represent another example of this:

> My son has learned a lot in his classroom, so he'll come home and give us facts, and we'll turn around and say . . . "You know when Grammy and Grampy were kids, they didn't get to go to school with Black kids; they only went to school with people who were their color! What do you think about that?" I wonder if we are erring too far on the side of "back then" that's what people did, and isn't that silly, and not being as aware of what we do today, but, I think for kids we're keeping it simple. So we've talked about MLK, and Medgar Evers . . . because of people like them, standing up for what they believed, now you get to go to school with, and he has a bunch of little friends that I'll name off by name.

Like many of the parents, Willa questioned her approach, in this case wondering if she focuses too much on "back then."

Discussions About Slavery

Three of the parents spontaneously brought up discussing slavery. However, there was a significant range in how they approached it. For example, Lila, who grew up in the South and is the mother of a 4-year-old girl, reflects on her own upbringing and what she is trying to do differently for her child:

We were white, so we didn't need to discuss the racism, we didn't need to discuss slavery. Which every now and then that's already come up with my daughter and I've tried to explain, "At one point people thought it was okay to own other people." . . . It was a long time ago, and then it was different. And that it was a different part of the country, but at one point, people thought they could tell other people what to do . . . and you had to do it, or else somebody could hurt you. But at the same time I can't make it too scary of a concept.

Lila, while trying to keep her explanation simple and developmentally appropriate, does not name race. Later in the interview, Lila passionately expresses more thoughts about slavery from an exclusively white perspective on the Civil War:

The Civil War—not all about slavery—primarily economics. And trying to explain that that's one of the reasons why it wasn't about "Oh you took my slaves from me" but it was "You took my only means of supporting my family away" and that . . . that still hits hard to this day in that area. You know? Families were just left devastated.

Rachelle, a community organizer, also mentioned trying to explain slavery to her young son while teaching him about race and ethnicity:

So I got this book on talking about race and culture, and where people came from and where he came from, from Ireland, and England, and we would start using a map talking about different children, and the teachers . . . and it was in some ways, maybe easier because a lot of the teachers and kids actually came from those countries. But when we got to African Americans, I was like, "Ok, we've got to say more about this" because people didn't come by choice. So . . . one day when he was like 4–4½ . . . and we hit on the Middle Passage, and you know, I thought, "What am I doing to my kid? I'm talking to my 4-year-old about slave ships?" And then I would turn it back on him and say, "What do you think about that? Does that sound like a fair thing to you?"

Like many parents interviewed here, Rachelle worries that talking openly and directly about racism will be harmful to her white child. And as many parents did, she ends by giving him the option of considering whether racism—and in this case *slavery*—is "fair" or not.

All of the parents who independently brought up slavery expressed that they found it challenging to strike the balance of providing truthful information in a way that they perceived to be developmentally appropriate.

How Aware of Race and Racism Do You Think Your Child Is?

As can be seen from Figure 8.3, the majority of parents believed that their children were not aware of racism, or only minimally aware. However, 5 parents (25%), all of whom had children ages 10 and above, stated that their children were "very aware" of race and racism. For example, Laura states:

> I think she's very aware of it, really aware of it. . . . When she was in 4th grade she made this newspaper . . . and she had some articles in there about racism, so yeah, she was already thinking about it and articulating it then, but really it wasn't until she was in high school that I feel like she was able to . . . really get it. I feel like she's really using the analysis now, she can articulate that.

Figure 8.3. How Aware of Race or Racism Is Your Child?

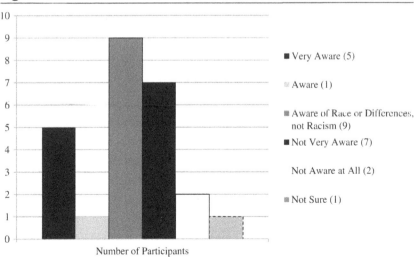

Legend:
- Very Aware (5)
- Aware (1)
- Aware of Race or Differences, not Racism (9)
- Not Very Aware (7)
- Not Aware at All (2)
- Not Sure (1)

Number of Participants

Similar to Laura, one other parent stated that her older child had integrated antiracist values into her life. At the same time, these parents did not mention discussing the racism that their children had internalized or indicate that they were engaged in an ongoing process of self-reflection; their focus in answering this question was on their children speaking out about other people's racism.

THEMES

White Children Expressing Racism Against Black Children

Several participants gave examples of times their children expressed that they didn't like Black children or thought they were mean or bad. One parent—Leanne—discussed her son's statement about African American boys in his public school elementary class:

> There are a few Black kids, not very many in that school, mostly African immigrants but some American Black, and uh, [sighs] Tom hasn't made particular friends with them, and he says, "They're mean" and so I started thinking about how Black kids are suspended more, and get in trouble for being boisterous in the classroom, and how much of that is teacher perception, and how much of that is student behavior. Because I don't think Tom is making stuff up, he's too little to be doing that stuff.

While Leanne is aware of some of the ways racism impacts the educational experience of Black elementary school children, she still suspects that the Black kids may actually be acting out more than other children—rather than responding to their environment. She doesn't mention the possibility that racism informs why Tom perceives the same behavior from the Black boys in his class as more aggressive.

Willa also commented on her 3-year-old daughter's negative statement about a Black child in her school:

> My 3-year-old said something a few weeks ago like, "I don't like that kid because he's brown" and my husband and I were freaked out, and we were trying not to

react too much, but we'd be like, "Why? What do you mean? Daddy's kinda pinkish, and I'm kinda yellowish, what do you think about that?" But she gets there's some kind of cultural difference there. I don't know why for her that means she doesn't like them. But we're trying to work with that.

In keeping with the assumption of racial innocence in children, Willa states that she doesn't understand why her daughter would have these feelings. She also doesn't question what might be going on in the classroom environment as a whole.

White Children Internalizing Entitlement or Superiority

Several of the parents gave examples of their white sons being given some sort of "special status" or being treated well. Jana told a poignant story about her son, Aiden, who is in a Mandarin immersion program. He is the only white child in the class, which is otherwise attended by Chinese and Korean American students:

> This is the *Chinese Weekly*, and they took out a full page ad and of course they put the one white child's picture . . . God . . . it almost made me feel guilty like why did you pick my one kid? . . . It made me feel like . . . I don't know . . . he was singled out because of his race and because she [teacher] feels like that's what people want to see."

Jana shared two more examples of Aiden's experiences in school, involving the school Christmas program:

> They make him Rudolph the red-nosed reindeer . . . so then all the other kids were the other reindeer, and then he was Santa, in the second part too. And then they had some sort-of baby Jesus, and he was baby Jesus.

In one final example, Jana shared a picture from Aiden's yearbook, in which Aiden has on a pair of fake reading glasses and is next to a Chinese girl. The caption says, "Follow me I can read for you." Jana states they call him "Dr. Wilson" and while she acknowledges that he is a good reader, she wonders why the teachers in the school think he can teach the other children. She is uncomfortable with the idea that her son has been given a special status, but has not discussed her discomfort with the teachers. In an environment run by women of color, she is surprised her son would be treated better than the other children.

Jana was not the only parent who mentioned the portrayal of Christian figures impacting the sense of self of a white son. Leanne shared an example of her son expressing white supremacy:

> I remember we were walking right near here down the street, and he said something about God being *white*. Well first of all, we're not a religious household, we don't talk about God, he probably hears it from friends, or relatives, but *God being white?* And I lit into him, like where did you get this!? You know, when Jesus is pictured, he's almost always white and he extrapolated from that.

Many parents talked about their white children as being particularly intelligent. Leanne described Tom's experiences in school, which are similar to those described by Jana, above:

> Tom, he's smart, he tested into the APP programs, we've known ever since he was very little, that he's bright and he's socially adept too, which is a nice combination. And he's pretty. So Tom's the golden child . . . he has been on the front page of the city paper . . . he's picked, partly because he's white. . . . There are Asian kids in his class too, but they'll never get picked. Because he's pretty and he has blond hair [sigh]. I haven't wanted to say, "You're just getting the attention because you're white" because it's much more than that.

While both Leanne and Jana recognize that their sons are receiving white privilege, neither mother has taken steps to address this in their child's school.

Gentrification

Gentrification was another theme that spontaneously arose in the data. The majority of participants—65%—stated that neighborhood choice was an aspect of integrating antiracism values into their parenting, and many of them cited it first, indicating it is the primary way in which they identify their antiracism values in practice. Thirteen of 19 (65%) also stated they lived in diverse neighborhoods and within the conversations 45% described gentrification (see Figures 8.4 and 8.5). Lila was one such parent:

> I like where we are, we're actually a very diverse neighborhood, although really it's a lot of gay white men [laughs].

Lila's contradiction between stating her neighborhood is diverse and then stating that it's really a lot of gay white men illustrates the difficulty in assessing white people's perceptions regarding racial diversity. Jess described her neighborhood this way:

> Our neighborhood is very clearly white ... not entirely but primarily and culturally it's like white middle-class, um. . . . But then it's like three blocks

Figure 8.4. Racial Makeup of Children's Neighborhoods

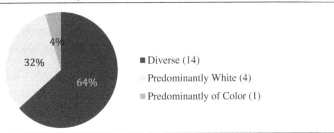

Figure 8.5. Gentrification

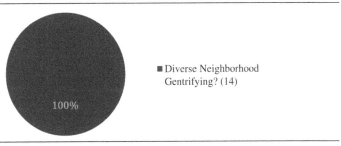

down the street is primarily African American, you know? It's only three blocks, right? But it feels like a very far distance . . . the places we go are the other places in the area that are still primarily white and . . . so the larger neighborhood is actually pretty racially diverse, but there's a way that we're able to choose to stay in a very white part of that neighborhood.

These parents identify how segregation manifests within the context of diverse neighborhoods. Three participants also specifically mentioned the zip code of their neighborhood and two of them made the point that it was the most diverse zip code in the country. However, this zip code is steadily gentrifying as many Black-owned businesses are being driven out. The narratives here support the data that there is a trend for white people to seek out these neighborhoods and co-opt them rather than integrate themselves into the community and patronize businesses owned by people of color.

Women of Color and Early Child Care

Several participants brought up having a child-care worker in their home or noted racism in the behavior of other white parents' choices for child care and early childhood education. One mother simply noted that she had a "mother's helper" from Mexico for 1 year to teach her child Spanish. Here Nora wonders about the potential impact of having an au pair who is a woman of color:

Our recent au pair she was from Brazil . . . they really saw her as a family member . . . on the other hand . . . she did a lot of work around the house . . . and I didn't want them to think like, you know, "We're all white, and this Asian girl . . . I can tell her what to do and she does our laundry." I didn't want them to define race that way. And they probably didn't, but I made sure she wasn't the only one doing the laundry; we all had a lot of work to do around the house.

Rachelle described her observations of the white parents in her son's school program:

We chose a day-care center that was run by a nonprofit for refugee women. And a lot of other white parents were choosing it for infant and toddler care. . . . About half his class was white kids and as the kids moved up beyond the toddler program to the preschool, all except two other white families moved their kids to different preschools . . . I have the sense that for many of the other white folks . . . taking care of a baby or toddler, they saw it as a perfectly appropriate role for women of color. . . . But the point at which they saw their kids as needing to be *learning* and needing to be in an academic environment . . . a couple parents said, "Well I want to make sure my kid speaks English properly" and "Well you know, they won't get the right kind of preparation for kindergarten and things." And . . . even . . . with all the work I've done, it was one of those stunning moments for me.

Rachelle observes that white parents—even those she assumes hold anti-racist values—still enact racist relations with women of color whom they see as qualified to care for but not to teach their children.

DISCUSSION

This research shows that white parents who identify with antiracism values are almost universally contradicting their value system in significant ways. The most noteworthy contradictions that we will discuss here were related to school choice and denial of their children's racial awareness.

School and Neighborhood Choice

The majority of parents stated that they chose a school based on diversity. However, most also spontaneously discussed the racial makeup of their child's program within the school, and these programs tended to be whiter and included many more middle- to upper-income families. The "school within a school" phenomenon is well known; honors programs are often completely different from mainstream school programs, which are typically under-resourced and taught by inexperienced teachers, amounting to de facto segregation (Oakes, 2008).

Johnson and Shapiro (2003) showed that "average" white parents' school and neighborhood decisions were based on race and served to secure education and economic advantage for their children. In terms of neighborhood choice, the antiracist white parents interviewed here differed from the non-antiracist-identifying parents in Johnson and Shapiro's study in that they exposed prodiversity values and chose to live in neighborhoods with people of color. Yet, as Johnson and Shapiro note:

> Ultimately, no matter how conflicted they are, the end result is the same. white families choose to live in, and are rewarded for living in, white neighborhoods . . . the social structure rewards white families for perpetuating segregation through their racialized decisions. (pp. 182–183)

For many of the parents interviewed here, neighborhood choice was stated as the main way they incorporated antiracism values into their parenting. Still, there weren't any that reported that their neighborhood was predominantly of color; most were in diverse neighborhoods that were gentrifying. While they stated that they ideally wanted a school that was both diverse and "good," the perceived quality of the program trumped racial diversity almost exclusively—and quality was consistently associated with race. There were a few rare examples in which the parents in this study identified school environments that were predominantly children of color to be high- or higher-quality than the whiter programs, but several of these parents expressed concern that their white child would have a negative experience, and/or lose their academic edge in a "traditional" (aka non-Montessori, non-honors) and less white environment. Thus, they avoided these academically strong programs.

These parents' choices happen within a highly inequitable context, and in this context they have options their counterparts with less race and class privilege do not. On one hand, despite having race (and for the most part class) privilege, these parents are going against the white norms in that they generally teach their children about racism, talk about white privilege, sometimes model activism for them in their school or their community, and in some cases are highly involved in racial justice movement work. On the other hand, they want to ensure privilege for their children, and their antiracism work—where it occurs—does not challenge their own children's racial advantage.

Some parents commented that institutional racism and tracking were in place in their school and expressed concern about programs being skewed along race and class lines as a result. The group who was concerned with racial disparities in their child's school struggled more with the decision about whether or not they should enroll their child in the non-honors or traditional program that was majority children of color. However, whether or not the parent felt conflicted about it, virtually all of them chose to place their child in the program that was considered "better" academically (if the better program was also whiter). Most did not think it was possible for the non-honors program to be high quality, yet it was unclear what they based this assessment on (however, coded racism is inherent in white discourses about schools as "good" or "bad" largely based on the mere presence of students of color in any significant number). Some of these parents discussed the alternative programs as a "better fit" for their children; the concept of fit may signify white middle/upper-class cultural values or norms (Sensoy & DiAngelo, 2012).

Several parents acknowledged that being middle- or upper-middle-class, they could remove their child at any time and place them in private school. Teresa described her son Darren's experience in a predominately Black after-school program, and her response:

> He never used race, like he never said, "Mommy I don't like it here" but often, like when I'd go pick him up, he'd be alone on the playground, playing by himself. 'Cause a lot of the kids were older, playing kickball and a lot of other really physical games, and you know he was a kindergartner. For me I really wanted him in the program, because it was so diverse. But the quality of the program wasn't good enough for me to feel good about the second year. I'm like, I can't really do this to my child for the sake of getting him exposed to diversity. . . . I didn't tell him why I was taking him out, I just said, "We're gonna get a nanny now."

Teresa was not atypical in her expression of valuing diversity while being unwilling to let her child struggle with the social difficulties of being in the minority. Shayla talked openly about the contradiction between her anti-racism values and her school choices:

> I looked for co-ops that had some racial and socioeconomic diversity and there is some in the one we went to but they're certainly white-dominated places. I made sure to check and make sure that there were African American kids in those classes, and there were, but it certainly wasn't the regular classes at the school, which was almost all African American, and I wasn't willing to go there. Not because of it being all African American, in fact that would be a great experience for Elijah, but it didn't have a reputation for being a program that was good for those kids, never mind my kid . . . and so I've been thinking about moving my son into the contemporary program. . . . So I really struggled with that, right? Do I move him because I want him to have that experience of being not in the majority, as a male, as a white male, and learning from an African American woman in particular, in a historically Black neighborhood? We have gentrification in the area I live, so all the people like me are looking for "Where's the safe place to send my child?" So I want to be able to say, "The contemporary program is a really good program, and we want everybody to be in every program, please send your kids!" But how can I do that if my kid isn't in it?

Further intensifying Shayla's internal conflict about program choice, her husband and other family members don't understand why she would even consider the main program.

It is also worthy of note that Shayla consulted the school principal (a white woman) about moving her child into the contemporary program, and the principal told her not to do it.

Maria also clearly described the contradictions between her own values and behaviors around school choice:

> We live in a really diverse neighborhood, more diverse when we moved in than it is now, but . . . our neighborhood middle school, it just really felt . . . like a prison or something. . . . You're welcomed by signs on the window that say things like, "3 Tardies = Suspension and 3 Suspensions = Expulsion." I want my kids to be excited about learning, not feeling like it's punishment.

So ... it was clear that it was like, "God this is not what I want my kids to be exposed to" and so I visit a bunch of other middle schools around the city ... *the best* was actually in [white neighborhood] and so low-and-behold, it's not a very diverse middle school, and so *trying* to balance.... You know that mama-bear kicks in. And for me as a parent who was trying to be cognizantly antiracist, it becomes really complicated, where it feels like there's a choice between sort-of a "good" education, vs. a "sucky" education that's more diverse. As a white middle-class parent ... in the middle of trying to change the system, you're also a part of the system.

Five parents described engaging in antiracism activism within their child's school. Some had worked to fight the closure of the under-resourced neighborhood school their children attended; others worked with parents of color to push for racial equity within their schools. Many described reaching out to parents of color to try and create relationships across racial and class lines. All of these activities are the self-report of white parents— how the parents of color they interacted with felt about their efforts is unknown. The majority of the narratives are more consistent with aversive racism—the type of racism well-intentioned, educated, progressive people are more likely to enact (Hodson et al., 2004). Aversive racism exists under the surface of consciousness because it conflicts with consciously held beliefs of equality and justice among racial groups. This form of racism allows white people with a progressive identity to enact racist practices while still maintaining that identity. For example, the pride expressed in choice of neighborhood ("the most diverse zip code in the country"), yet the maintenance of racial separation within that neighborhood.

Denial of Child's Racial Awareness

A significant number of parents (45%) reported they do not believe that their children notice difference, or notice it only minimally and/or have not yet assigned value to it. In fact, parents of younger children tended to express pleasure in their assessment that their children were not aware of race and racism; several stated that they were very happy or "loved it." For example, Lila said this about her 3-year-old daughter:

Right now most of this is just floating over her head, and I don't know how much to really draw attention to it yet. I like the fact that she is still not—it's not a thing to her, I don't think she's even identifying people as being of different races and ethnicities, I think she's just figuring, "Oh this person's my friend" and I'm very happy about that.

At the same time and often within the same response, parents reported that their children *have* noticed racial differences and *have* assigned a lesser value to people of color. Thus, they are in active denial of the racial awareness and racism their children exhibit. Further compounding this denial is that many of the parents—and all of those who brought up the issue of slavery in the interviews—worried about discussing racism in a developmentally appropriate way. This worry is significant because in their false belief that children are racially unaware, their assessment of what is developmentally appropriate is necessarily skewed. Thus, these parents are ill-equipped to address the racism of their children.

Anti-Black Tendencies

Of particular concern are the anti-Black tendencies that emerged in the data. Parents who believed that their children were not aware of race also provided clear evidence that their children had absorbed racism toward Blacks, and when parents described adverse experiences their children had with race, they usually involved a Black child. In addition to the examples discussed earlier, Rachelle shared her 5-year-old son's comments:

> They opened up a new classroom, and it ended up being like four African American kids in that classroom, and there hadn't been any other African American kids at this school . . . and my son came home, like talking trash about some of the African American kids and saying things like "I don't like those kids" and I would push and say, "let's talk about why you don't like them." . . . And he was probably four at the time, and what he could articulate is, "I don't like their hair . . . they don't look like me or any of my friends."

After this incident, Rachelle took action at home and met with her son's teacher to talk about her observations and help promote antibias curricula in the program. However, she stated that she couldn't imagine admitting "even to politicized friends" that her son had expressed explicit racism. It is of note that her shame kept her from sharing the comment with her antiracist-identified white friends. Antiracism principles hold that all white people (including children) internalize racism and it must be acknowledged and then addressed. Thus, Rachelle lost the opportunity to model to other parents in her community the power of racist conditioning on children and ways to handle such an incident when it occurs.

The presence of anti-Black sentiment was suggested in several other ways, including the preference for and increased comfort with people of Asian heritage over African Americans; the specifically anti-Black comments children made; the reality that even when living in racially mixed neighborhoods most parents did not integrate with Black neighbors or businesses; and when parents suggested that "reverse racism" had occurred, it was always between their children and Black children. Very few parents commented on the anti-Black racism that emerged throughout the data, and most seemed to deny it completely. This is in keeping with research that shows that on the continuum of racism, Blacks are on the bottom in the white mind (Baron & Banaji, 2006).

Recommendations

To address the contradictions between the self-identity of white parents as antiracist and their actual practices, we recommend the following. First, awareness must be raised within the community of white antiracist parents as to how many of their behaviors reinforce—rather than challenge—white supremacy. Given the courage it takes to identify as antiracist, we are hopeful that if these parents were more aware of the concrete manifestations of their racial privilege—particularly in the area of school and program choices—it is possible that they might act differently. As Farley and Frey (1994) state, we must lessen the "gap between attitude and behavior" (p. 40). What this might mean is that rather than simply ensuring their children are in a school or program they view as of "good" quality or desirable, white parents challenge the school systems that perpetuate racial and economic inequalities. They could do so by keeping their children in mainstream programs in city schools. In collaboration with parents, administrators, and educators of color, they could work to improve these programs while demanding that all children have access to a quality public education. This would yield multiple positive outcomes: change in the school system, modeling allyship for their white children, teaching by action rather than words, and building authentic cross-racial relationships in their communities.

In addition to awareness of their own behavior and modeling through action, white parents must be educated about the degree to which young children internalize messages about race. The trend in research over the past 2 decades indicates that children are vastly more sophisticated in their awareness of race than most Americans want to believe (Derman-Sparks & Ramsey, 2006; Quintana, 2008; Van Ausdale & Feagin, 2001). The parents interviewed here supported this research. Further, there is a growing body of research demonstrating that both white children and children of color internalize the dominant ideology of white as superior (DiAngelo, 2012). Just saying "everyone is equal" is not enough to address this internalization, as evidenced by the anti-Black sentiment that emerged in the data. With this understanding, parents may prepare themselves to talk openly and honestly about the history of and current manifestations of racism with their white children. Allport's (1979) seminal work on the nature of prejudice specified four conditions for optimal intergroup relations: equal group status within the situation, common goals, intergroup cooperation, and authority support. Efforts at neighborhood and school integration could open these conversations and address many of Allport's conditions.

CONCLUSION

The most hopeful finding regarded parents with older children. These children's friendship choices were reportedly "out of the dominant culture box" and included diversity in ability, religion, race, size, sexual orientation, and income. Parents reported that these teens were aware of racism and whiteness and engaged in antiracist action. However clumsy or inconsistent their parents' antiracist attempts, these children appear to have a cognizance of white racism that their parents did not have until much later.

This awareness translated into specific changes in behavior that were not typical for mainstream white people. For example, one child chose racism as a research topic, another was using racial diversity as a measure of value when choosing colleges, and most were reported to speak up about racism in general. It may be significant that all of the parents who talked about their teens' awareness were involved in organizing themselves. This suggests that seeing parents live in accordance with values (rather than just espousing them) may be the most effective antiracist parenting strategy.

However, with a few exceptions the main difference between parents who identify as antiracist white people and average white parents could be distilled down to an *awareness* of white privilege and racism. White Americans as a whole tend to have very little awareness of their own race and don't see racism as a serious social problem (DiAngelo, 2012; Wise, 2010). Thus, compared to average white Americans, most (but not all) of the parents interviewed here were taking intentional action to socialize their children to recognize and name difference. Yet the vast majority relied solely on addressing racism at an individual or interpersonal level. Only a few parents demonstrated a deep understanding of how embedded racism is in the structure of U.S. society and sought to convey this understanding and the action required to change it to their children. Perhaps the most disturbing finding was how much racism—and racism against Blacks in particular—the children had already absorbed. This is especially problematic in the face of the majority of parents' denial of their children's racial awareness. Further, hardly any of those who had a more sophisticated understanding of these dynamics took action against them.

Returning to the antiracist principles that opened this study—an ongoing process of understanding white privilege and supremacy; challenging color-blindness; countering internalized white superiority; being an ally to people of color; being accountable to people of color; and engaging in meaningful action against racism at a personal, interpersonal, and community level—these findings suggest that there is much work to be done within the white antiracism movement. According to the growing body of antiracism literature, awareness and discussion of racism and interruption at an interpersonal level are not sufficient; political action is necessary. As Stephanie wondered, "What could we do, if we really applied ourselves as white people? . . . How hard is that to do?"

REFERENCES

Adelman, L. (2003). *Race: The power of an illusion*. California Newsreel.

Akintunde, O. (1999). White racism, white supremacy, white privilege, and the social construction of race: Moving from modernist to postmodernist multiculturalism. *Multicultural Education, 7*(2), 2–8.

Allport, G. W. (1979). *The nature of human prejudice*. Perseus Books.

Baron, A. S., & Banaji, M. R. (2006). The development of implicit attitudes. *Psychological Science, 17*(1), 53.

Bonilla-Silva, E. (2006). New racism: Color-blind racism and the future of whiteness in America. In A. W. Doane & E. Bonilla-Silva (Eds.), *White out: The continuing significance of racism* (pp. 273–285). Routledge.

Clark, K., & Clark, M. (1939). The development of consciousness of self and the emergence of racial identification in Negro preschool children. *The Journal of Social Psychology, 10*(4), 591–599.

Clark, K., & Clark, M. (1950). Emotional factors in racial identification and preference in Negro children. *The Journal of Negro Education, 19*(3), 341–350.

Derman-Sparks, L., & Ramsey, P. G. (2006). *What if all the kids are white? Antibias multicultural education with young children and families*. Teachers College Press.

DiAngelo, R. (2006). My class didn't trump my race: Using oppression to face privilege. *Multicultural Perspectives, 8*(1), 51–56.

DiAngelo, R. (2012). *What does it mean to be white? Developing white racial literacy*. Teachers College Press.

Dyer, R. (1997). *White*. Routledge.

Frankenberg, R. (1997). Introduction: Local whitenesses, localizing whiteness. In R. Frankenberg (Ed.), *Displacing whiteness: Essays in social and cultural criticism* (pp. 1–33). Duke University Press.

Hilliard, A. G. (1992). Exceptional children. *Issues in the Education of African American Youth in Special Education Settings (Special Issue), 59*(2), 168–172.

Hodson, G., Dovido, J., & Gaertner, S. (2004). The aversive form of racism. In J. L. Chin (Ed.), *The psychology of prejudice and discrimination (Race and Ethnicity in Psychology)* (Vol. 1, pp. 119–136). Praeger.

Johnson, H. B., & Shapiro, T. M. (2003). Good neighborhoods, good schools: Race and the good choices of white families. In E. Bonilla-Silva & A. W. Doane (Eds.), *White out: The continued significance of racism* (pp. 173–187). Routledge.

Lipsitz, G. (1995). The possessive investment in whiteness: Racialized social democracy and the "white" problem in American studies. *American Quarterly*, *47*(3), 369–387.

Monteiro, M. B., de França, D. X., & Rodrigues, R. (2009). The development of intergroup bias in childhood: How social norms can shape children's racial behaviors. *International Journal of Psychology*, *44*(1), 29–39. https://doi.org/10.1080/00207590802057910

Oakes, J. (2008). Keeping track: Structuring equality and inequality in an era of accountability. *Teachers College Record*, *110*(3), 700–712.

Park, C. C. (2011). Young children making sense of racial and ethnic differences: A sociocultural approach. *American Educational Research Journal*, *48*, 387–420.

Quintana, S. M. (2008). Racial perspective taking ability: Developmental, theoretical, and empirical trends. In S. M. Quintana & C. McKown (Eds.), *Handbook of race, racism, and the developing child* (pp. 1–15). Wiley.

Raible, J. (2009). *Checklist for white allies against racism*. Retrieved from http://johnraible.wordpress.com/a-conversation-10-years-later-the-movie/checklist-for-allies-against-racism/

Roediger, D. (2008). *How race survived U.S. history: From settlement and slavery to the Obama phenomenon*. Verso.

Sensoy, Ö., & DiAngelo, R. (2012). *Is everyone really equal? Key concepts in critical social justice education*. Teachers College Press.

Tatum, B. D. (1997). *"Why are all the Black kids sitting together in the cafeteria?" And other conversations about race*. Basic Books.

Trepagnier, B. (2010). *Silent racism: How well-meaning white people perpetuate the racial divide* (2nd ed.). Paradigm.

Van Ausdale, D., & Feagin, J. R. (2001). *The first r: How children learn race and racism*. Rowman & Littlefield.

Wise, T. (2010). *Color-blind: The rise of post-racial politics and the retreat from racial equity*. City Lights Books.

NINE

◇◇◇◇◇◇◇◇◇◇◇◇◇◇◇◇◇◇◇◇◇◇◇◇◇◇◇

Respect Differences?

Challenging the Common Guidelines in Social Justice Education

ÖZLEM SENSOY AND ROBIN DIANGELO

Creating a democratic atmosphere in which everyone participates means both putting ourselves forward and including others. To do this we must understand the dynamics rooted in issues of power, and do things which counter them.

—Adair & Howell, 2001

IMAGINE ...

You are teaching a required teacher education course on social justice in one of its many forms (e.g., cultural diversity and social justice, multicultural education, or diversity in education). Typical of the teacher education student demographic in the United States and Canada, the majority of your class of 30 is white women who grew up in liberal, middle-class suburban contexts. Only a small percentage of the class represents other identities along lines of race, class, gender, ability, and so forth.

Originally published as Özlem Sensoy and Robin DiAngelo, Respect differences? Challenging the common guidelines in social justice education, *Democracy and Education*, 22(2). https://democracy educationjournal.org/cgi/viewcontent.cgi?article=1138&context=home. Reprinted with permission.

Knowing that the majority of students are new to discussions of social justice and seeking to create a supportive and democratic space that will encourage participation, you introduce a few standard discussion guidelines:

+ Speak for yourself instead of generalizing—use "I" statements.
+ Respect differences—everyone's opinion matters.
+ Challenge ideas, not people.
+ Stay open and engaged—be responsible for your own learning.

You ask students if they would like to add any additional guidelines to the list, and they suggest the following:

+ Don't judge.
+ Assume good intentions.
+ Don't attack people who disagree with you.
+ Treat others as you would like to be treated.
+ Don't take things personally.
+ Laugh with anyone, but laugh at no one.

After some discussion and clarification (e.g., "treat others as you would like to be treated" is modified to "treat everyone as that person would like to be treated," and "don't judge" is modified to "hold your judgments lightly"), everyone votes in agreement with the guidelines, and you post them on the wall or course website.

In subsequent weeks, several dynamics familiar to social justice educators begin to manifest. Students in dominant group positions (e.g., male, white, cisgender, able-bodied) repeatedly raise a range of objections to scholarly evidence that they have privilege by virtue of their social positions. Further, these students dominate the discussion and continue to use terms and phrases that you have repeatedly explained are problematic (e.g., colored people, Orientals, that's so gay, that's retarded, and that's ghetto). In response, other students are becoming triggered or withdrawn. From week to week, you notice that tensions increase in the classroom. And if you—as the instructor—represent a visibly minoritized group within academia (e.g., female, transgender, person of color, person with a visible disability), you sense that dominant students are invalidating you in ways they would not invalidate other instructors, and you are struggling to maintain your legitimacy as you try to facilitate these difficult dynamics.

Questioning the Common Guidelines

We teach courses with a social justice focus primarily for teachers or those who are becoming teachers in K–12 contexts. In addition to classroom teaching, we consult, conduct research, attend workshops and conferences, and contribute to social justice scholarly literature. From these sessions, research, and the literature, it is clear that building trust through an open, accepting, and "safe" space is an often taken-for-granted goal in our discipline (as an online search of syllabi will show). For example, almost every social justice–oriented education forum presents guidelines for discussion. These guidelines are either preformed and shared with the group, or elicited from the group and posted in the room. Guidelines typically include listen respectfully, don't judge, everyone's opinion counts, share the airtime, respect the right of others to disagree, and assume good intentions.

Guidelines are often viewed as fundamental to building the community and creating the democratic climate necessary for discussions of social justice content (Adams et al., 2007; Goodman, 2011). Indeed, so central is the goal of a supportive community that it is presumed that without it, the goals of the discussion cannot be achieved. These guidelines and the norms they engender are also embodied in assignments that invite students to connect personally to readings or other texts (e.g., What part of the reading did you relate to? What resonated for you? What didn't? Where have you seen these dynamics in your own life? What feelings came up for you as you read?). This indicates that the sharing of opinions and personal feelings and connections—and the elevation of this sharing through guidelines to respect, validate, and protect them—is a perceived cornerstone of social justice–oriented education.

Based upon having used such guidelines ourselves, we have come to believe that rather than creating an equitable and open classroom space, they actually increase unequal power relations in the classroom. They do so through an embedded assumption that it is possible to create a space that is experienced by all students as respectful, validating, and protective, regardless of their social locations. In recent years we have found it helpful to strategically constrain several of the most familiar community-building guidelines, including sharing opinions, affirming everyone's perspectives, assuring everyone feels heard, eliciting personal connections and feelings about the course material and emotional responses to course texts, co-constructing the curriculum, and sharing airtime. We refer to these familiar guidelines and community-building practices as *common guidelines*. In this essay we critique these common guidelines and explore four interrelated social justice concepts relevant to our critique. These concepts are

- knowledge construction,
- positionality,
- internalized oppression/internalized dominance, and
- safety.

Our argument is that the common guidelines intended to ensure support are often driven by the interests and needs of dominant groups (Lee & Johnson-Bailey, 2004; Leonardo & Porter, 2010; Sensoy & DiAngelo, 2012). Thus, these guidelines run counter to the goal of interrupting unequal power relations in service of social justice practice. We base our argument on scholarly work in the field as well as years of trial and error in our own struggles to set the most constructive context for social justice education in classrooms that are situated in an inherently inequitable sociopolitical context. Our goals in problematizing the common guidelines are twofold: to explicate how these guidelines function to reproduce dominant relations, and to unsettle the discursive authority that they hold.

CRITICAL SOCIAL JUSTICE PEDAGOGY

In mainstream discourse (in contrast to critical discourse), the term "social justice" is often employed loosely, devoid of its political commitments. Many who profess to support social justice do not acknowledge that all of us are complicit in systems of oppression and privilege. Indeed, being *for* social justice often seems to function as a disclaimer of any such complicity. Given this, we want to clarify that we define "social justice" as a recognition that

- all people are individuals, but we are also members of socially constructed groups;
- society is stratified, and social groups are valued unequally;
- social groups that are valued more highly have greater access to resources, and this access is structured into the institutions and cultural norms;
- social injustice is real and exists today;
- relations of unequal power are constantly being enacted at both the micro (individual) and macro (structural) levels;
- we are all socialized to be complicit in these relations;
- those who claim to be for social justice must strategically act from that claim in ways that challenge social injustice; and
- this action requires a commitment to an ongoing and lifelong process.

Anchored by these principles, social justice educators guide students in commitments along at least three fronts (Banks, 1996; Cochran-Smith, 2004; Kincheloe, 2008; Sensoy & DiAngelo, 2012).

First, social justice educators guide students in critical analysis of the presentation of mainstream knowledge as neutral, universal, and objective. For example, many social justice educators engage their students in examinations of various accounts of a given historical event, such as first contact between colonial settlers and Indigenous peoples (school accounts versus news media accounts versus pop culture accounts). The goals of this analysis are to uncover how the meaning given to various historical events always reflects a particular perspective and set of interests, and to understand how knowledge is socially constructed and never neutral or free of the social context that produced or circulates it (Banks, 1996; Loewen, 1995; Zinn, 1980/2005).

Second, social justice educators guide students in critical self-reflection of their own socialization into structured relations of oppression and privilege. They may do this through exercises such as My Culture Chest, Act

Like a Man/Act Like a Woman, and Step Forward/Step Back. These exercises help identify our placement in a matrix of unequally valued social groups and the messages received through those placements. Educators then ask students to examine how their positions in this matrix inform their action and practice (Adams et al., 2007; Johnson & Blanchard, 2008).

Third, social justice educators guide students in developing the skills with which to see, analyze, and challenge relations of oppression and privilege (Ayers et al., 2009; Goodman, 2011). For example, many educators encourage their students to participate in cultural events, work with case studies, and brainstorm strategies for working with youth on social justice action projects in their schools and communities (Nieto & Bode, 2007).

Thus, critical social justice pedagogues develop strategies in their classrooms that are responsive to omitted histories, positionality, and action. However, history has taught us that any resistive practice can come to serve the very interests it was developed to oppose (DiAngelo & Allen, 2006). In practice, the common guidelines purported to be important to building the kind of classroom climate that can support the commitments discussed above do not address the deeply patterned social and structural dynamics that are brought into the classroom. In other words, these guidelines can run counter to social justice pedagogical commitments. For example, assuming good intentions only goes so far when white students repeatedly use terms like "colored people." How do you respect differences and affirm everyone's perspectives when a student of color claims that racism doesn't affect him? How do you challenge a white student's claim that she didn't get a job or a scholarship because of "reverse" racism or sexism when she is speaking from her own experience? Does everyone's opinion matter when some people's opinion is that reverse racism is a valid concept? In the following sections, we explicate the limits of the common guidelines in relation to social justice education.

COMMON GUIDELINES AND KNOWLEDGE CONSTRUCTION

One of the key strategies of domination in mainstream society is the normalizing of particular knowledge as universal and applicable to all. Yet critical social justice pedagogues understand that knowledge is rooted in and shaped by specific positions and interests; in other words, knowledge is *socially constructed*. Further, these positions are constituted through relations of power (Banks, 1996; Dyer, 1997; Fiske, 1989; Frankenberg, 1997). Making those specific interests visible is a primary goal of the social justice classroom. To this end, educators work to reveal the values and interests embedded in dominant knowledge and to bring alternative knowledge claims to the fore. Meaning is constructed through the stories we tell and are told; we ascribe value by naming and, just as profoundly, by not naming. In light of this, many social justice educators invite speakers from minoritized groups to share experiences that are typically marginalized in the mainstream classroom.

Imagine you have been invited to a course on diversity as one of several queer-identified speakers representing a range of positionalities within that social identity. Along with the rest of the panel, you provide students with information, statistics, and research. You also share your experiences with oppression (transphobia, homophobia, parental rejection, school bullying, etc.). At the end of the presentation, the instructor asks the class for insights, connections, and/or questions. A student raises her hand and is called upon. She states that she disagrees with your lifestyle choice and believes it is immoral. She goes on to say that she should not be asked to accept homosexuality. The instructor allows her to finish and thanks her for sharing her perspective, then moves on to the next comment. You leave feeling very upset and angry—you did not volunteer your time and expose yourself only to be subjected to oppressive dominant narratives and microaggressions you already experience on a daily basis. You feel frustrated with the instructor for allowing that to happen.

In our view, this is exactly the type of context in which dominant knowledge claims must be silenced. The social justice classroom, because its goals include revealing and understanding marginalized voices and perspectives, is a rare setting. But when—in service to "fairness"—instructors give equal time to dominant narratives, we reinforce problematic discursive effects by legitimizing the idea that the conversation is equalizing only when it also includes dominant voices. This is why we have come to deny equal time to all narratives in our classrooms. Our intentions in doing so are to correct the existing power imbalances by turning down the volume on dominant narratives; to make space for dominant narratives in order to be "fair" assumes that these imbalances don't already exist or that equality of airtime is all that is needed to correct them. Because of this, we believe that restricting dominant narratives is actually *more* equalizing.

Making space for marginalized perspectives is also a strategy to make visible the dominant narratives that are unmarked (Kincheloe, 2008; Loewen, 1995). When nondominant perspectives are the mainstay approach (as is often the strategy in the social justice classroom), student demands to hear "the other side" obscure the reality that we get the other side in everyday mainstream media and schooling, unmarked and thus positioned as universal and neutral (Applebaum, 2009).

If the instructor is a woman of color and/or queer-identified, there are additional layers of complexity and power relations at play in this scenario. For these reasons, the common guidelines or other efforts defined as fairness and equality are not sufficiently constructive strategies. We believe that the socially just pedagogical move would be to stop the student from subjecting your guests (and other LGBTQ-identified people in the class) to this microaggression in the first place.

Efforts to make space for all views are often rooted in the desire for teachers to create an "open" dialogue that makes room for nondominant points of view and allows students to "unpack" or politicize their perspectives (Boler, 2004; Saunders & Kardia, 2013). Given this, an educator may ask, "But isn't it important to raise these issues in the classroom so that we can work through them and dispel these problematic ideologies?" While we agree that it is important to surface these perspectives so that they may be critically reflected upon, we do so only in controlled and structured ways (we offer an example of this strategy in the next section). We see at least three problems, in addition to those we have discussed above, related to openly raising these views in this context.

First, most students—regardless of their social identities—enter our classrooms attached to dominant ideologies (e.g., society is free from racism or sexism, the only thing preventing people from success is their lack of hard work, etc.). This attachment is extremely difficult to dislodge. Because of this, from the very first class session we work to unsettle the invisibility and authority of dominant ideologies. Thus, it is not likely that the student making homophobic comments can be moved without substantial and ongoing engagement, which the previous scenario does not allow for.

Second, these narratives can have the effect of hijacking the discussion. For example, were the instructor in this case to carve out time in that moment to challenge the student's claim, it would give it more airtime and hence more authority in the limited class period. Further, this homophobic and heteronormative comment is likely to trigger other comments, both of support and of rebuttal, which now have the effect of setting the agenda for the rest of the discussion time and further subjecting the panel (and any LGBTQ people in the class) to a debate on the morality of their lives.

Allowing the student to finish her erroneous claims (erroneous because they are not supported by social justice scholarship) has an equally problematic impact. In our view, the best way to handle this situation (based on our own trial and error) would be to halt the student as soon as what she is saying becomes clear ("I'm going to stop you there. This is an opportunity to hear the panelists' perspectives, so let's move on to another insight or question.").

Third, the common norm that *everyone's opinion matters* actually stands in the way of addressing the microaggression of the student's comments. The closest common norm for handling this moment might be to *challenge ideas, not people*, but this norm does not help us once the microaggression has already occurred.

While we may be able to point to another common norm—*assume good intentions*—to cope with this comment, it is the impact of our actions that are most relevant in these moments. All too often, claims of good intentions (or their converse, claims to have meant no offense) allow members of dominant groups to avoid responsibility for our transgressions. In the example above, if assuming good intentions is the rationale for not intervening, the homophobic voice is privileged above the minoritized voices of the panelists; while both "sides" are allowed a say through common norms such as *everyone's opinion counts* and *assume good intentions*, there is institutional weight, a history of violence, the ongoing threat of violence, and the denial of social rights behind the dominant narrative, making the impact of that "side's" voice very different.

Student efforts at the re-inscription of dominant knowledge claims within the context of social justice education call forth two other related discourses: First is the discourse of uninformed certainty—a kind of *willful ignorance* or refusal to know. de Castell (2004) has described this not knowing as a "right to be ignorant and the right to speak ignorantly" (p. 55). Resistance to the presentation of alternative knowledges is often embedded in the demand for further, better, and more "neutral" evidence. Dei et al. (2004) state, "There is usually little expression of humility in such 'knowledges' and, as a result, the power to 'know' often mutes the recognition that there is also power in not knowing" (p. xi). If new knowledge does not support existing knowledge, students often respond in one of several ways. They may

- invalidate the evidence based on ideological grounds or personal anecdotal evidence (such as the student to the queer-identified panel described above);
- invalidate the messenger of that evidence (the instructor, the author, the presenters) as having a biased or special interest or simply being a bad teacher ("He is so mean" or "She doesn't let anyone talk who doesn't agree with her");
- call for better or more data, expressing doubt at the small amount of evidence or isolated case presented ("This book is old. The dropout rate for Aboriginal students must be less today because there's so many programs to support them.");
- defend one another ("I thought Bob was really putting himself out there by sharing his belief that gender roles are natural."); or
- frame pushback as a personal assault ("You're attacking me!").

These responses are not simply the result of a lack of enough information or critical thinking skills; they are specific discursive moves that function to counter the challenge to institutionalized relations of power. Affirming everyone's perspective as equally valid supports the strategy for not-knowing (de Castell, 1993, 2004; Schick, 2000). Everyone's perspective is not equally valid when some are uninformed, unexamined, or uphold existing power inequities.

The second of the often cherished discourses in the social justice classroom is the language of experience. The discourses of *personal experience* and *speaking from experience* have figured prominently in a number of educational practices oriented toward social justice (Chor et al., 2003). This emerges in common norms via guidelines to personalize knowledge, wherein students are asked to speak for themselves and from their own experiences. This guideline is meant to prevent students from universalizing their perspectives via platitudes such as "Everybody knows that . . ." or "We should all just . . ." and to encourage awareness of positionality and the social locations from which they each speak. Although encouraging the use of experience was developed as a critical practice to undermine elite expertise (Schlegel, 2002) and to situate claims within the matrix of group identity positions in which they are located, the discourse of personal experience also can function to protect dominant voices (DiAngelo & Allen, 2006). This protection is accomplished by positing dominant participants' perspectives as the product of a discrete individual (outside of group socialization), rather than as the product of multidimensional social interactions. The individual is then responded to as a private mind in the Cartesian sense.

Allen and Cloyes (2005) identify the assumptions underpinning the discourse of personal voice. These assumptions are (1) only the individual has access to hir[1] own mind, and (2) s/he cannot be mistaken about what is going on in hir own mind (or, at least, there is no way to verify what occurs in someone else's mind). These assumptions function to make experience a kind of sacred text and to close experience-based claims from interrogation: How could one possibly question the personal experiences of others?

The discourse of personal experience has particularly significant consequences for dialogues in which the stated goals are to gain understanding of minoritized perspectives and to interrogate one's own privileges and (unwitting) complicity in upholding oppressions of others. The claim of personal experience removes the political dimensions and preserves conventional arrangements (Levine-Rasky, 2000). Similarly, the "right to my opinion" discourse (e.g., "I have the right to think and say what I want, and you don't have the right to challenge what I think and say") is another strategy that closes off "personal" experiences and perspectives. While the guideline to speak for oneself may be intended to prevent dominant groups from negating the perspectives of minoritized, in effect, it often protects dominant perspectives from critical analysis.

COMMON GUIDELINES AND POSITIONALITY

Understanding the concept of positionality is a specific dimension of understanding knowledge as socially constructed. In social justice practice, the concept of positionality is an assertion that all knowledge is partial knowledge and arises from a web of cultural values, beliefs, experiences, and social positions (Haraway, 1991; Harding, 1991, 1998; Kincheloe, 2008; Luke & Gore, 1992). Thus, who a person is (as knower) is intimately connected to that person's socialization into a matrix of group locations (including race, class, gender, and sexuality). As such, practicing seeing knowledge through the concept of positionality is a key pedagogical goal in the social justice classroom.

Consider the following examples of the complexity of positionality.

Instructor Positionality

Many instructors who teach social justice content have minoritized group identities that they tend to name and acknowledge, and thus face challenges not faced in other contexts. For example, an Asian female teaching biology will likely be viewed as more legitimate than an Asian female teaching social justice. While she will still experience dynamics of racism and sexism, she will likely not be seen as fundamentally biased or personally invested in her content area if it is (thought to be) objective science (a dominant knowledge paradigm). Conversely, a white male teaching biology or social justice, because of his positionality, will not have the same challenges related to how students read his identity, in either context. In the social justice class, even though he is teaching a nondominant knowledge paradigm, his dominant group identities (as a white male, especially if he is cisgender) will be read by most students as not biased but instead as objective and legitimate. Therefore, the strategies these two instructors take must account for how their bodies are read in the social justice classroom.

In our work we are often asked whether an instructor's positionality matters, given that that person has ultimate authority in the classroom. In thinking about instructor authority, there is a helpful distinction between *rank* and *status* (Nieto et al., 2010). "Rank" refers to social membership, which is not temporary and impacts all aspects of one's life (examples of rank include race, class, gender, sexual orientation, and ability). "Status" refers to a temporary position/job and is contextual. For example, research shows that women and people of color in positions of leadership are scrutinized more closely and judged more harshly than white men (Elsass & Graves, 1997; Green, 2003). Further, people of color are often assumed to be the recipients of special programs rather than to have earned their positions, and are often perceived as being biased, having special interests, and/or being troublemakers (Bonilla-Silva, 2006; Calliste, 1996; Pierce, 2003). In the context of schooling, female professors and professors of color often receive lower evaluations, impacting their tenure process and ultimately their wages and job security (Huston, 2012; Merritt, 2008). The common guidelines do not allow all instructors to take actions that are responsive to the interplay of rank and status in instructor positionality because they push instructors to affirm all perspectives as equally valid. In so doing, they don't provide minoritized instructors the structure and control they need to counter (rather than affirm) the extra resistance they receive as they push students past their comfort zones.

Student Positionality

The majority of college students are white and middle class, and the vast majority of teacher education students are white and middle class (Picower, 2009). This means that most educators are teaching a relatively homogeneous population with a specific racial, gender, and class positionality. When the social justice course is a required one as opposed to an elective, there are key implications for positionality. For those students with firsthand experiences with marginality via their race, class, sexuality, ability, or other positionalities, the course can be transformative in providing a language and framework through which to make sense of their lived experiences. As such, providing the time to reflect, to practice applying the concepts, and to grapple with the impact is an important part of the process. Simultaneously, for students in dominant positions, they may experience deep paradigm shifts in encountering concepts such as "privilege" and "internalized dominance" for the first time. They too need time to settle into the ideological, psychological, and emotional challenges occurring in a dual space of awakening. Because of these dynamics, the instructor in the social justice classroom bears additional layers of responsibility that are unique to teaching this content (Gallavan, 2000; Kincheloe, 2008) and as such is obligated to anticipate and be responsive to the inevitable disruption of traditional power relations and shifting paradigms that will occur. Developing the skill to dialogue across differences that are not directly addressed in other educational spaces is a central commitment of the social justice classroom.

Yet, the common guidelines do not take into account the different positionalities of students in relation to one another. Consider an assignment one of us (DiAngelo) uses in an education program that is 97% white as a concrete example of both positionality and why we do not affirm the free sharing of perspectives and experiences. On the first day of the semester students are asked to write anonymous reflections on the following questions:

Discuss what it means to be part of your particular racial group(s).

+ How racially diverse was your neighborhood(s) growing up?
+ What messages have you received about race from your family, friends, schools, and neighborhoods about race?
+ How has your race(s) shaped your life?

The following responses (reproduced in their entirety) are representative, both in content and in length. These students are in their third and fourth years of postsecondary education and will be going on to be teachers:

My first neighborhood, racially, was pretty (not meaning nice) diverse. These being apartments, you could find different races. My second neighborhood, where I live now, is not very racially diverse. Messages? Not really any. Impact? I don't know.

My neighborhood was not racially diverse at all growing up. Maybe freshman year of college was when diversity appeared, yet still very small. I am not sure [how race shapes my life]; I am white, and I feel like I am constantly hearing racial slurs or people using the race card, that it just makes me thankful for who I am, and don't have to deal with that.

My neighborhood wasn't very diverse at all, mostly white, middle class. From my parents and schools, I have been taught to be tolerant of other races and to accept others for their differences.

My neighborhood wasn't diverse at all. In my school of 500-plus students there was only a handful of non-white students. My family hasn't sent me messages on race. I guess my schools have sent the message that the non-white students have behavioral problems. Overall, race doesn't mean that much to me or my life.

These answers are not an anomaly; most white people live, love, worship, study, play, and work in racial segregation. This typical insistence that race doesn't matter comes from white students sitting in a virtually all-white classroom, who grew up in primarily white neighborhoods and attended primarily white schools, who were and are currently being taught by a virtually all-white faculty (including us). Given this starting point, these students do not have the skills yet to understand their racial positionality or to articulate a critical racial perspective (DiAngelo, 2012).

Nothing in mainstream society supports students to enter our classrooms with the ability to think critically about these issues, so their opinions are necessarily reflective of dominant paradigms. Given that the majority of our students are from dominant groups in key identities, their opinions, perspectives, and personal connections—taken at face value—are not constructive, as they only reinforce oppressive narratives. This is one reason why we restrict free sharing and affirmations of everyone's perspectives as equally valid. While we recognize that it is important to raise these perspectives (as this assignment does), we find it much more effective to do so in controlled ways. We then return to them after we have laid enough groundwork, via study of key concepts and literature, and begin to apply a critical analysis.

GUIDELINES AND INTERNALIZED DOMINANCE AND INTERNALIZED OPPRESSION

People practice *internalized dominance* when they internalize and act out (often unintentionally) the constant messages circulating in the culture that they and their group are superior to whichever group is minoritized in relation to theirs and that they are entitled to their higher position. Conversely, those who exhibit *internalized oppression* believe and act out (often unintentionally) the constant messages circulating in the culture that they and their group are inferior to whichever group is dominant in relation to theirs and that they are deserving of their lower position (Freire, 1970; Frye, 1983; Sue, 2003).

As social justice educators may well understand, much of oppression is invisible to and denied by those who benefit from it; a room that seems perfectly comfortable to dominant group members may not feel that way to minoritized group members. For example, given whiteness as the status quo, the more comfortable a space is for white people (often articulated as a "safe" space), the more likely it is to be harmful to people of color. Dominant group members are necessarily deeply invested materially, psychically, socially, and politically as the producers and beneficiaries of particular forms of privilege, and the system depends on our denial of these investments. Thus—and especially for the well-intended—the very behaviors we believe are supportive (and make us feel comfortable and "good") are likely to be the behaviors that are so toxic to minoritized groups; our identities as moral people rest on not seeing our own oppressive patterns. In other words, dominant group members work hard not to see their privilege, which is a key way we keep it protected and intact. As noted earlier, willful ignorance is a dynamic of internalized dominance; for those in dominant groups, the refusal to know protects power.

Conversely, there are several key reasons why members of a minoritized group may at times choose silence in a class discussion, including (1) responding to resistance or hostility expressed (consciously or not) by dominant participants; (2) feeling a lack of trust based on well-founded experience that they will be penalized for challenging dominant perspectives; (3) feeling hopeless in the face of dominant denial; (4) risking vulnerability by sharing their experiences and perspectives and then being met with silence, argumentation, or rationalization, all of which function as forms of invalidation; (5) being outnumbered by those in the dominant group and not seeing any allies; or (6) being acutely aware of the power differentials and choosing to protect themselves in the face of inevitable hurt. Given these and other dynamics, there are costs to minoritized students for speaking to their positionality. A lifetime of schooling that has denied acknowledging the significance of positionality and built on a collective history of denial is difficult to counter in a single course. The dynamics of internalized oppression, layered with the personal knowledge of minoritized groups, can also function to uphold the dominant framework the course is seeking to unsettle.

Another dimension of the dynamics of internalized dominance and internalized oppression is the *right to speak* discourse. This is the unspoken assumption underlying norms that encourage and affirm everyone's voice that all voices have been granted the right to speak and be heard equally in dominant society. However, as Boler (2004) notes, all speech is not free or equal, for institutionalized inequities in power ensure that not all voices carry the same weight. Given that inequity in weight, she asks, "If all speech is not free, then in what sense can one claim that freedom of speech is a working constitutional right?" (p. 3) Yet the right to speak discourse—which is a central feature of the presumed democratic classroom—assumes that the only reason some voices are not heard is that some students are exercising their rights by choosing not to speak (Applebaum, 2003; Chinnery, 2008; Li, 2004).

When dominant and minoritized groups come together, the pattern is that dominant group members will speak first and most often and will set the agenda where their dominant identities are salient. Yet this pattern is contextual—for example, white people who typically dominate discussions often choose silence when the topic is racism. Or, dominant group members may take up a lot of intellectual space but leave the emotional (or self-reflective) work to minoritized group members. Thus, minoritized group members often experience dominant group silence, regardless of what drives it, as hostile (DiAngelo, 2011; DiAngelo & Sensoy, 2014). Silence from mi-noritized group members can be an act of resistance, but silence from domi-nant group members can function as a power move and needs to be interrogated. These are examples of the complexities inherent in facilitating discussions across dominant and minoritized positionalities, and guidelines that seek to equalize the weight of all voices or ensure everyone's comfort are not adequate for navigating those complexities.

GUIDELINES AND SAFETY

In the social justice classroom, many educators try to not only establish a democratic space, but also a "safe" space. According to Adams et al.'s (2007) well-known sourcebook for teaching social justice education, "Establishing a safe environment in which students can discuss ideas, share feelings and experiences, and challenge themselves and each other to reevaluate opinions and beliefs is one of the primary facilitation responsibilities" (p. 283). Similarly, in Beverly Tatum's classic article (1992) "Talking About Race, Learning About Racism," she explains, "Many students are reassured by the climate of safety that is created by these guidelines and find comfort in the nonblaming assumptions I outline for the class" (p. 4). In approaches that are similarly informed by an anti-oppressive social justice frame-work (e.g., feminist pedagogy), there is also an embedded assumption that instructors should create a caring as well as safe environment (Lee & Johnson-Bailey, 2004).

As a response to the expectation that safety be a prerequisite for social justice discussions, some scholars have problematized the very definition of safety and questioned the premise that these spaces can or should be safe to begin with. For example, in the context of cross-racial dialogues that are explicitly about race and racism, what feels safe for white people is pre-sumed to feel safe for people of color. Yet for many students and instructors of color, the classroom is a hostile space virtually all of the time, and espe-cially so when the topic is race. The expectation of safety for dominant group members can be a symbolic form of violence toward minoritized groups, intensifying the real violence—physical, as well as structural and discursive—that they already bear in society at large.

For minoritized groups the social justice classroom has the potential to be one of the few environments in which they can feel somewhat protected, given their numbers and/or support of the instructor. While the feelings may be real for dominant group members struggling with a sense of safety, it may be useful to consider what safety means from a position of social, cultural, historical, and institutional power. Scholars have raised questions about whether, for example, antiracism education that does not perpetuate discursive violence toward students of color is even possible in cross-racial settings (cf. Chinnery, 2008; Crozier & Davies, 2008; DiAngelo & Sensoy, 2014; Jones, 1999, 2001; Leonardo & Porter, 2010). Their argument is that such spaces ultimately foreground the needs of white students and position students of color as "native informants and unpaid sherpas" (Thompson, 2004, p. 388) guiding white students into a racial awakening. This is why we do not believe that common guidelines intended to ensure a generalized safe space are a realistic goal at all, nor can they ever be a prerequisite for a democratic outcome. In practice, the expectation that safety can be created in the social justice classroom through universalized procedural guidelines is always about the dominant group's safety.

CONCLUSION: BEYOND THE COMMON GUIDELINES

The capacity to recognize the need for and engage in social justice activism is part of what it means to participate in a healthy democracy. Preparing students for active participation in a democratic society requires the development of specific skills. To this end, educators must guide students in

- engaging constructively with alternative perspectives,
- thinking critically,
- grappling with multiple perspectives,
- building stamina for engaging with new and challenging ideas,
- engaging with research,
- raising critical questions,
- tolerating ambiguity,
- recognizing the power relations embedded in positionality, and
- valuing collaboration over competition.

Without these skills, young people are ill-equipped to cultivate a just and democratic society. Further, the kind of space required to develop these skills often appears counter to commonsense notions of democracy. Because schools are among the most powerful institutions wherein social stratification is reproduced, they are also where it must be challenged. To do this, we must be willing to interrogate our notions of what fairness, safety, and participation look like.

As we have argued, social justice educators are facilitating deeply complex issues and dynamics. These dynamics are not purely theoretical—they are occurring in every moment in and out of the classroom, and social justice action depends on recognition of them. We won't always make the right call in all moments for all students, but using the common guidelines as a starting point, we have found the following less-orthodox adaptations to be more constructive to our goals:

+ Strive for intellectual humility. Be willing to grapple with challenging ideas.
+ Differentiate between opinion—which everyone has—and informed knowledge, which comes from sustained experience, study, and practice. Hold your opinions lightly and with humility.
+ Let go of personal anecdotal evidence and look at broader group-level patterns.
+ Notice your own defensive reactions and attempt to use these reactions as entry points for gaining deeper self-knowledge, rather than as a rationale for closing off.
+ Recognize how your own social positionality (e.g., race, class, gender, sexuality, ability) informs your perspectives and reactions to your instructor and those whose work you study in the course.
+ Differentiate between safety and comfort. Accept discomfort as necessary for social justice growth.
+ Keep focused on yourself: *What does this mean for me and my life?*
+ Identify where your learning edge is and push it. For example, whenever you think, *I already know this*, ask yourself, *How can I take this deeper?* Or, *How am I applying in practice what I already know?*

We design controlled opportunities for students to practice articulating a social justice framework (vocabulary and concepts) that moves them into humility, openness, and analysis rather than certainty, rebuttal, or refusal. For example, in addition to the guidelines above, we offer a list of Silence Breakers (adapted from course materials co-developed by DiAngelo and Anika Nailah, 2013). These are intended to recognize and respond to unequal power relations in the room, help more reticent students speak up, help more dominant students slow down, and guide open and humble entry into the conversation.

We also regularly ask students to turn their claims into the form of questions by offering Question Starters. For example, turn the claim "We had a student with a disability in my school, and no one treated her differently" into a question "We had a student with a disability in my school—what kind of privileges did I have that she didn't?" The intended effect of this is to engender a stance of humility, develop critical thinking skills, interrogate what students think they know, identify dynamics of oppression and privilege, and continually seek out new information.

The following are discussion starters that accomplish these multiple goals and operationalize the guidelines above. As may be noted, many of these are intertwined:

- I'm really nervous/scared/uncomfortable to say [X], but . . .
- From my experience/perspective as [identity], . . .
- I'm afraid I may offend someone, and please let me know if I do, but . . .
- It feels risky to say [X], but . . .
- I'm not sure if this will make any sense, but . . .
- I just felt something shift in the room. I'm wondering if anyone else did. . . .
- It seems like some people may have had a reaction to that. Can you help me understand why?
- Can you help me understand whether what I'm thinking right now might be problematic?
- This is what I understand you to be saying: . . . . Is that accurate?

+ I've been wondering about how we are using [term] in this discussion....
+ I have always heard that [X]. What are your thoughts on that?
+ The author is arguing that only [X; e.g., men can be sexist]. Can you help me understand that?
+ Is [X] a good example of what the author was saying?
+ How would you respond to [X] from a social justice framework?
+ I am having a "yeah, but" moment. Can you help me work through it?
+ Given the reality of inequitable power, would it be better if ...?
+ How does [X] effect relationships between [Y] and [Z]?
+ What is another example of [X]?
+ This perspective is new to me, but I'm wondering if it is accurate to say that ...?

Again, our goals are not to create fixed, rote formulae for engaging with the materials via these limited prompts. Rather, these prompts are strategies to help students *lean into* rather than *away from* difficult content. Leaning into a social justice framework does not require agreement or disagreement; it is simply—but powerfully—a way to practice critical engagement.

We share the goals of our social justice–oriented colleagues to create supportive, engaging, and transformative classrooms, and we do give guidelines in service of these goals. The development of our particular approach is adapted from those who have gone before us, as well as from our own struggles as educators who often have felt ineffective and unable to respond constructively to power relations in the classroom. We have found our guidelines to be helpful responses not only to the challenges of student positionality but to our own challenges regarding dynamics of rank and status. For example, when we need to interrupt dominant power moves, these guidelines offer us the backup to take unpopular measures that often appear unfair to dominant groups and thus elicit pushback.

All instructors channel their authority, but only some pedagogical strategies are read as authoritarian. Just as all curricula are political even if they are not marked as such, the pedagogies we deploy are also political, whether or not they are marked as such. As instructors, we are embedded in and facilitate complex relations of power in the classroom, and we want to address that power in intentional, strategic, and critical ways. We do acknowledge the "master's tools" dilemma (Lorde, 1984) inherent in the academic setting related to social justice education efforts. An academic course whose primary goal is to challenge social stratification is not without irony. As instructors, we recognize that our courses are ensconced within an institution whose default effect is the reproduction of inequality. In many ways we are a part of the very system we seek to challenge. Still, we stand in solidarity with others who choose to work within the constraints of academia in order to equip the elite that it produces with perspectives and tools that might ultimately challenge social inequality.

NOTE

1. We use the terms "hir" and "s/he" in order to be inclusive and challenge normative gender binaries.

REFERENCES

Adair, M., & Howell, S. (2001). Creating an atmosphere where everyone participates. In *A handout from Tools for Change*. Retrieved from http://www.toolsforchange.org/resources/org-handouts/social%20power.pdf

Adams, M., Bell, L. A., & Griffin, P. (Eds.). (2007). *Teaching for diversity and social justice: A sourcebook* (2nd ed.). Routledge.

Allen, D. G., & Cloyes, K. (2005). The language of experience in nursing research. *Nursing Inquiry, 12*(2), 98–105.

Applebaum, B. (2003). Social justice, democratic education and the silencing of words that wound. *Journal of Moral Education, 32*(2), 151–162.

Applebaum, B. (2009). Is teaching for social justice a "liberal bias"? *Teachers College Record, 111*(2), 376–408.

Ayers, W., Quinn, T., & Stovall, D. (Eds.). (2009). *Handbook of social justice in education*. Routledge.

Banks, J. A. (Ed.). (1996). *Multicultural education, transformative knowledge, and action: Historical and contemporary perspectives*. Teachers College Press.

Boler, M. (Ed.). (2004). *Democratic dialogue in education: Troubling speech, disturbing silence.* Peter Lang.

Bonilla-Silva, E. (2006). *Racism without racists.* Rowman & Littlefield.

Calliste, A. (1996). Antiracism organizing and resistance in nursing: African Canadian women. *The Canadian Review of Sociology and Anthropology, 33*(3), 361–390.

Chinnery, A. (2008). Revisiting "The Master's Tools": Challenging common sense in cross-cultural teacher education. *Equity & Excellence in Education, 41*(4), 395–404.

Chor, E. N., Fleck, C., Fan, G., Joseph, J., & Lyter, D. M. (2003). Exploring critical feminist pedagogy: Infusing dialogue, participation and experience in teaching and learning. *Teaching Sociology, 31*(3), 259–275.

Cochran-Smith, M. (2004). *Walking the road: Race, diversity, and social justice in teacher education.* Teachers College Press.

Crozier, G., & Davies, J. (2008). "The trouble is they don't mix": Self-segregation or enforced exclusion? *Race Ethnicity and Education, 11*(3), 285–301.

de Castell, S. (1993). Introduction: 6 December 1989/1993, Je me souviens. *Canadian Journal of Education / Revue canadienne de l'éducation, 18*(3), 185–188. http://www.jstor.org/stable/1495381

de Castell, S. (2004). No speech is free: Affirmative action and the politics of give and take. In M. Boler (Ed.), *Democratic dialogue in education* (pp. 51–56). Peter Lang.

Dei, G. J., Karumanchery, L. L., & Karumanchery-Luik, N. (2004). *Playing the race card: Exposing white power and privilege.* Peter Lang.

DiAngelo, R. (2011). White fragility. *International Journal of Critical Pedagogy, 3*(3), 54–70.

DiAngelo, R. (2012). *What does it mean to be white? Developing white racial literacy.* Peter Lang.

DiAngelo, R., & Allen, D. (2006). My feelings are not about you: Personal experience as a move of whiteness. *InterActions: UCLA Journal of Education and Information Studies, 2*(2), article 2.

DiAngelo, R., & Nailah, A. (2013). Unpublished course materials. *Racism in the United States: Implications for Social Work Practice.* Smith College School of Social Work.

DiAngelo, R., & Sensoy, Ö. (2014). Getting slammed: White depictions of interracial dialogues as arenas of violence. *Race Ethnicity and Education, 17*(1), 103–128.

Dyer, R. (1997). *White.* Routledge.

Elsass, P. M., & Graves, L. M. (1997). Demographic diversity in decision-making groups: The experiences of women and people of color. *The Academy of Management Review, 22*(4), 946–973.

Fiske, J. (1989). *Reading the popular.* Unwin and Hyman.

Frankenberg, R. (1997). Introduction: Local whitenesses, localizing whiteness. In R. Frankenberg (Ed.), *Displacing whiteness: Essays in social and cultural criticism* (pp. 1–33). Duke University Press.

Freire, P. (1970). *Pedagogy of the oppressed.* Continuum.

Frye, M. (1983). *The politics of reality: Essays in feminist theory.* The Crossing Press.

Gallavan, N. P. (2000). Multicultural education at the academy: Teacher educators' challenges, conflicts, and coping skills. *Equity & Excellence in Education, 33*(3), 5–11.

Goodman, D. (2011). *Promoting diversity and social justice: Educating people from privileged groups* (2nd ed.). Routledge.

Green, T. K. (2003). Discrimination in workplace dynamics: Toward a structural account of disparate treatment theory. *Harvard Civil Rights–Civil Liberties Law Review, 38,* 91–157.

Haraway, D. J. (1991). *Simians, cyborgs and women: The reinvention of nature.* Free Association Books.

Harding, S. (1991). *Whose science? Whose knowledge?* Cornell University Press.

Harding, S. (1998). *Is science multicultural? Postcolonialisms, feminisms, and epistemologies.* Indiana University Press.

Huston, T. A. (2012). Race and gender bias in higher education: Could faculty course evaluations impede progress toward parity? *Seattle Journal for Social Justice, 4*(2), article 34.

Johnson, B. C., & Blanchard, S. C. (2008). *Reel diversity: A teacher's sourcebook.* Peter Lang.

Jones, A. (1999). The limits of cross-cultural dialogue: Pedagogy, desire, and absolution in the classroom. *Educational Theory, 49*(3), 299–316.

Jones, A. (2001). Cross-cultural pedagogy and the passion for ignorance. *Feminism & Psychology, 11*(3), 279–292.

Kincheloe, J. L. (2008). *Knowledge and critical pedagogy.* Springer.

Lee, M., & Johnson-Bailey, J. (2004). Challenges to the classroom authority of women of color. *New Directions for Adult and Continuing Education, 102,* 55–64.

Leonardo, Z., & Porter, R. K. (2010). Pedagogy of fear: Toward a Fanonian theory of "safety" in race dialogue. *Race Ethnicity and Education, 13*(2), 139–157.

Levine-Rasky, C. (2000). Framing whiteness: Working through the tensions in introducing whiteness to educators. *Race Ethnicity and Education, 3*(3), 271–292.

Li, H. L. (2004). Rethinking silencing silences. In M. Boler (Ed.), *Democratic dialogue in education: Troubling speech, disturbing silence* (pp. 69–86). Peter Lang.

Loewen, J. W. (1995). *Lies my teacher told me: Everything your American history textbook got wrong.* New Press.

Lorde, A. (1984). The master's tools will not dismantle the master's house. In *Sister outsider: Essays and speeches by Audre Lorde* (pp. 112–119). Crossing Press.

Luke, C., & Gore, J. (Eds.). (1992). *Feminisms and critical pedagogy.* Routledge.

Merritt, D. J. (2008). Bias, the brain, and student evaluations of teaching. *St. John's Law Review, 82*(1), article 6. Retrieved from http://scholarship.law.stjohns.edu/lawreview/vol82/iss1/6

Nieto, L., Boyer, M., Goodwin, L., Johnson, G., Collier Smith, L., & Hopkins, J. P. (2010). *Beyond inclusion, beyond empowerment: A developmental strategy to liberate everyone.* Cuetzpalin.

Nieto, S., & Bode, P. (2007). *Affirming diversity: The sociopolitical context of multicultural education* (5th ed.). Allyn & Bacon.

Picower, B. (2009). The unexamined whiteness of teaching: How white teachers maintain and enact dominant racial ideologies. *Race Ethnicity and Education, 12*(2), 197–215.

Pierce, A. E. (2003). *Between worlds: The narration of multicultural/transnational identities of women working in a post-national space* [Doctoral dissertation, University of Texas at Austin]. Retrieved from http://repositories.lib.utexas.edu/bitstream/handle/2152/861/pierceae039.pdf

Saunders, S., & Kardia, D. (2013). *Creating inclusive college classrooms.* Center for Research on Learning and Teaching. Retrieved from http://www.crlt.umich.edu/gsis/p3_1

Schick, C. (2000). "By virtue of being white": Resistance in anti-racist pedagogy. *Race Ethnicity and Education, 3*(1), 83–102.

Schlegel, J. H. (2002). Flight from fallibility: How theory triumphed over experience in the West. *Journal of Economic History, 62*(2), 632–633.

Sensoy, Ö., & DiAngelo, R. (2012). *Is everyone really equal? An introduction to key concepts in social justice education.* Teachers College Press.

Sue, D. W. (2003). *Overcoming our racism: The journey to liberation.* Jossey-Bass.

Tatum, B. D. (1992). Talking about race, learning about racism: The application of racial identity development theory in the classroom. *Harvard Educational Review*, 62(1), 1–25.

Thompson, A. (2004). Anti-racist work zones. In K. Alston (Ed.), *Philosophy of education yearbook 2003* (pp. 387–395). Philosophy of Education Society.

Zinn, H. (2005). *A people's history of the United States: 1492–present*. Harper Perennial Modern Classics. (Original work published 1980)

TEN

Stop Telling That Story!
Danger Discourse and the
White Racial Frame

I am a white professor. I teach in a program that is 97% white. We are
located 10 miles away from Springfield, MA, a city that is approximately
57% Black and Latino. I am walking down the hallway toward the
classroom where I am teaching a course titled "Schools in Society." In
this course, we take an institutional perspective on schools as primary
sites of socialization and explore the role that schools play in the
maintenance and reproduction of social inequality. All my students are
white. On the second day of class, during an introductory exercise
wherein students share aspects of their frames of reference, a student
shared that she and her boyfriend had been "mugged by a Black man
in Springfield." I am dismayed that she is reinforcing racist representations by choosing to tell us this without following it with any point or
connection, but don't see how I can challenge her story so early in the
course. Now, 8 weeks later, we have finished reading James Loewen's
Lies My Teacher Told Me and are halfway though Michelle Alexander's
The New Jim Crow: Mass Incarceration in an Era of Colorblindness. My
students have responded very well to both texts and I am feeling
hopeful that they are beginning to understand the multi-dimensional
nature of racism and how it is structured into society. As I walk toward
the classroom, a group of students are sitting in the hall and as I
approach, I hear their conversation. "I grew up in a really sheltered
neighborhood so I am scared to do my placement there." "Oh, I used to

From Lea, V., Lund, D. E., & Carr, P.R. (eds.). (2018). *Critical Multicultural Perspectives on Whiteness:
Views from the Past and Present.* Peter Lang. pp. 265–271. Reprinted with permission.

211

live in New Haven where I heard gunshots at the dance club, so Springfield doesn't scare me." "Wow! Growing up in a small town, I've never had anything like that happen to me." The conversation continues in this vein.

This chapter applies critical discourse analysis to uncover an aspect of white racial framing and the role it plays in the maintenance and reproduction of white supremacy. I term this aspect *danger discourse*; narratives that reinforce the association of people of Color—and Blacks in particular—as inherently dangerous, while simultaneously reinforcing whites and the spaces associated with whites as the embodiment of safety and innocence. Using the theoretical concepts of white racial framing, and white solidarity—I apply discourse analysis to examine the discursive effects of these narratives and the racial capital they accrue. I conclude by asking white people to give up their investment in this racial capital and stop telling stories that reproduce racism and white supremacy.

THE WHITE RACIAL FRAME

After conducting extensive research on racism, sociologist Joe Feagin coined the term *white racial frame* to describe the deeply internalized racist framework through which whites make meaning of race and racial difference (2009). This framework includes images, interpretations, perceptions, evaluations, emotions, and actions that position Whites as superior and that are passed down and reinforced throughout society.

The white racial frame has several levels. At the most general level, the racial frame views whites as superior in culture and achievement and views people of Color as generally of less social, economic, and political consequence. People of Color are seen as inferior to Whites in the making and keeping of the nation. At the next level of framing, because social institutions (education, medicine, law, government, finance, and military) are controlled by white people, white dominance is unremarkable and taken for granted. That white people are disproportionately enriched and privileged via these institutions is also taken for granted; we are entitled to more privileges and resources because we are "better" people. At the deepest level of the white frame, negative stereotypes and images of racial others as inferior are reinforced and accepted. At this level, corresponding emotions such as fear, contempt, and resentment are also stored.

The white racial frame is deep and extensive, with thousands of stored "bits." These bits are pieces of cultural information that are collected and passed along from one person and group to the next, and from one generation to the next. They circulate both explicitly and implicitly, through movies, television, news, and other media, and stories told to us by family and friends. The frame includes both negative understandings of people of Color and positive understandings of white people and white institutions; the justification of inequality involves two complementary strategies: the positive representation of the dominant group, and the negative representation of the marginalized group. Whites typically combine racial stereotypes (the cognitive aspect), metaphors and concepts (the deeper cognitive aspect), images (the visual aspect), and emotions (feelings like fear, contempt, or curiosity), to assess and respond to people of Color. By constantly using the white racial frame to interpret society, events, and relations, by integrating new bits, and by applying learned stereotypes, images, and interpretations in discriminatory actions, whites reinscribe the frame ever deeper into our consciousness.

It's important to note that the absence of people of Color in one's environment (workplace, school, neighborhood) also fortifies the white racial frame, as other white people reinforce the concept that these spaces are of a higher quality precisely because people of Color are absent (DiAngelo, 2012). This framing is so internalized that it is rarely consciously considered or challenged by most white people. The concept of the white racial frame may be useful for explaining several white racial patterns, including the preference for racial segregation, unconscious racial discrimination, the lack of interest in people of Color's perspectives or in challenging racism, feeling entitled to our position of dominance in society, and defensiveness when white privilege is questioned.

WHITE SOLIDARITY

White solidarity is the tacit agreement among whites not to talk openly and honestly about race and to avoid causing another white person to feel racial discomfort by confronting them when they say or do something racially problematic. Sleeter (1996) describes this solidarity as white "racial bonding": ". . . interactions in which whites engage that have the purpose of affirming a common stance on race-related issues, legitimating particular interpretations of groups of Color, and drawing conspiratorial we–they boundaries" (p. 149). White solidarity requires silence about anything that exposes the meaning of race, as well as the implicit agreement to remain racially united in protection of white privilege and white supremacy. By maintaining this silence, we maintain group solidarity. To break the silence is to break rank.

White solidarity also requires an agreement not to "embarrass" other white people when we make racist statements or engage in racist behaviors. We see this at parties, at the dinner table, and in work settings. Most white people can relate to hearing another white person say something racially offensive, but not challenging them in order to avoid conflict or being told to "lighten up." In the workplace setting, we avoid naming racism for the same reasons, in addition to the fear that we may jeopardize our employment. But silence, regardless of its conscious motivation, functions to maintain white solidarity—a united front in the protection of racism and white supremacy.

DANGER DISCOURSE

Toni Morrison (1993) uses the term "racetalk" to capture the explicit insertion into everyday life of racial signs and symbols that have no meaning other than positioning African Americans into the lowest level of the racial hierarchy. Casual racetalk is a key component of white racial framing because it accomplishes the interconnected goals of elevating white people while demeaning people of Color; racetalk always implies a racial "us" and "them." How we *think* and *speak* about people of Color is a fundamental foundation for how we *treat* people of Color. Discourse that specifically positions people of Color as inherently dangerous while simultaneously positioning white people as inherently innocent has material consequences in the larger society. My goal here is not to add to the body of evidence for racetalk, but to make a clear and compelling case, based on a familiar and representative example, for white people to *stop* racetalk.

As I consider the effects of my students' racial narratives as examples of those that circulate daily among whites, it is important to note that these comments do not stand alone. They represent a vast network of similar comments, images, and representations that white people are exposed to and circulate daily. For example, Picca & Feagin (2007) asked 626 white college students at 28 different colleges across the United States to keep journals recording every instance regarding racial issues, images, and understandings that they observed or were part of over the course of 6–8 weeks. They received over 7,500 accounts of blatantly racist comments and actions by the white people in their lives (friends, families, acquaintances, strangers). These accounts come from the generation most likely to claim they were taught to see everyone as equal. This study provided empirical evidence that racism continues to be explicitly expressed by white people, even those who are young and profess to be progressive. What had changed since the pre–Civil Rights era was that whites are more likely to be careful to only make these statements when no people of Color are present.

Returning to the vignette of danger discourse that opens this chapter, we can see white racial framing and white solidarity at play in several familiar, albeit more or less racially explicit statements. While the opening claim of the student in the hall: *"I grew up in a really sheltered neighborhood . . ."* is less explicit than the mugging story, it is still clearly racially coded and a necessary component of white racial framing. It is a very important narrative for whites, as illustrated by its familiarity as an opening to many white narratives. It is also relentlessly reinforced by news stories that position any primarily white suburban community in which a major crime occurs as "sheltered." It is a claim that begs the question, "Sheltered from what and in contrast to whom?" Of course sheltered is always in contrast to spaces that are not sheltered, which are by default urban and filled with dangerous people of color (Black and Brown in particular).

Conversely, positioning white spaces as sheltered and those who are raised in them as racially innocent taps into classic discourses of people of Color as *not* innocent. The second part of the claim reinforces the first, "... *so I am scared to do my placement there.*" Racist images and resultant white fears can be found at all levels of society, and myriad studies demonstrate that white people believe that people of Color (and Blacks in particular) are dangerous (DiAngelo & Sensoy, 2014; Feagin, 2006; Johnson & Shapiro, 2003; Myers, 2005). These beliefs are fueled by the mass media via relentless representations of people of Color associated with criminality. Indeed, much of white flight and the resulting segregation in housing and schooling can be attributed to this representation. This discourse distorts reality and perverts the actual direction of danger that has historically existed between whites and people of Color. Thus the history of extensive and brutal explicit violence perpetrated by whites and their ideological rationalizations are all trivialized through white claims of racial innocence. The power and privilege whites wield and have wielded for centuries is thus obscured.

The discourse of innocence is powerful in part because it rests not only on the current structure of white supremacy, but also on this vast backdrop of historical white supremacy. Whites rarely consider how sheltered and safe their spaces may be from the perspective of people of Color (e.g., Trayvon Martin's experience in a gated white community). Because it perverts the actual direction of racial danger, this narrative may be one of the most perniciously clever of racist discourse.

The opening claim is followed by this statement: "*Oh, I used to live in New Haven where I heard gunshots at the dance club, so Springfield doesn't scare me.*" Contrary to the first speaker, this speaker is positioning herself as jaded rather than innocent. She isn't afraid to go to an urban space because she has been initiated; she has ventured outside of sheltered communities, been exposed to the threat of the racial Other, and survived. Her narrative works powerfully to reinforce the belief in the inherent danger of Black and Brown spaces for those who have no cross-racial experience—she has witnessed the danger firsthand and can confirm it. She has been to places *even worse than Springfield*, and she is not afraid. But her lack of fear does not come because she can now testify that there is nothing to be afraid of. She has not built relationships with the inhabitants of these spaces; she has no stories to tell that would humanize them. This is not a narrative of integration. No, her social capital is generated from the fact that she has seen the danger and can attest to it firsthand. Her narrative, while in contrast to the first speaker, still positions her firmly inside of whiteness as she testifies for the white collective gathered there that their fears are legitimate.

"*Wow! Growing up in a small town, I've never had anything like that happen to me.*" The "wow!" indicates that our second speaker has indeed accrued the social capital of "racial experience." Her narrative is met with a kind of white racial awe. This third speaker has been reinforced in her fear of racial others. The statement that follows the "wow!" brings us back to the narrative of white racial innocence and the reinforcement of white spaces as inherently safe by virtue of the absence of people of Color—these things happen "out there" where *they* are but not "in here" where *we* are (I feel compelled to point out that we are located 75 miles from Newtown, CT). These students bond over their collective recognition of spaces inhabited by Black and Brown people as *other* to their own, simultaneously reinforcing racist images and weaving the threads of White solidarity.

The statement made by a student on the second day of class, "*My boyfriend and I were mugged by a Black man in Springfield*" functions similarly to that above, but holds perhaps more shock value and thus more social capital; racetalk has a "certain allure" and "spices up conversations in enjoyable ways" (Myers, 2005, p. 4). While I assume that this is a true statement (and that her boyfriend is white), discursively it is deeply problematic in this context. It is shared in an exercise in which students have been asked to articulate how various aspects of group identity shape their perspectives. This student does not talk about being white; that a Black man mugged her is the sum of her racial narrative. Yet it is critical to this student's story that she name the mugger's race. This naming happens in a context in which many whites (and younger white people in particular) insist that they don't see color, or that it has no meaning for them (Bonilla-Silva, 2009; DiAngelo, 2012).

The one-sided racial naming of this story powerfully highlights the racial binary while serving as a cautionary tale. Through her narrative, she reinscribes the white racial frame, reinforces Black danger and white innocence, reinforces we–they boundaries, and maintains white solidarity in this all-white space. She too gains the white racial capital accrued from surviving Black space. Her testimony is unmarred by evidence that could disrupt the narrative of Black danger.

These stories are told in a context of extreme segregation. The most profound message of racial segregation for whites may be that there is no real loss in the absence of people of Color. No messages in our daily lives convey that there is loss in racial segregation, that we lose anything by not having people of Color in their lives. In fact, my students' life trajectories (as with most middle-class/upwardly mobile whites) almost certainly ensure that they will have few, if any, enduring relationships with people of Color. They have met some people of Color when playing sports in school, or there "just happened" to be a person of Color or two in their classes, but when they are outside the context of a class or game, the vast majority do not have any authentic, long-term cross-racial relationships; many Whites who describe having a friend of Color in childhood rarely keep them into adulthood (DiAngelo, 2012). Pause for a moment and consider the magnitude of this message: We lose nothing of value by not having cross-racial relationships. In fact, the absence of people of Color in our lives is in large part what defines our schools and neighborhoods as "good." Segregation is justified and reinforced by danger discourse.

There is nothing special about these students (although it is important to note that they will go on to become teachers). These narratives have been well documented across many white contexts (see Bonilla-Silva, 2009; Johnson & Shapiro, 2003; Myers, 2003; Picca & Feagin, 2007). I have been to countless conferences wherein white teachers preface their comments with a description of their schools as "rough" or in "bad neighborhoods." These are only slightly more racially coded forms of danger discourse, and while they are socially acceptable, they are also highly reductive and paint whole communities with a very broad and negative brush. These narratives carry discursive capital that rests on and connects to countless supporting narratives stretching across history and kept alive and in circulation. The examples here provide a momentary freeze-frame of the on-going and adaptive racial (and racist) social context we are all immersed in. As Myers (2003) states, "Dominant ideologies help whites to maintain power by manufacturing consent . . ." (p. 144). Danger discourse links and reinforces the ideology of white supremacy with the resultant practices of segregation, white flight, and resource hoarding.

I understand that aspects of the stories my students and colleagues tell may be true, but I want to make a case for them to stop telling them in contexts in which they can only function to reinforce white solidarity and white supremacy. Of course one may tell about a mugging to the police and to one's family when in need of emotional or physical support. But in a predominately white public forum (and with no antiracist analysis), sharing this story is deeply problematic. Challenging whiteness requires breaking white solidarity and giving up the social capital accrued from the oppression of people of Color. It requires us to think intentionally and strategically about what we are doing and how that functions to either maintain or reinforce racism. We must ask ourselves, "What do I lose by not telling this story?" and use the answer to that question as an entry point into examining and breaking our investments in racism and white supremacy.

REFERENCES

Bonilla-Silva, E. (2009). *Racism without racists: Color-blind racism and the persistence of racial inequality in America.* Rowman & Littlefield.

DiAngelo, R. (2012). *What does it mean to be white?: Developing white racial literacy.* Peter Lang.

DiAngelo, R., & Sensoy, Ö. (2014). Getting slammed: White depictions of cross-racial dialogues as arenas of violence. *Race & Ethnicity in Education, 17*(1), 104–128.

Dyer, R. (1997). *White.* Routledge.

Feagin, J. (2009). *The white racial frame: Centuries of racial framing and counter-framing.* Routledge.

Fine, M. (1997). Introduction. In M. Fine, L. Weis, C. Powell & L. Wong (Eds.), *Off white: Readings on race, power and society* (pp. vii–xii). Routledge.

Frankenberg, R. (1997). Introduction: Local whitenesses, localizing whiteness. In R. Frankenberg (Ed.), *Displacing whiteness: Essays in social and cultural criticism* (pp. 1–33). Duke University Press.

Jacobson, M. (1999). *Whiteness of a different color.* Harvard University Press.

Johnson, H. B., & Shapiro, T. M. (2003). Good neighborhoods, good schools: Race and the "good choices" of white families. In A. W. Doane & E.

Bonilla-Silva (Eds.), *White out: The continuing significance of racism* (pp. 173–187). Routledge.

Leonardo, Z., and R. Porter. 2010. Pedagogy of fear: Toward a Fanonian theory of 'safety' in race dialogue. *Race Ethnicity and Education, 13*(2), 139–157.

Mills, C. W. (1997). *The racial contract.* Cornell University Press.

Morrison, T. (1993). On the backs of Blacks. *Time* (Fall) 57.

Myers, K. (2005). *Racetalk: Racism hiding in plain sight.* Rowan & Littlefield.

Myers, K. (2003). White fright: Reproducing white supremacy through casual discourse. In W. Doane & E. Bonilla-Silva (Eds.), *White out: The continuing significance of racism* (pp. 129–144). Routledge.

Omi, M., & Winant, H. (1994). *Racial formation in the United States: From the 1960s to the 1990s.* Routledge.

Picca, L., & Feagin, J. (2007). *Two-faced racism: Whites in the backstage and front-stage.* Routledge.

Schick, C. (2000). "By virtue of being white": Resistance in anti-racist pedagogy. *Race, Ethnicity and Education, 3*(1), 83–102.

Sensoy, Ö., & DiAngelo, R. (2012). *Is everybody really equal?: An introduction to key concepts in critical social justice education.* Teachers College Press.

Sleeter, C. E. (1996). White silence, white solidarity. In N. Ignatiev & J. Garvey (Eds.), *Race traitors* (pp. 257–265). Routledge.

Van Dijk. T.A. (1992). Discourse and the denial of racism. *Discourse and Society, 3*(1), 87–118.

ELEVEN

Leaning In

A Student's Guide to Engaging
Constructively With Social Justice Content

ROBIN DIANGELO AND ÖZLEM SENSOY

> The struggle has always been inner, and is played out in
> outer terrains. Awareness of our situation must come before
> inner changes, which in turn come before changes in society.
> Nothing happens in the "real" world unless it first happens in
> the images in our heads.
>
> —Gloria Anzaldúa, 2009, p. 310

If you are reading this essay, you are likely enrolled in a course that takes a critical stance. By *critical stance* we mean those academic fields (including social justice, critical pedagogy, multicultural education, as well as antiracist, postcolonial, and feminist approaches) that operate from the perspective that knowledge is socially constructed and that education is a political project embedded within a network of social institutions that reproduce inequality.

In your course, you will be studying key concepts such as *socialization, oppression, privilege,* and *ideology* and doing coursework that challenges your worldview by suggesting that you may not be as "open-minded" as

Originally published as DiAngelo, Robin & Sensoy, Özlem. (2014). Leaning in: A student's guide to engaging constructively with social justice content. *Radical Pedagogy, 11.* Reprinted with permission.

you may have thought. You are encountering evidence that inequality not only exists but is deeply structured into society in ways that secure its reproduction. You are also beginning to realize that, contrary to what you have always been taught, categories of difference (such as gender, race, and class), rather than merit alone, *do* matter and contribute significantly to people's experiences and life opportunities.

When confronted with evidence of inequality that challenges our identities and worldviews, we often respond with resistance; we want to deflect this unsettling information and protect a worldview that is more comforting. This is especially true if we believe in justice and see ourselves as living a life that supports it. Forms that resistance takes include silence, withdrawal, immobilizing guilt, feeling overly hopeless or overly hopeful, rejection, anger, sarcasm, and argumentation. These reactions are not surprising because mainstream narratives reinforce the idea that society overall is fair, and that all we need to overcome injustice is to work hard and treat everyone the same. While comforting, these platitudes are woefully out of sync with scholarly research about how society is structured. Yet the deeply held beliefs that inform our emotional responses make studying and teaching from a critical stance very difficult. Further complicating the challenges of facilitating social justice content, many instructors who teach these courses occupy marginalized identities, which adds more complications that we will discuss later in the chapter (cf. Dlamini, 2002; King, 1991; Schick & St. Denis, 2003; Williams & Evans-Winters, 2005).

In addition to being asked to question ideology that is deeply internalized and taken for granted, critical engagement rarely provides concrete solutions. This ambiguity can lead to frustration, for our K–12 schooling (especially in Canada and the United States) has conditioned us to seek clear and unambiguous answers. In other projects, we have taken on some of these forms of resistance and provided strategies for responding to them (cf. DiAngelo & Sensoy, 2009, 2010, 2012; Sensoy & DiAngelo, 2012). In this chapter, we pull these various strategies together and offer an overall framework for critical engagement. We draw on research and our years of practice teaching social justice content and share the vignettes and guidelines that have been most effective for our own students. A vocabulary list of key terms used can be found at the end of this chapter.

AN OPEN LETTER TO STUDENTS

Courses that address social justice and inequality through a critical lens often challenge mainstream understandings and thus bring to the surface patterns and tensions that other courses do not (Gallavan, 2000; Kincheloe, 2008). We believe that this is due, primarily, to two key reasons.

The first is that many of us are *underprepared to engage in the course content in scholarly ways*. Basic study habits, reading comprehension, writing skills, vocabulary, and critical thinking are often underdeveloped in college students. Ironically, much of this is due to structural inequalities that courses like these try to address. For example, political and economic pressures on schools to focus on standardized testing have resulted in moves away from intellectual curiosity, critical thinking, and engagement with ambiguity and toward creating conforming and compliant students who can memorize the "one right answer" to pass the test. Differences in the kinds of schooling we receive and the differential futures they prepare us for (e.g., *to* manage versus *to be* managed) are based on structural inequalities related to our race, class, gender, and other social locations. These differentials affect our preparation for college and university-level engagement and are examples of the kind of inequalities that social justice–oriented courses address. The ultimate goal of social justice education is to enable us to recognize structural inequalities in ways that prepare us to change them. However, the socio-political context of schooling makes critical engagement challenging for many students, and this challenge is heightened when the topics under study are politically and emotionally charged.

This leads to the second reason that courses that address social justice and inequality bring to the surface patterns and tensions that other courses do not: *most of us have very strong feelings and opinions about the topics examined in social justice courses* (such as racism, sexism, and homophobia). These opinions often surface through claims such as these:

"People should be judged by what they do, not the color of their skin."
"I accept people for who they are."

"I see people as individuals."

"It's focusing on difference that divides us."

"My parents taught me that all people are equal."

"I was always taught to treat everyone the same."

"I've been discriminated against so I don't have any privilege."

"Our generation is more open-minded."

"I have friends from all races and we are all fine with each other."

"I don't think race and gender make any difference—as long as you
 work hard."

"It's white males who are the minority now."

"Women are just as sexist as men."

While these opinions are deeply held and appear to be "common sense" truth
(and not mere opinion at all), they are predictable, simplistic, and misinformed, given the large body of research examining social relations. Yet, the
relentless repetition of these ideas in the mainstream makes them *seem* true,
and allows us to form strongly held opinions without being particularly educated on the issues (Sensoy & DiAngelo, 2012). Indeed, where we are members of dominant groups (e.g., if we are men, white, cisgender, able-bodied),
we will almost certainly have a superficial understanding because that is the
primary message made available to us through *mainstream* society. Where
we are members of minoritized groups (e.g., if we are women, people of
color, transgender, people with disabilities), we may have a deeper personal
understanding of social inequality and how it works, but may not have the
scholarly language to discuss it in an academic context.

Further, it is a rare individual who is dominant in all key social groups,
or conversely is minoritized in all key social groups. Yet messages that circulate in mainstream society do not prepare most of us to conceptualize or
develop the language to discuss our intersecting identities in any depth.
Take for example the intersection of race and class and consider a white
woman who lives in poverty. While she will face many *class* barriers, she
will not face *racism*. Yet a poor white woman—while not facing *racism*—
will face barriers related to her gender—*sexism*—that a poor white *man* will
not. For example, she will be more likely to be held responsible for the care
of her children, she will be more likely to earn less than a man, and she will
be more at risk for male violence, all of which increase the burden of

poverty. Yet mainstream culture tends to present poverty as if there is a collective and shared experience of "the poor."

Without practice and study beyond what we absorb in our daily living, we are ill-prepared to understand social group injustices. Therefore, our perspectives on issues like poverty and social inequality are necessarily lacking—and especially so if we ourselves are not poor. These perspectives include the idea that if we don't *believe in* things such as social inequality, then we don't *participate in* them. Mainstream culture prevents us from understanding a central tenet of social justice education: Society is structured in ways that make us all complicit in systems of inequality; *there is no neutral ground*. Thus, an effective critical social justice course will unsettle mainstream perspectives and institutional discourses, and challenge our views about ourselves and what we think we know about society, how it works, and our place in it.

Unfortunately, when we are new to the examination of social relations, we only know one way to respond to ideas studied in the course: "If the professor is saying that I participate in systems of injustice (such as racism), s/he is saying that I am a bad person (a racist)." Later, we should come to understand that this is *not* what our professors are saying, and that binary ways of conceptualizing these issues (good/bad, racist/not-racist) are part of what prevents us from seeing them.

In sum, the combination of underdeveloped academic skills brought to difficult theoretical concepts and highly charged political content that is absent of complex analysis in mainstream culture, all of which is embedded within an institutional context that is structured to reproduce inequality, make these courses very challenging for most of us. Yet basing our knowledge on such sources as personal opinions, self-concepts, anecdotal evidence, hearsay, intuition, family teachings, popular platitudes, limited relationships, personal experiences, exceptions, and mainstream media is insufficient for understanding and responding constructively to social injustice.

Therefore, to maximize our learning of social justice content, we offer the following guidelines:

1. Strive for intellectual humility.
2. Recognize the difference between opinions and informed knowledge.

3. Let go of personal anecdotal evidence and look at broader societal patterns.

4. Notice your own defensive reactions, and attempt to use these reactions as entry points for gaining deeper self-knowledge.

5. Recognize how your own social *positionality* (such as your race, class, gender, sexuality, ability status) informs your perspectives and reactions to your instructor and those whose work you study in the course.

In what follows, we explain these guidelines in more depth and show how they can help you engage constructively with social justice content.

A STORY: THE QUESTION OF PLANETS

Imagine: You are in a course that fulfills a university science requirement. The professor holds a PhD in astronomy. He has written several books, is widely published in academic journals, and has a national reputation in his field. The course objectives include defining terms used in modern astronomy and exposure to the practices, methodology, and concepts of the discipline. The professor is reviewing the assigned readings, which present the most established theories in the field. He overviews the scientific community's discussion of the number of planets and states that based on the criteria for what constitutes a planet, only eight planets are officially recognized in our solar system.

One of the students raises his hand and insists that there are actually nine planets because that is what he learned in school. He has seen many books with pictures of the planets, and there are always nine. As further evidence, he recites the mnemonic he learned to pass all his science tests: "My Very Educated Mother Just Served Us Nine Pizzas." He states that he had map of the sky in his bedroom as a child and it showed nine planets. Further, he says, his parents taught him that there were nine planets and many of his friends also agree that there are nine. He spent his childhood camping out and looking up at the sky and identifying constellations, so he has experience in astronomy. The professor tries to explain to the student that to engage with the planet controversy one must first demonstrate understanding of the criteria for what constitutes a planet, but he is cut off by the student, who declares, "Well, that's your opinion. My opinion is that there are nine."

The professor tries once more to explain that what he presents in regard to the number of planets is not his opinion, but knowledge based on the scholarly community's established criteria for what defines a planet. Although at one time astronomers believed that Pluto qualified as a planet, as with all disciplines, their knowledge evolved. With the discovery of new information and further study they now understand that Pluto doesn't meet the criteria for a planet, in large part due to its shape. This is not an opinion, the professor repeats, but astronomical theories that have resulted from ongoing research and study. The student replies, "I don't care if Pluto is square, diamond-shaped, or shaped like a banana, it's a planet, and there are nine planets."

How likely is it that the majority of the class thinks our hypothetical astronomy student is raising a credible point? Would the class admire him for standing up to the professor and expressing the same understanding they had (and were too hesitant to bring up)? Even if his peers did share his view, that would not make his argument valid. It is more likely that he would be seen as having some academic challenges, as somewhat immature, and perhaps even as disrespectful. It may even be assumed that he might have trouble passing the class.

GUIDELINE 1: STRIVE FOR INTELLECTUAL HUMILITY

Our hypothetical student is representative of many of students we encounter; he has not done the readings or has trouble understanding what he's read, he has limited knowledge but is resistant to increasing it, he clings to the same opinions he came into the course with, and he is overly confident about his position. Scholars have referred to these patterns as a form of *willful ignorance* (Baker, 1990; de Castell, 1993, 2004; Dei et al.,

2004; Schick, 2000). In our experience, students who have trouble under-standing what they read seldom re-read, read more slowly, use a dictionary to look up new words, or ask their professors to explain difficult passages. Standardized testing and the punishment and reward system of grades are major contributors to these habits, as they have created a school culture that rewards conformity and single, correct answers over intellectual curi-osity and risk-taking. Yet critical social justice education demands a differ-ent kind of engagement than most of us have been prepared for in our previous schooling.

Another challenge to intellectual humility is that many of us see social science content as "soft science" and therefore *values laden* and *subjective*. On the other hand, the natural sciences such as astronomy are seen as "hard science" and therefore *values neutral* and *objective*. Because of the presumed neutrality of the natural sciences, we are unlikely to argue with astronomy findings until we have some mastery in the field—knowing that we might not fully understand the concepts and theories presented. We are more likely to focus on gaining a basic understanding and not on whether we agree or disagree. If we perform poorly on tests, we might feel frustrated with the professor or material as being "too hard," but still rec-ognize our own lack of knowledge as the primary cause of the poor performance. Yet in the study of the social sciences—and particularly when the topic is social inequality—the behavior of our imaginary astron-omy student is not unusual. In fact, it is common for students to argue with professors prior to achieving mastery of the concepts and theories presented. Furthermore, students frequently cite anecdotal evidence to support their arguments and dismiss course content prior to engaging with the research. And unfortunately, students who "disagree with" social justice content *are* often taken seriously by classmates—even seen as a kind of hero for speaking up to the professor. Seeing the study of social inequality as a form of subjective scholarship, they put it on par with their own personal opinions and often dismiss it out of hand.

In academia (including the social and natural sciences), in order for an argument to be considered legitimate (such as how many planets there are, and whether or not structural racism exists), it must stand up to scrutiny by others who are specialists in the field. This scrutiny is called *peer review*. Peer review is the process by which theories and the research they are

based on are examined by other scholars in the field who question, re-
fine, expand, challenge, and complicate the arguments, expanding the collective knowledge base of the field. Just as the astronomy professor's teachings
are more than his "personal opinions," social justice professors' teachings are more than their personal opinions. Both instructors are presenting ideas and theories that have undergone peer review. The overall evidence,
theories, arguments, and analysis presented in class are rooted in the peer
review process.

Most of us—especially when in introductory critical social justice
courses—have seldom previously encountered—much less understood
enough to "disagree with"—the scholars we read. Although some of us
may bring important firsthand experiences to the issues (such as being a
member of a particular *minoritized* group under study), we too can benefit
from grappling with any theoretical framework before debating it. For the
beginner, grappling with the concepts is the first step. To facilitate doing
so, practice the following:

+ Read the assigned material carefully. Look up vocabulary words
  and terminology that are new to you. Accept that you may need
  to read all or part of the material more than once. Consider
  reading passages out loud or taking notes of key points as you
  read. Practice using new terms in class.
+ If there are terms or concepts you are still unsure about, raise
  them in class. It is likely that you are not alone in your confusion.
  Assume that your instructors appreciate questions that
  demonstrate engagement and curiosity, rather than apathy and
  silence that make it difficult to assess student needs.
+ Strive to see the connections to ideas and concepts already
  studied. This will help with your recall, critical thinking, and
  ability to see the "big picture."
+ Focus on *understanding* rather than *agreement*. Consider whether
  "I disagree" may actually mean "I don't understand," and if so,
  work on understanding. *Remember, understanding a concept does
  not require you to agree with it.*
+ Practice posing questions. Because most students have been
  socialized to care more about getting the answers right and less

about comprehension, we may fear that asking questions might reveal that we don't know the answers. Thus, we may make bold statements that lack intellectual humility. These statements could be more usefully framed as questions.

+ Be patient and willing to grapple with new and difficult ideas. "Grappling with" ideas means to receive, reflect upon, practice articulating, and seek deeper understanding; grappling is not debate or rejection. The goal is to move us beyond the mere sharing of opinions and toward more informed engagement.

One place where grappling often falls short is in small-group work. For most instructors, the goal of small-group work is for students to spend time thinking through difficult ideas with others in order to deepen understanding and share insights. In addition to the specific prompts and questions that the instructor has given, all of the following could be taken up in small-group work:

+ Asking clarifying questions of each other
+ Making connections to other readings
+ Identifying key concepts and defining terms
+ Generating examples that illustrate the concepts under study
+ Identifying patterns
+ Developing questions
+ Questioning relationships between concepts
+ Discussing the implications for your own life and work
+ Practicing articulating the ideas introduced in the course in order to clarify and increase your comfort discussing them with others
+ Identifying and discussing challenging passages

Yet instructors often encounter small groups who are merely reinforcing their previous opinions, have moved on to engage in off-topic social banter, or are sitting in silence, checking email or texting because they are "finished" discussing the topic at hand. From an academic perspective, a small group should never be "done" talking about any topic they are given. Scholars have spent their careers developing these concepts, and a limited number of class minutes is not adequate to finish working through and understanding them. If you find yourself at a standstill, work through the bulleted list above, or ask your instructor for some prompts and check in about how you are doing in your comprehension.

GUIDELINE 2: EVERYONE HAS AN OPINION. OPINIONS ARE NOT THE SAME AS INFORMED KNOWLEDGE

One of the biggest challenges to attaining Guideline 1—intellectual humility—is the emphasis placed in mainstream culture on the value of opinion. Mainstream culture has normalized the idea that because everyone has an opinion, all opinions are equally valid. For example, local news and radio shows regularly invite callers to share their opinions about questions ranging from "Do you think so-and-so is guilty?" to "Should immigration be restricted?" Reality shows invite us to vote on the best singer or dancer, implying that our opinions are equal to the opinions of professional dancers, singers, choreographers, and producers. While we *might* have an informed opinion, our response certainly does not depend on one. Thus, we can easily be fooled into confusing *opinion* (which everyone has) with *informed knowledge* (which few have without on-going practice and study).

Because of this socialization, many of us unwittingly bring the expectation for opinion-sharing into the academic classroom. However, in academia, *opinion is the weakest form of intellectual engagement*. When our comprehension is low and critical thinking skills underdeveloped, expressing our opinion is the easiest response. All of us hold opinions on a topic before we enter a course (as our astronomy student did), and these opinions don't require us to understand the issues or engage with the course readings at all. Therefore, expressing these opinions simply rehearses what we already think and doesn't require us to expand, question, or go beneath our ideas. If we aren't interested in reading what we have been assigned, or do not understand what we have read, the easiest thing to do is to point to a passage in the text and give a personal response to it (e.g., "I loved it when the author said that men dominate because it reminded me of an experience

I had . . ."), or use it to reject the reading out of hand (e.g., "The author said white people have privilege. I totally disagree with that because I know someone who didn't get a job because he was white!").

When we make academic claims based on *anecdotal evidence* with regard to the concepts studied—for example, claiming, "Now there is reverse racism"—we are in effect expressing an opinion that is not supported by scholarly evidence. We would not use opinion in astronomy class and believe it unlikely that a student arguing that she or he disagrees with Stephen Hawking on a matter of astronomy would have her or his position taken seriously, much less feel free to make such a claim to begin with. Yet in the social justice classroom, scholars such as Peggy McIntosh, Michel Foucault, and Beverly Tatum are regularly "disagreed with" well before comprehension of their work is mastered. Consider how our astronomy student's understanding of planets—as well as his understanding of science as an ever-evolving field—could deepen if he was able to engage with current theories about what constitutes a planet. Unfortunately, our hypothetical student's attachment to his previously held beliefs precludes this possibility.

Because of these tendencies, professors who teach from a critical social justice stance sometimes "shut down" opinion-sharing. However, curtailing the sharing of opinions in class is often perceived as breaking a social rule: "I have the right to my opinion and denying me that right is unfair." Of course we have a right to our opinions. But our academic goals are not to simply share our pre-existing opinions; our goals are to engage with scholarly evidence and develop the theoretical tools with which to gain a more complex understanding of social phenomena. Yet let us be clear—we *do* want students to offer opinions in order to *reflect on and examine* them; opening one's opinions to examination is not the same as simply sharing them.

In order to move beyond the level of previously held opinions, practice the following:

+ Reflect on your reasons for pursuing higher education. Many students would say they are going to university or college in order to secure a good career. However, your longevity and success in that career will depend on your critical thinking skills and the depth and breadth of your general knowledge base. How might allowing your worldview to be stretched and challenged actually serve your future career interests?

+ Recognize that you do not have to agree with what you are studying in order to learn from it. Let go of the idea that you must agree with a perspective you are studying in order for it to be valid or "worth learning."

+ Practice posing open-ended questions rather than closed questions that invite yes/no responses or debate. Closed questions often begin with "Should" or "Do you agree" (e.g., "Should schools ban soda machines?" or "Do you agree that opportunity is not equal?"). The limitation of these questions is that the debate format does not leave much room for examining grey areas—the space between an either/or, yes/no frameworks. Closed questions can also be answered with an easy yes or no, which prevents a nuanced engagement with complex issues.

+ Practice developing quality questions. For example, using John Taylor Gatto's "The Seven Lesson Schoolteacher" (1992), strong questions could include "Consider Gatto's argument that all teachers teach the 7 lessons. On a continuum from 'Yes absolutely' on one end, to 'No absolutely not' on the other, position yourself in relation to his argument. Explain why you have positioned yourself there." Use phrases such as "Under what conditions . . ." and "To what extent . . ."; for example, "*Under what conditions* might we avoid teaching Gatto's lessons?" "*To what extent* does the school curriculum influence teacher autonomy?" Use the course readings to support your position. Questions connected to texts should require familiarity with the text to answer. For example, "Identify two of Gatto's 7 lessons and find examples you have seen in schools." If someone can respond to the question without ever having read the text, it is not a strong question. Questions may also ask people to *re-imagine*. For example, "Using the readings, design the ideal classroom. Describe the guidelines for student engagement in this ideal classroom. How would the curriculum and pedagogical activities be organized? How would you assess your goals?"

GUIDELINE 3: LET GO OF ANECDOTAL EVIDENCE
AND INSTEAD EXAMINE PATTERNS

Anecdotal evidence is evidence drawn from hearsay or only personal experience, and thus anecdotal evidence is superficial, limited to personal interpretation, and not generalizable. For example, many of us have heard something similar to "My cousin tried to get a job, but they hired an unqualified Black guy instead because they had to fill a quota." Because mainstream education and media seldom teach us how social inequality works, most of the evidence we rely on to understand issues of social justice is anecdotal.

But the goals of college and university classes are to expand one's ability to make sense of everyday events, issues, and incidences—in other words, to offer new and more complex sense-making systems. One of the more important academic skills we can develop is the ability to apply a new sense-making framework to something we currently make sense of using another framework.

To illustrate this concept of *frameworks*, imagine that you have pain in your leg and go to your doctor. Your doctor would likely examine your leg, feel the bones and muscles, and perhaps take X-rays to identify the source of the pain. If, however, you went to an alternative (from a Western perspective) medical practitioner, such as a doctor of traditional Chinese medicine (TCM), she might have a completely different way of examining your body and identifying the source of the pain. She may begin by looking at your tongue and examining other parts of your body. A chiropractor might not examine your leg at all, but instead begin work on your spine.

If we are taking a course studying how humans understand the body and conceptualize healing, then we are less interested in which practitioner is "right" and which is "wrong" in their approach to identifying the source of your pain. We are more interested in the various frameworks each practitioner uses, the scholarly community that informs the ideas that practitioner draws on, and what each framework offers us in terms of understanding how the body works and how humans conceptualize illness and healing. Just as the TCM doctor offers a new way of understanding how your body works, the critical social justice framework offers us a new way of understanding how society works.

Another popular approach many of us take when we encounter a new and unfamiliar framework is to focus on one or two exceptions in order to disprove the framework under study. For example, when reading scholarship describing racism as structural, we may cite sensational examples such as Barack Obama as proof that "anyone can make it." We may also use personal stories to "prove" that structural oppression doesn't exist (or has now "reversed" direction), such as in the story above about the cousin who didn't get a job and believes this is because the company had to fill a racial quota. Although it is a common white myth that people of color must be (unfairly) hired over white people, it is false and problematic for at least three reasons. First, it's misinformed, because hiring quotas are actually illegal. Affirmative Action in the United States or Employment Equity in Canada are not hiring requirements programs, but a system of *goals for the hiring of qualified people who are underrepresented in a given field*. Second, all of the evidence demonstrates that people of color are *discriminated against* in hiring, not preferred (Alexander, 2010; Bertrand & Mullainathan, 2004; Dechief & Oreopoulos, 2012). Third, the story above rests on an embedded racist assumption that the only reason a person of color *could* have been hired over the cousin is because of a quota and not because the person of color was in fact more qualified, or equally qualified but brought a needed perspective that the cousin did not.

Focusing on exceptions or unanalyzed personal experiences prevents us from seeing the overall, societal patterns. While there are always exceptions to the rule, exceptions also *illustrate* the rule. Yes, people from oppressed groups occasionally rise to the top in dominant society. But the historical, measurable, and predictable evidence is that this is an atypical occurrence. If we focus exclusively on those exceptional occurrences, we miss the larger structural patterns. Focusing on the exceptions also precludes a more nuanced analysis of the role these exceptions play in the system overall.

The following questions offer a constructive way to engage with the course content and support Guideline 3:

+ How can using a critical framework expand my understanding of this phenomenon? For example, let's say you are white and have spent time abroad. You have enjoyed the food and cultures of places such as China, Mexico, or Morocco, but have also felt discriminated against (ignored, stereotyped, made fun of) because you are white and from the United States or Canada. Why, you might wonder, aren't the locals more open to you when you are being so open to them—maybe even learning a bit of their language? You offer this anecdote as an example that illustrates that everyone is racist in some ways. Now imagine that you are grappling with a new framework to make sense of your experience. You are studying key concepts such as *whiteness*, *globalization*, and *hegemony*. How can using this framework help you contextualize your experience within larger macro-dynamics?

* Am I able to identify the larger group patterns at play in any individual example? In other words, if my best friend lives with a disability, how can my friendship provide me with a view into the broader patterns of external, structural, internal, and attitudinal barriers faced by persons with disabilities? I may assume that I am outside of ableism because I am open to this friendship when others are not. Yet how can considering overall patterns help me recognize how my friendship is situated in relation to broader social dynamics—dynamics that intentions and individual practices alone cannot overcome?

* Do I recognize that when I claim that my friend's disability is not an issue in our friendship, I am sharing my own limited perspective, because my experiences are interpreted from my positionality as someone who is considered able-bodied? What might the risks be for my friend to disagree with me or try to give me feedback on unaware ableist assumptions I may be making? Do I have the skills to respond to this feedback without defensiveness and denial? Using another example, we often hear heterosexual students make claims such as "There was one gay guy in our school and no one had an issue with him." Yet we can assume that that "one gay guy" has a very different story. Indeed, when we have students in our classes from minoritized groups, they invariably tell us of the misery of high school and all of the unconcious attitudes and behaviors from the dominant group that they had to endure. Our anecdotes are not universal, they are

from a particular perspective; they will necessarily be filtered through our blind spots and on their own are not sufficient evidence.

GUIDELINE 4: USE YOUR REACTIONS AS ENTRY POINTS FOR GAINING DEEPER SELF-KNOWLEDGE

Because social justice courses directly address emotionally and politically charged issues, they can be upsetting. For many of us, this is the first time we have experienced a sustained examination of inequality—especially where we are in dominant groups. Further, much of what is presented is counter to everything we have previously been taught. In addition, these courses typically ask us to connect ourselves personally to the issues under study, triggering patterns of resistance such as those previously discussed. For those of us who have experienced inequality in key dimensions of our lives, it can be painful to see the explicit resistance and hostility of classmates.

Although the frameworks used in these courses do not claim that people in dominant groups are "bad," many of us hear it that way because our current sense-making framework says that participation in inequality is something that only bad people do. Until we have a critical social justice framework—which requires a whole new paradigm of sense making—we often find it difficult to remain open, especially if we are a member of a dominant group under study. Defensiveness, cognitive dissonance, and even feelings of guilt, shame, and grief are not uncommon. In some ways, these kinds of feelings indicate movement and change, and although unpleasant, they are not necessarily problematic. The key to whether these feelings play a constructive or destructive role lies in what we do with them. We can, of course, use them as "proof" that the class content and approach is "wrong" and reject all that we are being taught. But there is no growth for us in this reaction. Rather than allow these emotions to block our growth, we can use them as entry points into greater self-knowledge, and content knowledge.

Conversely, where we belong to minoritized groups, these courses can surface emotions for different reasons. Feelings such as anger, frustration, shame, grief, and that we are under a spotlight are common and can also get in the way of our academic development. However, the analysis, evidence, and conceptual language offered by social justice education can provide the tools with which to challenge the relations of oppression that lead to these feelings. Indeed, the evidence and analysis presented should reveal that the challenges you have faced are not due to your own individual shortcomings but are in large part the product of socially organized, structural barriers. As such, these barriers can be identified and acted against. In this way, rather than increase a sense of hopelessness and immobilization, courses such as this have the potential to empower.

Returning to our astronomy student, we can see that upon receiving information that challenged his worldview, he was unable to use his emotional reactions constructively. Instead, he categorically rejected the information, ending with a somewhat nonsensical claim that Pluto was still a planet, even if it was shaped like a banana. This is the equivalent to claiming that "I treat people the same regardless of whether they are 'red, yellow, green, purple, polka-dotted, or zebra-striped.'" Simplistic platitudes often surface when we are faced with evidence that fundamentally challenges our worldviews. For example, the evidence that racism not only exists, but is systemic and implicates everyone, is a difficult idea for many of us. But popular platitudes such as "I don't care if you're purple" are problematic for at least two reasons: First, color-blindness is not actually possible—we *do in fact* see race and it *does have* social meaning and consequences; second, people do not come in these colors, so claims about green, purple, and polka-dotted people render race ridiculous and trivialize the realities of racism.

Social justice content can trigger strong reactions, but these reactions can be constructive if we use them as entry points to deeper self-awareness, rather than as exit points from further engagement.

Practice the following approaches to the course content in support of Guideline 4:

+ How does considering the course content or an author's analysis challenge or expand the way I see the world?
+ How have I been shaped by the issues the author is addressing? For example, if the author is talking about the experiences of the

poor and I was raised middle class, what does their perspective help me see about what it means to have been raised middle class?

+ What about my life in relation to my race/class/gender might make it difficult for me to see or validate this new perspective?

+ What do my reactions reveal about what I perceive is at risk were I to accept this information?

+ If I were to accept this information as valid, what might be ethically required of me?

GUIDELINE 5: RECOGNIZE HOW YOUR SOCIAL POSITION INFORMS YOUR REACTIONS TO YOUR INSTRUCTOR AND THOSE WHOSE WORK YOU STUDY IN THE COURSE

Positionality is the concept that our perspectives are based on our positions within society. Positionality recognizes that where you stand in relation to others in society shapes what you can see and understand. For example, if I am a considered an able-bodied person, my position in a society that devalues people with disabilities limits my understanding of the barriers people with disabilities face. I simply won't "see" these barriers, in large part because I don't have to—society is structured to accommodate the way I use my body.

Guideline 5 addresses the perception that the content of the class is subjective, values based, and political, while the content of mainstream courses is objective, values neutral, and unpartisan. We discussed this perception under Guideline 3 as it relates to common views on the social sciences. Here, we want to consider this perception using the lens of positionality, and as it relates to the instructors of these courses. Because instructors of critical social justice content are more likely to *name* their positionality and encourage students to do the same, they are often seen as more biased. Mainstream courses rarely if ever name the positionality of the texts they study (e.g., the idea that Columbus *discovered* America is from the colonizer's perspective, but certainly not from the perspective of Indigenous peoples). Unfortunately, because acknowledging one's positionality is a rare occurrence in mainstream courses, doing so reinforces students' perceptions of mainstream courses as *objective* and critical social justice courses as *subjective*. Yet all knowledge is taught from a particular perspective; the power of dominant knowledge depends in large part on its presentation as neutral and universal (Kincheloe, 2008).

In order to understand the concept of knowledge as never purely objective, neutral, and outside of human interests, it is important to distinguish between discoverable "laws" of the natural world (such as the law of gravity), and "knowledge," which is socially constructed. By *socially constructed*, we mean that all knowledge understood by humans is framed by the ideologies, language, beliefs, and customs of human societies. Even the field of science is subjective (the study of which is known as *the sociology of scientific knowledge*). For example, consider scientific research and how and when it is conducted. Which subjects are funded and which are not (the moon's atmosphere, nuclear power, atmospheric pollution, or stem cells)? Who finances various types of research (private corporations, nonprofits, or the government)? Who is invested in the results of the research (for-profit pharmaceutical companies, the military, or nonprofit organizations)? How do these investments drive what is studied and how? How will the research findings be used? Who has access to the benefits of the research? As you can see, these are not neutral questions—they are political, and they frame the way in which knowledge is created, advanced, and circulated. Because of this, knowledge is never values neutral.

To illustrate the concept of knowledge as socially constructed and thus never outside of human values and subjectivity, consider an example of a tree—a seemingly neutral object whose existence is simply a physical fact that can be observed. Yet notice that how we *see* the tree is connected to our meaning-making frameworks (and thus is not neutral at all). First, consider our perceptions of its *size*. A tree that looks big to someone who grew up on the East Coast might not look big to someone who grew up on the West Coast.

Next, consider our perceptions of its *meaning* or *purpose*; these will be shaped by our perspectives and interests. For example, an environmentalist might see a limited resource. A member of the Coast Salish nation might see a sacred symbol of life. A logger or a farmer might see employment. A scientist might see a specimen to be dissected and studied. Further, while it may appear that the logger and the farmer have shared interests, in fact their interests are opposite; the logger would see employment only if the tree is cut down, while the farmer would see employment only if the tree is not cut down. Now let's add the layer of *political power*. Who owns the tree? Who has "the right" to cut it down and profit from it? Would the logger, tribal member, environmentalist, and scientist all agree on this matter of ownership? Whose interests are served by the concept that nature can be owned at all? And who's in the position to impose this concept on others? Who takes the idea of ownership for granted, and who doesn't? What kind of resources, institutions, and larger interests are behind each of these individuals, and how do they influence whose interests will prevail?

Finally, how are these interests informed by the specific time and place in which they occur? In other words, what is considered "valid" scientific research today (from a Western perspective) is not the same as what was considered valid in the past. So while a tree may be an objective, factual, and "real" object that exists independently of humans, our understanding of—and thus our interaction with—it cannot be separated from the cultural context we are currently embedded in. In other words, humans can only make meaning of the tree from the cultural frameworks into which they have been socialized. And so it goes for history, physics, and all fields studied in academia. Knowledge is always culturally informed and thus cannot be values neutral.

Many educators use the metaphor of a fish in water to capture the all-encompassing dimensions of culture. A fish is born into water and so simply experiences the water as one with itself; a fish has no way of knowing that it is actually separate from the water. And although the fish *is* separate, it still cannot survive without water. In the same way that a fish cannot live without water, we cannot make sense of the world without the meaning-making system that our culture provides. Yet this system is hard to see because we have always been "swimming" within it; we just take for granted that what we see is real, rather than a particular perception of reality. For these reasons, social justice educators name our positionality (the currents and waters we swim in) in order to make the socially constructed nature of knowledge visible and to challenge the claim that any knowledge is neutral. Yet ironically, that naming is often used to reinforce the idea that social justice content and those who present it are driven by personal agendas and special interests, and thus less legitimate.

Because instructors who teach critical social justice courses often be-long to minoritized groups, and because they name these groups, they are often perceived as having a personal bias. In other words, they are viewed as if they only teach these courses because they are "minorities" and have an "axe to grind." Because the instructors are seen as simply pushing their personal agendas, students often feel more comfortable to explicitly dis-agree with the curriculum and pedagogy. Indeed, this challenge further illustrates how unimaginable our example of the astronomy student is. The instructor in our scenario is most likely a white male, as is the vast majority of higher education faculty. White males overall hold more social authority and are seen as more objective, and thus students are less likely to argue with them (Rudman & Kiliansky, 2000). In other words, the po-sitionality of the white male professor usually remains unnamed. That, along with the presumed neutral content of a subject like astronomy, means students respond to this instructor and the course as though they were values neutral. In contrast, because the positionality of a woman of Color professor teaching a social justice course is named, both she and the course are presumed to be values driven.

Ultimately, one or two courses in our academic career are not enough to "brainwash" us or deny us the ability to think freely. In fact, the opposite is true: The more depth, perspective, and complexity we can bring to bear on how we and others view and understand the world, the clearer, more nuanced, and ultimately freer our thinking can become. Returning to our astronomy student, it isn't necessary for his positionality to align with that of the instructor in order for him to consider the framework the instructor is using.

The following practices support Guideline 5:

+ Identify your social positionality and stay attentive to how it informs your response to the course context (e.g., your race, class, gender). What "blind spots" might you have as a result of your social groups? In other words, what are the things you can and can't see based on the social positions you hold or don't hold?
+ Recognize the perspective embedded in all texts (such as textbooks, newspaper articles, and TV news), especially those

that don't explicitly name them. Are the ideas presented as if they have no perspective and apply universally to all people, regardless of social positionality? If so, practice seeking out and considering alternative perspectives informed by a range of positionalities.

* As you study the content of your course, it is important for you to continuously consider the interplay between your positionality and that of your instructor. If the instructor represents perspectives and/or experience with key minoritized groups (women, people of color, persons with disabilities, gay, lesbian, or trans people), you could welcome the opportunity to hear perspectives seldom represented in mainstream education. Support the course for the opportunity it offers, rather than undermining it because the concepts are unfamiliar, uncomfortable, or difficult.

GRADING

Grading in a course whose primary goal is to challenge *social stratification* is not without its irony. Activist and scholar Audre Lorde (1984) captures this irony when she states that "The master's tools will never dismantle the master's house." By this she means that in using the tools of the system we are more likely to uphold that system than to challenge it. As instructors, we recognize that by grading, we are upholding an institutional system that ranks students hierarchically, and such rankings are part of the very systems we seek to challenge. Still, many of us choose to work within the system, despite its constraints, in order to challenge the system. The traditional grading system is one of those constraints we must work with.

Mainstream schooling places a tremendous emphasis on grades, and the prevalence of high-stakes testing has only intensified this emphasis. Grades convey powerful ideas about our presumed intellectual abilities and these ideas influence what education we will have access to (through tracking into "gifted" or "special" programs and ability grouping). We are placed into academic tracks as early as 1st grade, and these tracks have very real consequences for the kinds of careers we will have access to later in life

(Oakes & Guiton, 1985). Thus, an understandable but regrettable outcome of tracking based on grades in K–12 schooling is that we may care more about the grades we receive than about the knowledge we gain.

The focus on grades often shapes our very identities and sense of self-worth, further complicating the dynamics of grading. This identity is often reinforced outside of schools as we earn praise or punishment from our families based on our grades. While some of us who have not been successful within this system come to feel fortunate just to earn a C, those of us who have generally been successful by the measure of grades often feel *entitled* to As. It is not uncommon for these students to claim, "I am an A student!" Students with such an identity may feel frustrated—even personally slighted—when receiving grades that challenge this identity.

Although we as instructors are aware of the complexities and contradictions of grading, we are also deeply invested in student comprehension of the course concepts. The grading system is one of the primary tools we must use to both measure and communicate our assessment of this comprehension. We encourage students to keep the following two points in mind when considering the dynamics of grading:

In Order to Grade Comprehension, Instructors Must See Demonstration of Comprehension

Whether in assignments or in class participation and discussion, we must *demonstrate* understanding. Comprehension can be demonstrated in written, verbal, and active forms (such as presentations and projects).

Assessing our comprehension verbally is generally done through class discussions and question-and-answer sessions. However, assessing comprehension verbally can be challenging for instructors if we don't speak up in class. For example, how many times have you witnessed your instructor posing a question to the whole class only to be met by silence? Looking out into a room full of students, most of whom are not responding, instructors are left to assume that these students cannot answer the question. Students sometimes say later that they did not respond because the answer was "so obvious" that it did not require a response. Yet how can our instructors know that we understand if we do not respond when questions are posed in class, even if the answers to those questions seem obvious?

Another common explanation for silence is that someone has already said what we were thinking. Yet from an instructor's perspective, it is fine to repeat (or better yet, to build on) an idea that another student has already stated. No two people will say it exactly alike, and it is important to practice articulating these concepts in your own words in order to develop your critical social justice literacy. Any statement can be expanded, deepened, or in other ways supported. At the minimum, if students repeat what others have said, instructors can gain a sense of how many students are thinking similarly, or struggling with understanding key ideas. This is valuable information for instructors in terms of assessing the collective understanding of the group as well as the comprehension levels of individual students. For these reasons, we encourage students to give some kind of verbal response when asked questions in class, even if it is to say that one does not know, is not sure, or only has a partial answer.

In regard to demonstrating understanding in written work, we evaluate this work by assessing how well written, organized, and clear it is, and how well the submitted work meets the goals of the assignment. The work should (at minimum) be proofread for errors, use academic language, avoid colloquialisms, conform to a standard style of citation, use inclusive language, and stay within the guidelines of the assignment description. These are all *baseline* indicators of the degree of student achievement in a written assignment. Perceptive integration of course readings and lectures in a student's own words, relevant use of examples, and insightful connections can transform an adequately written assignment into an excellent (or A) assignment. These criteria are usually communicated to students in either the course syllabus or assignment description. Thus, in order to most accurately grade comprehension we must see evidence of comprehension in both verbal participation and written work.

Effort is Not The Same as Understanding

When students are worried about their grades or are making a case for the grade they believe they should receive, they often claim that they "worked really hard." These students feel that they should be rewarded for that hard work with an A. The reason this argument rarely makes much headway with instructors is because we are grading student *demonstration of understanding* of content, not the perceived degree of effort expended to achieve it.

Consider this story as analogy: I am taking swimming lessons. My goal is to compete in an upcoming match. I see myself as putting in a lot of effort by making the time to show up for practice, following my coach's instructions, and swimming the number of laps I am assigned. My coach, however, *expects* that I will show up and complete my practice sessions; thus, s/he is focused on other things such as how I hold my body while swimming, my breathing pattern, hip and shoulder movements, smoothness of stroke, and speed. In the end, my coach will determine whether I am ready to compete. This determination will be made based on my demonstrated ability that I am ready, regardless of the degree of effort it takes me to reach that point, and certainly not on the mere fact that I showed up for my lessons and got in the pool.

In a similar way, we are grading students on the degree of demonstrated understanding of studied concepts and not on perceptions of effort, especially because what we as instructors see as effort and what a student sees as effort are often not the same. For some students, showing up to class, listening, and handing in assignments are viewed as evidence of effort. For instructors, this level of effort qualifies as the *minimum* expectation for all students. Still, we are not grading on how "hard" a student works but on the *outcome* of that work.

The following are common (yet not relevant) student rationales for why they should get a grade higher than what was earned:

- "I worked really hard."
- "I am an A student."
- "I came to all the classes."
- "I listened."
- "I spent hours doing the readings."
- "I talked in class discussions."
- "I handed in all my assignments."
- "I have never thought about these things before."
- "I'm really interested in these issues."
- "I've had other courses like this one so I already know all this."

- "I have to get a good grade or I will have to drop out."
- "I have been going through a lot of personal issues this semester."
- "I learned so much in this class."

Student rationales such as these are familiar to many instructors, and we understand that they are driven by real anxieties about grades. However, we urge our students to challenge this anxiety because it thwarts the process of authentic learning.

A final note on grading: Students often believe that the reason they received a poor grade was because the instructor didn't like something they said in class, or because they disagreed with the instructor. Every institution has an appeal process for students who feel they have not been graded fairly by an instructor. This makes it very difficult to lower a student's grade just because of something they said. While classroom assessments have some degree of subjectivity, an instructor has to be able to account for a grade they gave in terms of guidelines for the assignment, as well as in terms that are clear to a mediating third party. Because of this accountability, an instructor's grading criteria are usually clearly stated in the syllabus or on assignment sheets.

CONCLUSION

Many college and university courses provide opportunities that are rare in any other dimension of life: critical engagement with new ideas; the opportunity to hear and consider multiple perspectives; the expansion of one's capacity to understand and talk about complex social issues; guidance in the examination of our identities, socialization, and meaning-making frameworks; and the tools to build a more just society. Unfortunately, the focus on grades minimizes these opportunities.

We find that students who let go of their attachment to grades and put their energy into sincerely grappling with the content tend to do well. Worrying about grades detracts from the ability to focus on content and can become a kind of self-fulfilling prophecy. The following reflection questions may be useful in lessening this attachment:

- Am I willing to consider that I may not be qualified to assess my performance in a course, especially one in which new concepts are being introduced?
- Do I expect an A in all of my courses, and if so, why? Is it because I have always received As, or is it because I have demonstrated mastery of course concepts?
- When I ask my instructor, "How am I doing?" am I asking them to provide me with valuable feedback about what my performance conveys about my comprehension and how it might be improved, or am I asking them to tell me what grade I will receive?

We sincerely hope that our students find our courses valuable in terms of the knowledge and insight gained. It has been our experience that this is most likely achieved when we focus more on mastery of content than on the final grade.

GENERAL REFLECTION QUESTIONS TO MAXIMIZE LEARNING OF SOCIAL JUSTICE CONTENT

1. If I wasn't worried about my grade, how would my engagement in this class shift?
2. Which of the various guidelines detailed in this essay are the most challenging to me, and why? How can I meet these challenges?
3. What degree of responsibility am I willing to take for getting the most out of this course (e.g., coming to class prepared and having completed the reading, engaging in large-group discussions, not dominating discussions, asking questions for clarity, speaking respectfully in class, and using academic rather than colloquial discourse)?
4. What degree of responsibility am I willing to take to support my peers in getting the most from this course (e.g., engaging in discussions, not dominating discussions, listening respectfully when others speak, taking the small-group discussions seriously, coming to class prepared, and having completed the reading)?

5. Many students think about higher education solely as a stepping stone to employment, and thus the only knowledge that is worthwhile is knowledge they see as directly connected to getting a job. We ask you to consider what other kinds of skills higher education can provide, and how these skills are also connected to future employment. If you think beyond a strictly vocational approach, what skills do citizens in a global democracy need? How are these skills also important to any future work you do?

VOCABULARY LIST

Anecdotal Evidence: Evidence that is based on personal stories and single, isolated, or nonrepresentative examples—e.g., "I know a guy that . . . and that proves that. . . ."

Cisgender: Persons whose gender identity matches their biologically defined sex; their identity aligns with the sex category assigned to them at birth (male or female).

Dominant Group: The group at the top of the social hierarchy. In any relationship between groups that define each other (men/women, able-bodied/person with disability), the dominant group is the group that is valued more highly (avoid referring to the minoritized group as "non" dominant group, e.g., "non-white"). Dominant groups set the norms by which the minoritized group is judged. Dominant groups have greater access to the resources of society and benefit from the existence of the inequality.

Framework: A fundamental theory, paradigm, or thought pattern through which we make meaning of a given phenomenon; a particular way of seeing and knowing.

Globalization: The process by which corporations and other large enterprises exert international influence. In exerting this influence, they channel resources away from local communities and usually erode local industry, culture, environment, and identity.

Hegemony: The imposition of dominant group ideology onto everyone in society. Hegemony makes it difficult to escape or to resist "believing in" this dominant ideology, thus social control is achieved through conditioning rather than physical force or intimidation.

Ideology: The big, shared ideas of a society that are reinforced throughout all of the institutions and thus are very hard to question or avoid believing. These ideas include the stories, myths, representations, explanations, definitions, and rationalizations that are used to justify inequality in the society. Individualism and meritocracy are examples of ideology.

Intersectionality: The term used to refer to the reality that we occupy multiple social groups. Some of these groups are dominant in society and some are not. For example, one may be minoritized as a female but privileged as white, minoritized as a person with a disability but privileged as male, and so on. Thus, while all persons with disabilities suffer under ableism, they will have a different experience interacting with dominant society based on whether they are male or female, white or a person of color—for example, a person of color with a disability will *also* be dealing with racism, while a white person with a disability will not.

Mainstream Society: The dominant framework for making sense of society that is circulated across all institutions and that all members are exposed to. The dominant framework includes everyday films, TV shows, advertisements, public school curriculum, holidays, and the stories, myths, representations, explanations, definitions, theories, and historical perspectives that are used to rationalize and hide inequality.

Minoritized Group: A social group that is devalued in society and given less access to resources. This devaluing encompasses how the group is represented, what degree of access to resources it is granted, and how the unequal access is rationalized. Traditionally, a group in this position has been referred to as the minority group. However, this language has been replaced with the term "minoritized" in order to capture the active dynamics that create the lower status in society, and also to signal that a group's status is not necessarily related to how many or how few of them there are in the population at large.

Objective: Perceiving something as factual and not informed by social or cultural interpretations; a universal truth outside of any particular framework. Thus, a person or position that is seen as objective is seen as having the ability to transcend social or cultural frameworks and analyze without bias or self-interest.

Peer Review: The evaluation of scholarly work—often done anonymously to ensure fairness—by peers with expertise in the same field in order to maintain or enhance the excellence of the work in that field and to advance knowledge.

Platitude: A trite, simplistic, and meaningless statement, often presented as if it were significant and original; for example, "*I didn't own slaves*" or "*People just need to take personal responsibility.*"

Positionality: The recognition that where you stand in relation to others in society shapes what you can see and understand about yourself and others.

Social Stratification: The concept that social groups are relationally positioned and ranked into a hierarchy of unequal value (e.g., people without disabilities are seen as more valuable than people with disabilities). This ranking is used to justify the unequal distribution of resources among social groups.

Subjective: An individual's personal perspective, feelings, beliefs, interests, or experience, as opposed to those made from a source considered independent, unbiased, universal, and objective. A person or position that is considered subjective is assumed to be biased and/or self-interested, while a person considered to be objective is seen as unbiased and outside of any cultural influences.

Transgender: A person whose gender identity does not match the sex category assigned at birth (male or female); they may feel themselves to be neither like a woman or a man, that they are a combination of both genders, or that their gender is opposite to their sex. A transgender person can appear to others to partially, occasionally, or entirely perform their gender in a way that does not conform to traditional gender roles.

Whiteness: The academic term used to capture the all-encompassing dimensions of white privilege, dominance, and assumed superiority in society. These dimensions include ideological, institutional, social, cultural, historical, political, and interpersonal.

REFERENCES

Alexander, M. (2010). *The new Jim Crow: Mass incarceration in the age of color-blindness*. The New Press.

Anzaldúa, G. (2009). La conciencia de la mestiza: Towards a new conscious-ness. In R. Warhol-Down & D. Price Herndl (Eds.), *Feminisms redux: An anthology of literary theory and criticism* (pp. 303–313). Rutgers University Press.

Baker, H. A., Jr. (1990). Handling "crisis": Great books, rap music, and the end of Western homogeneity (reflections on the humanities in America). *Callaloo*, *13*(2), 173–194.

Bertrand, M., & Mullainathan, S. (2004). Are Emily and Greg more employable than Lakisha and Jamal? A field experiment on labor market discrimination. *American Economic Review*, *94*(4), 991–1013.

de Castell, S. (1993). Introduction: 6 December 1989/1993, Je me souviens. *Canadian Journal of Education / Revue canadienne de l'éducation*, *18*(3), 185–188. http://www.jstor.org/stable/1495381

de Castell, S. (2004). No speech is free: Affirmative action and the politics of give and take. In M. Boler (Ed.), *Democratic dialogue in education* (pp. 51–56). Peter Lang.

Dechief, D., & Oreopoulos, P. (2012). *Why do some employers prefer to interview Matthew but not Samir? New evidence from Toronto, Montreal, and Vancouver.* Canadian Labour Market and Skills Researcher Network; Working Paper No. 95. Electronic copy available at http://ssrn.com/abstract=2018047

Dei, G. J., Karumanchery, L. L., & Karumanchery-Luik, N. (2004). *Playing the race card: Exposing white power and privilege*. Peter Lang.

DiAngelo, R., & Sensoy, Ö. (2009). We don't want your opinion: Knowledge construction and the discourse of opinion in the equity classroom. *Equity and Excellence in Education*, *42*(4), 443–455.

DiAngelo, R., & Sensoy, Ö. (2010). OK! I get it! Now tell me how to do it: Why we just can't tell you how to do critical multicultural education. *Multicultural Perspectives, 12*(2), 7–12.

DiAngelo, R., & Sensoy, Ö. (2012). Getting slammed: White depictions of race discussions as arenas of violence. *Race & Ethnicity in Education, 17*(1), 103–128. https://doi.org/10.1080/13613324.2012.674023

Dlamini, S. N. (2002). From the other side of the desk: Notes on teaching about race when racialized. *Race, Ethnicity, and Education, 5*(1), 51–66.

Gallavan, N. P. (2000). Multicultural education at the academy: Teacher educators' challenges, conflicts, and coping skills. *Equity & Excellence in Education, 33*(3), 5–11.

Gatto, J. T. (1992). The seven-lesson schoolteacher. In *Dumbing us down: The hidden curriculum of compulsory schooling* (pp. 1–19). New Society Publishers.

Kincheloe, J. L. (2008). *Knowledge and critical pedagogy.* Springer.

King, J. E. (1991). Dysconscious racism: Ideology, identity, and the miseducation of teachers. *Journal of Negro Education, 60*(2), 133–146.

Lorde, A. (1984). The master's tools will never dismantle the master's house. In *Sister outsider: Essays and speeches by Audre Lorde* (pp. 110–113). Crossing Press.

Oakes, J., & Guiton, G. (1995). Matchmaking: The Dynamics of High School Tracking Decisions. *American Educational Research Journal, 32*(1), 3–33. https://doi.org/10.3102/00028312032001003

Rudman, L. A., & Kilianski, S. E. (2000). Implicit and Explicit Attitudes Toward Female Authority. *Personality and Social Psychology Bulletin, 26*(11), 1315–1328. https://doi.org/10.1177/0146167200263001

Schick, C. (2000). White women teachers accessing dominance. *Discourse: Studies in the Cultural Politics of Education, 21*(3), 299–309.

Schick, C., & St. Denis, V. (2003). What makes anti-racist pedagogy in teacher education difficult? Three popular ideological assumptions. *Alberta Journal of Educational Research, 49*(1), 55–69.

Sensoy, Ö., & DiAngelo, R. (2012). *Is everyone really equal? An introduction to key concepts in social justice education.* Teachers College Press.

Williams, D. G., & Evans-Winters, V. (2005). The burden of teaching teachers: Memoirs of race discourse in teacher education. *The Urban Review, 37*(3), 201–219.

TWELVE

◇◇◇◇◇◇◇◇◇◇◇◇◇◇◇◇◇◇◇◇◇◇◇◇◇◇◇◇◇

Showing What We Tell

ROBIN DIANGELO AND DARLENE FLYNN

We are a cross-racial facilitation team and have led antiracist education together for many years. We are leading a work group in an antiracist training. The group of 40 participants is racially diverse (approximately half people of color and half white) and tightly packed into a small training room. It is just before lunch and we are one-third of the way through an all-day session. The white facilitator has finished an in-depth presentation on white privilege that appears to have gone well; the group listened attentively and no challenges were raised. She has traded places with her co-facilitator, a Black woman who is now standing in front of the group with the white facilitator sitting next to her. The facilitator of color is leading the group in the corollary section to the previous one: the impact of racism on people of color. She has prefaced her talk with the statement, "I will now be specifically engaging the people of color in the room on the topic of how systematic white racism impacts us. This is a very sensitive conversation for us to have in the presence of white people, and I ask the white participants to simply listen." Yet as she begins moving down a list of ways that people of color are impacted by racism, a white woman repeatedly questions her. The facilitator does her best to speak to the woman's questions, but the interruption continues. Finally, in response to an example given by the facilitator of color of how

Originally published as Robin DiAngelo and Darlene Flynn (2010), "Showing What We Tell: Facilitating Antiracist Education in Cross-Racial Teams." *Journal of Understanding and Dismantling Privilege*, 1(1). Reprinted with permission.

internalized oppression manifests for people of color, the white woman states to the facilitator of color, "I think it's more complex than that." At this point, the white facilitator leans in and quietly asks her co-facilitator if she would like her to intervene. The facilitator of color says yes, and the white facilitator steps in and points out to the white participant what is racially problematic about the way she is engaging. The white woman is shocked and expresses outrage at the "accusation" that her actions could have a racist impact. The room immediately divides along the lines of whether the woman has been "mistreated" or not, with many people speaking at once. Other participants nervously withdraw. A Black man calls out that the white facilitator has treated the white woman unfairly. A Black woman calls out in response that the Black man is acting on his internalized racial oppression by "rescuing" the white woman. The room erupts in emotional reaction to their charges.

THEORETICAL FRAMEWORK: ANTIRACIST EDUCATION

There are many models used in social justice education, including diversity training, antiracist education, multicultural education, and cultural competency training. While all of these models appear to be similar in that they address cultural difference, they may or may not rest on shared tenets. For example, cultural competency training seldom names racism, theorizes power, or critiques systems of institutional oppression (Pon, 2009).

Antiracist education, however, by design names racism and seeks to recognize and challenge differentials in access to social and institutional power among white people and people of color[1] (Derman-Sparks & Ramsey, 2006; Mullaly, 2002). Deliberately avoiding the "celebrating differences" approach common to much of diversity and cultural competency training, antiracist education centers the analysis on the social, cultural, and institutional power that so profoundly shapes the meaning and outcome of racial difference (Nieto & Bode, 2007). The leadership model explored in this chapter is based on the framework of antiracist education, which conceptualizes racism as a multilayered, multidimensional, ongoing, adaptive process that functions to maintain, reinforce, reproduce, normalize, and render invisible white power and privilege.

Antiracist education seeks to interrupt relations of racial inequality by educating people to identify, name, and challenge the norms, patterns, traditions, structures, and institutions that keep racism and white supremacy in place. One norm and tradition of racism that antiracist practice seeks to interrupt is white leadership. This chapter will provide a rationale for leading in cross-racial teams as a means to challenge racism, address common pitfalls when leading cross-racially, and offer tools and techniques to address these challenges.

WHY LEAD IN CROSS-RACIAL TEAMS?

Put simply, a cross-racial team interrupts racism by providing a new model of leadership. In a white supremacist society, few of us have been given images of role models for the leadership of people of color. For example, if our first image of ultimate power and authority beyond our parents were images of God or Jesus, we most likely saw white men. If religion did not play a large role in our lives, or if we were raised in religions who did not value iconography (such as Jews or Jehovah's Witnesses), other key role models were our teachers (the teaching force is over 90 percent white and this percentage is actually increasing) (National Center for Education Statistics, 2004). When we watched the news; visited statues in parks and museums; were shown our heroes and heroines in books, movies, and television, all of us, regardless of our own race, were presented with images for leadership in the overarching culture that were white. In this context, to lead in a cross-racial team (in which the white member does not dominate and the leader of color does not assist) is to interrupt racial norms and expectations and provide the powerful real-life images and modeling of cross-racial leadership that we have been denied. This interruption of typical norms for leadership is key for the participants being led, but also for the leadership team itself. In that regard, it is a powerful "laboratory" for cultivating cross-racial skills and the opportunity to practice interrupting socialized patterns of racism.

A cross-racial team will invariably be stretched as traditional racial patterns of leadership are broken. Authentic cross-racial leadership requires sustaining honest and courageous dialogue across race about how racism manifests, solving problems, coordinating efforts, responding to racial mistakes, and resolving conflicts. These requirements necessarily bring us to the limits of our skills in that they compel commitment from each team member to deal with racial tensions—a commitment that the culture at large does not require and that few of us are practiced in. Through the process, however, we can build the authentic relationships that are critical for effective team leadership. Of course, bringing us to the limits of our skills is precisely what gives cross-racial teams such potential for growth, but at the same time, our skill limits can also operate to lull us back into familiar and comfortable (albeit racist) patterns of engagement. The next section addresses some of the challenges and dynamics of racism that often manifest when leading in cross-racial teams.

CHALLENGES OF CROSS-RACIAL TEAMS

In the context of the white supremacy in which we are embedded, changes in our racial socialization don't come easily and our roles in the racist structure, regardless of where we are positioned in the racial hierarchy, take a lifetime of committed practice to unravel. For people of color, this means actively challenging the internalization of messages of inferiority (referred to as internalized racial oppression, or IRO). For white people this means actively challenging the internalization of messages of superiority (referred to as internalized racial dominance, or IRD). Both IRO and IRD result in patterns of behavior that may seem natural. Given how racist norms and patterns are obscured (particularly for white people) and the ways in which racism mutates and adapts while it continues to accomplish its work (i.e., dominant discourse about a "postracial" society at the same time that segregation is increasing), we can never relax about challenging racism in general and our own IRO or IRD in particular.

It is a basic premise of antiracist education that racism is operating at all times and in myriad ways; racism is not isolated in discrete incidents that some individuals may or may not "do," but is embedded in all aspects of society, including our very identities (DiAngelo, 2006a). Patterns of racism *will* manifest and can reinforce racism for the team and the participants if the team is not vigilant. We discuss common dynamics and challenges of interracial teams in general racial terms. Intersecting identities will impact and complicate these dynamics, such as gender, ability, sexuality, age, and so on. For example, navigating gender differences in the team will add another layer to the challenges of leading and to the ways in which participants respond to the team. It is beyond the scope of this chapter to address these intersections, but they should be explored among team members.

COMMON DYNAMICS: WHITE PARTNER

Because all white people who are raised in white supremacist culture have internalized, to varying degrees, white superiority, which is often coupled with a lack of practice in *authentic*[1] cross-racial relationship building, there are many problematic patterns that the white partner may manifest. A strong white member of a cross-racial team must stay alert and resist complacency, as these patterns reinforce racism and white dominance for the members of the team as well as the participants. These patterns include

- The white partner assumes the lead, takes over the lead, interjects comments, summarizes the partner's points or otherwise has the last word, dominates the session, and/or recenters him- or herself.
- The white partner abandons the partner of color when the training gets challenging (e.g., by sitting at the back of the room and leaving the partner to lead alone, or by distancing him- or herself from the partner of color if she/he says something "provocative" and/or is being challenged by the group). Distancing can occur through silence, engaging in negotiation with the group about the point the partner made, modifying or softening a point made by the partner in order to appease the group, or explicit disagreement or questioning of the partner in front of the group.

- The white partner defaults to socialization to avoid racial conflict and evades addressing issues on the team. When working with a group, the white partner avoids or smoothes over conflict, maintains comfort, or plays it safe, which dilutes the objectives of the work and thus coddles the racist status quo. If the facilitator of color is taking risks, smoothing over conflict undermines that facilitator by setting the white facilitator up as the "good" facilitator.
- The white partner doesn't use his or her position and power to challenge racism or leaves the facilitator of color to do it. The white partner doesn't use his or her position to back up points made by the facilitator of color.
- The white partner trusts his or her own ability to think about racism in isolation from people of color, and makes decisions without consulting the partner of color. He or she may also override decisions made by or in consultation with the partner of color. The white partner does not make his or her decision-making process transparent to the partner of color.

When working with difficult and resistant groups, the white partner uses the partner of color to process how "hard" the group is, which functions to minimize and invalidate the profound differences in how the room impacts each facilitator based on his or her race, and the ultimate direction that racism flows (no matter how difficult the group is, in the end, their resistance will benefit white supremacy, and thus the white facilitator).

- The white partner assumes that his or her partner is having the same experience and is impacted in the same way that he or she is ("What a great group!"). However, a group that feels open and welcoming to a white facilitator can feel very hostile to a facilitator of color, for precisely the same reasons it feels welcoming to the white facilitator (white liberalism is a pernicious form of racism, and a group perceived as "open" to the white facilitator may seem very inauthentic and dangerously oblivious to a facilitator of color).

+ The white partner doesn't give the partner of color constructive feedback—white guilt causes him or her to feel too uncomfortable guiding or "correcting" a person of color, so the partner doesn't get the feedback that is essential to professional growth.

+ The white partner doesn't check in to see how it is going for the facilitator of color and doesn't cultivate cross-racial curiosity.

COMMON DYNAMICS: PARTNER OF COLOR

People of color in leadership inevitably bring a lifetime of experiences with institutional racism that can result in a complex mix of survival and striving patterns (Bivens, 1995; Mullaly, 2002; Sue, 2003). These patterns result in an internal tension that can be difficult to unravel. While one's parents or other supportive role models may have conveyed one's value, the larger society in which we are all embedded does not. On the one hand, there is the message that one is smart, capable of anything, and has the right to expect to be treated well. On the other, there are the ubiquitous messages that surround us when we open our textbooks in school, receive discipline from white people in authority, have our intelligence assessed by white teachers, watch TV and movies, play with other children, etc. As a result, people of color often find themselves leading without reliable touchstones regarding their ability and right to lead and because society denies that this is a result of systematic racism, attributing that lack to some deficiency in themselves. Working in an antiracist cross-race training team provides an opportunity to explore and strategize to interrupt the internalized patterns that limit us through the process of building a relationship with a committed white co-facilitator.

The mere appearance of a person of color in a role not socially assigned—in this case, as an authority figure on equal footing with a white authority figure—challenges the accepted "order." Through this challenge, there is a rich opportunity for leaders of color to identify and work through the various layers of internalized oppression that could be limiting them. A team member of color can intentionally maximize this opportunity by staying alert to the patterns he or she carries that work to collude with racism. These patterns include

+ *The partner of color doubts his or her ability to lead*, which may manifest in feeling more comfortable in the background, avoiding challenging content, waiting to be asked to step up even when he or she is the most qualified, or trying not to take up "too much" or equal space.
+ *The partner of color feels like an imposter.* He or she has a distracting fear that people will find out that he or she has knowledge gaps. The partner of color sells him- or herself short (undercharging or working for less pay than others with the same or less experience) or prefaces his or her leadership with apologies as though he or she were not entitled to lead.
+ *The partner of color doesn't trust his or her own perspective.* He or she routinely needs outside validation, is hesitant to share his or her thinking, or waits to find out what the co-leader (whom he or she sees as the expert) thinks or wants.
+ *Caretaking.* The partner of color takes on or accepts disproportionate responsibility/work (emotional and/or physical) to make the team "work," and lets problematic dynamics go to avoid making the white partner "feel bad."
+ *Conflict avoidance.* The partner of color feels "lucky" to have the work so avoids "rocking the boat" by confronting the white partner on racist patterns. He or she doesn't give honest feedback to the co-facilitator to avoid creating tension.

It is important to note that many of the patterns on these two lists collude perfectly with each other. For example, while the white partner has been socialized to see him- or herself as the lead and will lean toward assuming the lead, the partner of color has been socialized to doubt his or her ability to lead and may easily (and even with relief) hand off leadership to the white partner. In this way, both internalized racial dominance and internalized racial oppression are reinforced, while seeming to occur "naturally"— simply as a function of each facilitator's unique "preference." The white partner may even see him- or herself as being supportive to the partner of color by taking on aspects of leadership his or her partner finds difficult. Sometimes the white partner taking on key aspects of leadership is strategically wise, for example, when deciding who should challenge white participants or make the most direct statements about white power and privilege. But these decisions should always be explored within the context of internalized racial oppression and internalized racial dominance. A team that is not on top of its own internalized patterns will necessarily model traditional (and often subtle) racist dynamics and inadvertently *reinforce* racism for the group, rather than challenge it.

GROUP DYNAMICS

A primary objective of antiracist education is to interrupt the traditional norms, policies, practices, and procedures that reinforce and reproduce white racism. These norms include not talking openly about race and not having role models for cross-racial leadership. The mere presence of a cross-racial team, coupled with the explicitness of the discussion on race, will challenge and unsettle everyone's racial socialization. As the session unfolds, the concepts and exercises presented become even more challenging. In addition, the racial identities of the facilitators will trigger participants and impact how each facilitator is perceived, heard, and responded to. Unfortunately, we are seldom aware of the socialized racial filters through which we view people; most people see themselves as objective and will insist that race has nothing to do with their assessments of the facilitators. Adding to this complexity, participants often make unconscious moves intended to ward off feelings of racial disquiet and regain racial comfort. In other words, they respond with white fragility (DiAngelo, 2006a). As illustrated in the opening story, the unconscious nature of racism makes these reactions highly charged, and addressing them head-on usually invokes defensiveness.

Another key challenge of antiracist education is that most white people conceptualize racism as occurring only in individual acts that only bad people do. This way of thinking about racism makes it very hard to talk honestly with a group about how racism is manifesting because, for many white people, identifying racist patterns in their behavior is akin to saying that they are bad people. When white people get upset about a challenge to racist norms, people of color can be triggered into survival patterns and, based on their history of harm from white people, work to diffuse the conflict to pacify white people, and thus inadvertently undermine the goals. All of the patterns of internalized racial dominance and internalized racial oppression that play out for the facilitators can play out for the group.

Our opening story illustrates many of the dynamics discussed for facilitators, playing out for the participants. Internalized racial dominance can be seen in the white woman's disregard of the facilitator of color's request to just listen, her continual interruption and interrogation of the facilitator of color but not the white facilitator, her dismissal of the facilitator of color's expertise as simplistic, and her defensiveness, sense of being accused, and rejection of the feedback when her impact was pointed out to her. These dynamics then triggered survival patterns of internalized racial oppression for the people of color. By claiming that the white woman had been mistreated, the Black man moved into caretaking of her, seeking to smooth over her anger. This caretaking functioned to diffuse the impact of the white facilitator's comments, and in so doing, left the facilitator of color unsupported. In turn, a Black woman challenged him (the Black woman's public charge that the Black man was acting on his internalized racial oppression). At this point, other people of color in the room starting working hard to explain or play down the conflict, or nervously withdrew. This allowed white participants to focus on tensions between people of color and avoid looking at themselves. Yet as intense and racially familiar as all of these reactions were, virtually none of the participants consciously intended to undermine anyone.

The team needs to anticipate that the same dynamics they struggle with can be triggered at any time in the room. The team's ability to get a handle on these triggers among themselves will enable them to effectively deal with them when manifesting among the participants. A strong cross-racial team recognizes that from the moment participants enter the room (and often before, as they anticipate the session), they will be racially unsettled. As the content unfolds, this racial disquiet increases and complicates the traditionally problematic patterns of engagement already present in mixed-race groups. A united cross-race team becomes a kind of container or holding environment for the group, and thus needs to be clearly united.

BEING STRATEGIC: PRESESSION PLANNING

In this section we offer a guide to strategic cross-racial leading of workshops on antiracism. While there is extensive literature on the dynamics of cross-racial dialogue (DiAngelo, 2006a, 2006b; DiAngelo & Allen, 2006; Hyers & Swim, 1998; Miller & Donner, 2000; Powell, 1997; Roman, 1993; Shelton & Richeson, 2005), there is very little on the *specific* dynamics of leading these dialogues cross-racially (see Adams et al., 1997; Arnold et al., 1991; Nagda & Zúñiga, 2003). Thus, this guide is based on our experience leading cross-racially over the past seven years. It is important to note that while this may read as a "how-to" guide, and many may find it useful precisely for this reason, teams need to be flexible and "organic," adapting any framework used to the unique dynamics of each individual team.

Given the unique and complex dimensions of antiracist training in a cross-racial team, the following are essential issues to explore in planning a session:

+ *Talk through previous challenges.* What worked? What didn't? What, if anything, would you change for the next time?
+ *Decide the speaking order* from the framework of challenging white dominance and intentionally use each facilitator's position in the racial hierarchy. *Also take into consideration the racial demographics of your group.* For example, generally the person who starts the training is seen as the leader, so having the facilitator of color introduce the session can interrupt the expectation for white leadership. However, having the white facilitator cover ground rules during the introduction with a predominately white group may be wise because this is a potential place for white resistance and the white partner covering ground rules can minimize having that resistance directed towards the facilitator of color from the start. With a group that is predominantly people of color, having

the facilitator of color cover the ground rules can minimize reinforcing the effect of a white person giving rules.

* *Decide the agenda order*, being attentive to the dynamics of pacing and who will end up doing which parts if presenters are alternating covering agenda items. *Take into consideration the balance of airtime* and who is leading which topics and why.
* *Discuss what support might be needed from one another* to be the most effective leaders during the session.
* *Discuss how each presenter will check in with the other*. What signal will be used to attract the co-presenter's attention when the presenter needs assistance or needs to call a break?

BEING STRATEGIC: DURING THE SESSION

If unexpected challenges arise during the session that require flexibility and attention, use your prearranged check-in technique to quickly maneuver. If the issue doesn't require immediate attention, a check-in can occur during a break. You will need to decide

* *Who will do the intervention?* Issues to consider are the racial dynamics involved in the issue and which facilitator's racial position will be most effective in the intervention, the skills of each partner, and how the issue is affecting each partner.
* *When and how will you do the intervention?*
* *What might you need from each other?*

Techniques:

* *Take a break to check in*. A break can be called spontaneously, or participants can be put in pairs or small groups to discuss a topic while you consult together.
* *Make decisions transparently*. For example, tell the group what the challenge is and what you are going to do and why.
* *Call a caucus*. Within the context of antiracist education, caucuses are same-race groups who meet together to discuss aspects of

racism that are specific to their group. Caucuses provide the opportunity for each group to discuss their issues or feelings and their next steps without the pressure of the presence of the other racial group. A strong leader who shares the race of the caucus should facilitate each caucus. For example, when we lead together, Darlene leads the caucus for people of color and Robin leads the caucus for white people. When we are working with a larger and more diverse team, we can break off into more specific caucuses, such as whites, Asian heritage, Latina/o, bi-/multiracial, and so forth. Caucuses are an especially powerful intervention when tension and conflict across racial divides are high.

+ *Do a handoff*, passing the lead to the other facilitator if his or her racial identity makes him/her more effective with the issue or if the facilitator leading feels overwhelmed, out of ideas, and so forth. For example, if a facilitator of color is leading a section and is getting continually challenged by a white participant, she may pass the lead off to the white facilitator, who can use her shared white identity to push back on the participant with more authority and less personal and political risk.

+ *As much as possible, stay physically close together*. It's usually fine to have the facilitator who is leading a particular section standing while the co-facilitator sits to the side, but it is not recommended for one of the facilitators to sit in the back of the room while the other presents. Doing so reinforces several problematic dynamics. If the facilitator sitting in the back is white, she leaves the facilitator of color alone in front and unsupported. Given the dynamics of white racism, an isolated facilitator of color is an easy target for white resistance. When the white facilitator is clearly visible and at the side of the facilitator of color, he or she conveys that he or she is in support of what his or her co-facilitator is saying (of course, it is critical that he/she does not cut in and "take over" from the sidelines). Conversely, when a facilitator of color sits in the back, the image of a white person leading alone and in front is reinforced for participants, and traditional representations of white leadership are reinforced.

BEING STRATEGIC: STAYING HEALTHY AS A MEMBER OF A CROSS-RACIAL LEADERSHIP TEAM

A basic premise of antiracist education is that it is lifelong work; the process of identifying and challenging patterns of racism is always evolving and never finished. It is essential that each facilitator continue to do his or her own racial work outside of the leadership relationship. While many white co-facilitators may believe that if their partners of color are not raising issues of racism that are manifesting on their team, then there aren't any. But, from an antiracist framework, a lack of issues should be viewed as a red flag. In the context of white supremacy, it is not possible for racism not to be manifesting on a cross-racial team, and if issues are not coming up for discussion, it is likely due to a range of related dynamics, including a sense that the white partner will not be receptive to them (a common white pattern). The following suggestions can help each member identify areas in need of skill-building and continued growth:

- *Have a circle of same-identity support.* For example, leaders of color should be involved in an ongoing people-of-color caucus, and white leaders in a white caucus.
- *Resist complacency.* Check in with each other consistently, and frequently ask for feedback.
- *Stay involved in continuing education* through reading, workshops, conferences, support groups, and other forums.
- *Make a commitment to stay in the work and stick by your partner.*
- *Commit to each other's growth.*
- *Give honest, specific, and detailed feedback,* balancing positive feedback with feedback that is more difficult to hear.
- *Remember your shared purpose/vision when things get hard.* Remind your partner of this vision when he or she feels hopeless. A note of caution: If you are white, be sensitive to your privileged position when encouraging your partner of color. Ask him or her early on how you can support him or her when he or she feels discouraged, rather than assume that what you find encouraging will have the same impact on your partner of color.

+ *Take risks in the service of your own growth,* putting your own liberation and the liberation of your racial group first. When white people take on antiracist work in order to "help" people of color, they reinforce paternalistic, missionary, and colonialist relations between white people and people of color. For people of color, doing this work increases their effectiveness in the larger society and with other people of color, and ultimately reduces the effort required to challenge the racist system.

+ *Be aware of your other identities and how they intersect with your race* and can work to undermine your antiracist practice. For example, for white, middle-class women, the class and gender socialization to "look good," save face, and avoid conflict can interfere with the ability to take risks and confront racism in oneself and other white people. For people of color, class and gender differences can set up divides and patterns that undermine the goals of working together to challenge institutional racism.

We recommend that teams create worksheets to guide them through these discussions. The worksheet we use is divided into pre- and postsession sections. Each section has a series of questions that are designed to address many of the points discussed in this chapter. Some questions address specific issues, such as how we will communicate to one another, who will do what sections and why, and so forth. Other questions speak to more personal issues of support and self-awareness, such as how each facilitator's other social identities (class, gender, sexual orientation, ability status, religion, etc.) intersect with race and what their partners should understand about these intersections, emotional trigger points for each facilitator, and so forth. When planning for a session, the questions help guide the way we develop the curriculum for each group. After training, the questions guide our debriefing session and ensure that we discuss some of the more sensitive (and thereby more tempting to avoid) dimensions of our work together. Questions here will include how well supported each facilitator felt by his or her partner, what aspects of racism each facilitator recognized manifesting on the team, what new insights he or she gained about how race works, and what skills he or she wants to continue to develop.

CONCLUDING THE STORY

For many facilitators, the opening vignette is one of the worst imaginable scenarios when leading antiracist education cross-racially. And while it was indeed among the more challenging situations we have ever dealt with, there was not a moment in which either of us felt we had lost control of the group. In fact, it was a very powerful session for almost everyone involved, including us. No amount of explanation, presentation of theory, or group exercises could match the degree of learning and self-awareness that participants gained that day. Through their own and their peers' spontaneous reactions to the highly charged racial dynamics, they gained a rare glimpse into many aspects of their racial socialization. So, what did we do to turn the tide from looming disaster to constructive learning? As we return to the story, we will use our real names.

Darlene (the facilitator of color) quickly checked in with Robin (the white facilitator) and then called for racial caucus groups, with people of color staying in the same room with Darlene and white people moving with Robin to an adjacent room. Each caucus gave members a place to explore what had happened and their reactions to it, specifically from the perspective of their racial identity and without the pressure of the presence of the other racial group. As emotions were expressed and abated, more reflection occurred and the participants moved toward deeper understanding; they were able to apply their reactions to the framework we had presented. Many of the dynamics we had been discussing were illustrated in action. Each facilitator was able to map out for the participants (and with the participants' help) the complex web of racial dynamics that were at play, from their particular racial group's perspectives. After about 45 minutes in caucus, the groups reunited and reported out the highlights of their caucuses. We co-led the discussion and shared with the participants our analysis of the situation and our decision-making process. The facilitated debriefing of the incident both in and following the caucus increased their insights, as participants were guided through a sustained analysis of their reactions from an antiracist framework.

One of the questions that came out of this larger group discussion was whether Robin had acted to "rescue" Darlene by stepping in and naming the

Table 12.1. Strategies Taken

Action	Pattern(s) Challenged	Advance Team Prep	Learning
Darlene handled initial interruptions from white participant	Doubting her own ability, expertise, or right to lead	Both agree that Darlene is a highly competent leader and when she is leading, she is in front—it's her call.	Handling interaction in which her power is challenged affirmed her ability and increased her confidence.
Robin holds back, waits, watches, and asks before making a move	Assuming she is the only one who can manage the situation. Making decisions unilaterally. Taking over.	Both aware of how white dominance plays out. Robin has educated herself on how privilege functions in herself and among her racial group.	Robin's commitment to adhering to guidelines of allyship affirmed in practice and reinforced through Darlene's sense of support. Always remember to ask before stepping in.
Robin steps in. Uses her white privilege in the service of interrupting racism.	Avoiding conflict, maintaining white solidarity by staying silent, playing it safe, not challenging other white people. Leaving people of color on their own to deal with racism.	Team clarity on racial roles and how to use racial position most strategically. Team has discussed signals.	Participant reactions can't be controlled. No single perfect way to handle a situation, but team needs to be firm in their integrity, and able to articulate clearly what decisions they make and why.
Darlene steps in and resumes leadership. Calls for caucuses.	Not trusting her own thinking. Withdrawing or turning decisions over to "expert." Avoiding the difficult work of caucusing. Not holding firm with other people of color on internalized oppression.	Both are familiar with a range of facilitation strategies. Understand how caucuses work and are both competent to lead them. Trust each other's thinking and capabilities.	Darlene is a capable expert. Can think flexibly under pressure. Leaning into conflict pays off.

(continued)

Action	Pattern(s) Challenged	Advance Team Prep	Learning
Co-led after caucus. Stayed physically close and unified in decisions/content. Transparent with the group on our decision-making process and rationale.	Allowing group to divide team. Lose team cohesiveness. Physically separate. Try to move on and avoid staying with hard issues.	Deep trust built. Advanced strategizing on key issues, including room setup, our physical positions, who would lead which sections, and so forth. Both have done our "homework" and are strong in antiracist theory.	Transparency is important for a group's learning. Team alignment is first priority—an aligned team can hold a group together.
Debriefed afterward. Shared each step of the training from our racial position and perspective. Gave and received feedback. Wove insights together. Discussed lessons learned.	Avoid giving or receiving difficult feedback. Assume that if you don't talk about issues, then there are none. Give in to guilt and anxiety about perceived mistakes.	Routinely use our worksheet to guide the conversation and ensure it happens. We schedule in time to talk about training while it is still fresh. We revisit as often as needed.	The patterns for white people and people of color are not the same, but they hook together powerfully. White people acting out racism trigger survival patterns in people of color. A strong cross-racial team is critical!

woman's behavior. This question allowed us to be transparent about some of the key dimensions of the intervention that assured us that this was a case of strategic support and alliance, and not rescue. First, Darlene was initially willing to entertain the woman's questions, and Robin did not step in. However, given that Darlene had asked white participants to listen, the questions were problematic, and Robin watched closely for signs that Darlene might need support. While Darlene wasn't making headway with the woman, it was her curriculum piece and she wasn't signaling a need for backup. But at the point that the woman's dismissal of Darlene became overt, Robin felt it was time to use her white position and privilege and speak to "one of her own" about how racism was playing out. However, she would not have stepped in and risked undermining Darlene's leadership without checking first (had Darlene said no when asked if she needed her to step in, Robin would have deferred, and then consulted with Darlene over break about how best to return to the exchange as a teachable moment from her white perspective). Once one person of color challenged another, Darlene was the appropriate person to step back in and call for a caucus. The following table illustrates the actions taken and how they functioned for the team.

As should be clear, the racial dynamics were complex and shifted quickly. We believe that the deep relationship we have built by intentionally working together as a cross-racial team enabled us to think clearly and work collaboratively under great pressure. Each facilitator knew the other well, had a good grasp of the dynamics of racism, and trusted each other to "have her back." Although we have certainly struggled through situations in which Darlene has not felt supported by Robin as a woman of color, our commitment to continuing the work has enabled us to move through these challenges. We have found no deeper or more authentic way to practice the lifelong work of ending racism than leading antiracist work cross-racially.

NOTE

1. While many white people know some people of color, we use "authentic" to indicate cross-racial relationships that have at their core an understanding of white power and privilege, that recognize the inevitability of the dynamics of white power and privilege surfacing, and that explicitly and intentionally work towards interrupting white power and privilege in their relationship.

REFERENCES

Adams, M., Bell, L., & Griffin, P. (1997). *Teaching for diversity and social justice: A sourcebook*. Routledge.

Akintunde, O. (1999). White racism, white supremacy, white privilege, and the social construction of race: Moving from modernist to postmodernist multiculturalism. *Multicultural Education, 7*(2), 2–8.

Arnold, R., Burke, B., James, C., D'Arcy, M., & Thomas, B. (1991). *Educating for a change*. Between the Lines and the Doris Marshall Institute for Education and Action.

Bivens, D. (1995). *Internalized racism: A definition.* Women's Theological Center. Retrieved from http://www.thewtc.org/publications.html

Derman-Sparks, L., & Ramsey, P. (2006). *What if all the kids are white? Anti-bias multicultural education with young children and families.* Teachers College Press.

DiAngelo, R. (2006a). "I'm leaving!": White fragility in racial dialogue. In B. Mc-Mahon & D. Armstrong (Eds.), *Inclusion in urban educational environments: Addressing issues of diversity, equity, and social justice* (pp. 213–240). Centre for Leadership and Diversity, Ontario Institute for Studies in Education of the University of Toronto.

DiAngelo, R. (2006b). My race didn't trump my class: Using oppression to face privilege. *Multicultural Perspectives, 8*(1), 51–56.

DiAngelo, R., & Allen, D. (2006). "My feelings are not about you": Personal experience as a move of whiteness. *InterActions: UCLA Journal of Education and Information Studies, 2*(2), article 2. Retrieved from http://repositories.cdlib.org/gseis/interactions/vol2/iss2/art2

Feagin, J. (2001). *Racist America: Roots, current realities, and future reparations.* Routledge.

Fine, M. (1997). Introduction. In M. Fine, L. Weis, C. Powell, & L. Wong (Eds.), *Off white: Readings on race, power, and society* (pp. vii–xii). Routledge.

Goldberg, D. T. (1993). *Racist culture.* Blackwell.

Hilliard, A. (1992). *Racism: Its origins and how it works* [Paper presentation]. Mid-West Association for the Education of Young Children, Madison, WI.

Hyers, L. L., & Swim, K. J. (1998). A comparison of the experiences of dominant and minority group members during an intergroup encounter. *Group Processes & Intergroup Relations, 1,* 143–163.

Miller, J., & Donner, S. (2000). More than just talk: The use of racial dialogues to combat racism. *Social Work With Groups, 23*(1), 31–53.

Mills, C. (1999). *The racial contract.* Cornell University Press.

Mulally, R. (2002). *Challenging oppression: A critical social work approach.* Oxford University Press.

Nagda, B. (R.) A., & Zúñiga, X. (2003). Fostering meaningful racial engagement through intergroup dialogues. *Group Processes & Intergroup Relations, 6*(1), 115–132.

National Center for Education Statistics. (2004). *The condition of education 2004.* U.S. Department of Education, Institute of Education Science. Retrieved January 5, 2010, from http://nces.ed.gov/pubsearch/pubsinfo.asp?pubid=2004077

Nieto, S., & Bode, P. (2007). *Affirming diversity: The sociopolitical context of multicultural education* (5th ed.). Pearson, Allyn & Bacon.

Pon, G. (2009). Cultural competency as new racism: An ontology of forgetting. *Journal of Progressive Human Services, 20*(1), 59–71.

Powell, L. (1997). The achievement (k)not: Whiteness and "Black underachievement." In M. Fine, L. Powell, C. Weis, & L. Wong (Eds.), *Off white: Readings on race, power and society* (pp. 3–12). Routledge.

Roman, L. (1993). White is a color! White defensiveness, postmodernism, and antiracist pedagogy. In C. McCarthy & W. Crichlow (Eds.), *Race identity and representation in education* (pp. 135–146). Routledge.

Shelton, J. N., & Richeson, J. A. (2005). Intergroup contact and pluralistic ignorance. *Journal of Personality and Social Psychology, 88,* 91–107.

Sue, D. W. (2002). *Overcoming our racism: The journey to liberation.* Jossey-Bass.

Van Ausdale, D. (2002). *The first r: How children learn race and racism.* Rowman & Littlefield.

THIRTEEN

"We Are All for Diversity, But . . ."

How Faculty Hiring Committees Reproduce Whiteness and Practical Suggestions for How They Can Change

ÖZLEM SENSOY AND ROBIN DIANGELO

> The reason we don't have more faculty of color among college faculty is that we don't want them. We simply don't want them.
>
> —Marybeth Gasman, 2016, "The Five Things No One Will Tell You About Why Colleges Don't Hire More Faculty of Color"

As university workers, we find ourselves in a critical social moment. We are in the midst of the Black Lives Matter movement and global student protests (in Chile, South Africa, and Taiwan, among other countries) against government austerity and authoritarian state structures, the 2017 protests led by Indigenous students against Canadian celebrations of 150 years of the colonial state, and the high-profile 2015 resignations of the University of Missouri's president and chancellor over racial tensions they could not manage. The deep racial divides exposed by the 2016 election in the United States and the subsequent rise in hate crimes on campuses illustrate that racism has been and will continue to be a central issue

Used with permission. Sensoy, Ö., & DiAngelo, R. (2017). "We Are All for Diversity, but . . .": How Faculty Hiring Committees Reproduce Whiteness and Practical Suggestions for How They Can Change. *Harvard Educational Review* 87(4), 557–580. https://doi.org/10.17763/1943-5045-87.4.557

in higher education. It is no longer justifiable for academia to remain racially illiterate. Interviews with student protesters repeatedly show that a key demand is increased racial diversity among the faculty and racial literacy among the white faculty (Chessman & Wayt, 2016; We The Protestors, 2015). These calls are not new; generations of activism and scholarship have reiterated the demand to diversify and decolonize predominantly white university campuses (Kayes, 2006; Smith et al., 2004). Yet, while most universities have responded with declarations of "valuing diversity" and some with pledges and specialized programs, why have they overwhelmingly still not achieved these goals?

While racial diversity among students has increased, faculty diversity has not. In the fall of 2013, among full-time professors in the United States, 84 percent were white (58 percent males and 26 percent females), 4 percent Black, 3 percent Hispanic, and 9 percent Asian/Pacific Islander. Making up less than 1 percent each were professors who were American Indian/Alaska Native and of two or more races(National Center for Education Statistics, 2015). Similarly, in a comprehensive diversity accounting of Canadian universities made public in 2016, Malinda Smith and colleagues (Academic Women's Association [AWA], 2016a) report that despite two-plus decades of equity policies, the Canadian university professoriate remains overwhelmingly white (81 percent) and male (66 percent). The numbers are even more bleak as one looks up the ladder of university leadership: 73 percent of universities have all-white leadership teams, and "in 2016, not a single university had a visible minority woman, or Aboriginal man or woman on their presidential leadership teams" (AWA, 2016b, para. 4).

At the same time, position calls that "encourage" and "invite" underrepresented groups and especially visible minority applicants are ubiquitous. In Canada, publicly funded universities have a legal obligation through the Employment Equity Act to include statements that demonstrate their commitment to equitable hiring practices. In the United States, federal law requires equal opportunity and reasonable accommodation. Yet, in the face of these legal and stated commitments to diversity, the above statistics speak to the urgent need for predominantly white academic institutions to identify the persistent barriers that prevent greater racial diversity among their faculty and to develop strategies to address them. In this chapter we focus on one such entry point: the faculty hiring process.

We argue that through a range of discursive moves, hiring committees protect rather than unsettle whiteness. In so doing, they actively close the gates against racial diversity (Canadian Association of University Teachers, 2010; Gutiérrez y Muhs et al., 2012; Henry et al., 2017; Matthews, 2016; Ng, 1993; Schick, 2000). These moves include the so-called objective scrutiny of applicant CVs, the discourse of "fit," the token committee member, the additive nature of diversity-related interview questions, and the acceptability of candidate ignorance on issues of race/gender. By analyzing these elements, we offer a thematic examination of both well-meaning and outright obstructionist actions that block efforts to increase racial diversity within the academic labor force.

We explicate these familiar moves and also reflect on our own efforts to increase faculty diversity as white women who have served on numerous university hiring committees in both Canadian and U.S. contexts (Sensoy & DiAngelo, 2009). While we are situated within the field of education, these dynamics have been documented across these national borders and in a range of disciplines, including education, law, humanities, social sciences, and nursing (Beard & Julion, 2016; Henry, 2015; Henry et al., 2017; Smith et al., 2004; Vick & Furlong, 2012; Ware, 2000). Drawing from this research and the generous mentorship of colleagues of color and our own struggles to advance racial equity in our spheres of influence, we speak explicitly to our fellow white colleagues who serve on these committees and offer strategies that might authentically open the gates to greater faculty diversity.

We are white academics whose work is indebted to the generations of scholarship on race by Indigenous scholars and scholars of color. In addition to this academic foundation, we have benefited from the personal mentorship of many colleagues of color and Indigenous colleagues. While we centralize the example of race in our discussion, we do so using an intersectional race analysis. At times, we use race interchangeably with the common institutional language of diversity. In isolating race (to the exclusion of intersectional identities, for example), we do not intend to minimize the importance of gender, sexuality, class, or ability on how people experience racialization. Nor do we intend to make invisible the history of white settler society that has erased Indigenous bodies for generations (Barker, 2009; Razack, 2002; Wolfe, 2006). For both brevity and accessibility, we use race as a familiar entry point for predominantly white institutions to begin to problematize a range of unnamed and exclusionary institutional practices. We recognize that we may seem at times to be essentializing racial categories. But our objective is not to reify these categories but to make common racial patterns and assumptions visible in an accessible way.

WHITENESS IN HIGHER EDUCATION

Ruth Frankenberg (1997) describes whiteness as multidimensional: "Whiteness is a location of structural advantage, of race privilege. Second, it is a 'standpoint,' a place from which white people look at ourselves, at others, and at society. Third, 'whiteness' refers to a set of cultural practices that are usually unmarked and unnamed" (p. 1). Thus, to name whiteness is to refer to a set of relations that are historically, socially, politically, and culturally produced and intrinsically linked to dynamic relations of white racial domination (Frankenberg, 1997; Roediger, 2007). In other words, whiteness is deeply embedded in sociocultural practices, and disentangling whiteness from these practices requires a multifaceted approach.

As Eduardo Bonilla-Silva (2015) explains, white-oriented and -led institutions reproduce whiteness through their curriculum, culture, demography, symbols, and traditions, while they simultaneously pass as neutral spaces free of race and racialized perspectives. Only peoples of color are racialized and seen as "bringing" race into race-neutral (white) spaces. If there are no peoples of color present, race remains unnamed and is not presumed to be an organizing institutional factor. Bonilla-Silva surfaces this normative invisibility through his deliberate naming of non–Historically Black Colleges and Universities (HBCUs) as Historically White Colleges and Universities (HWCUs). He terms this normative invisibility "the white racial innocence game," in which white people claim to have no racial knowledge and therefore no awareness of the structures of racism that reproduce white advantage. Similarly, Indigenous scholar Susan Dion (2009) refers to the stance of "perfect stranger," wherein white teachers claim a racial innocence about Indigenous peoples despite having received a lifetime of formal and informal pedagogy on the stereotypical "imaginary Indian" (p. 330).

HWCUs have, for decades, articulated a desire for integration and lamented the difficulty of achieving that goal (Gasman, 2016). Yet these lamentations do not address whiteness itself as a fundamental barrier to integration (or to racial equity, which goes far beyond mere integration). As Sara Ahmed (2012), Bryan Brayboy (2003), Eduardo Bonilla-Silva (2012), Frances Henry and colleagues (2017), and others have explained, for many white/settler-colonial institutions, the implementation of university-wide diversity initiatives and policies is problematic for at least three reasons. First, they tend to view diversity as a stand-alone policy that is conceptualized as the adding of students or faculty of color to the existing makeup of the institution and do not address the fundamental whiteness of the university's policies and practices. Second, the conceptualization and implementation of diversity initiatives in this manner nearly always add workload to the most junior faculty of color and the few numbers of senior faculty of color who can mentor them. Third, diversity initiatives render their underlying logic of whiteness invisible and thus normalize the everyday discourses that racialize only faculty of color. In these ways, the everyday "grammar of whiteness" (Bonilla-Silva, 2012) remains unaddressed.

Additionally, the labor of diversity work is often devalued at the highest-tier institutions, where research in the form of peer-reviewed journal publications and the acquisition of grant monies are the longstanding barometers of the most-valued work driving salary and career progression. In this context, faculty of color are positioned at the frontlines of implementing HWCUs' diversity policies, since they are seen as "the face" of these initiatives and are often among the few who understand the stakes associated with them (Henry et al., 2017). They are expected to do this work in spite of deep white resistance and at a cost to their own research programs. Further, they must make the diversity work palatable for white colleagues when even pressure to attend a stand-alone diversity workshop is a cause for animosity. If a stand-alone session names white advantage and challenges presumed white racial neutrality, the backlash of white fragility often ensues. DiAngelo (2011) defines white fragility as the result of the white subject position—moving through a wholly racialized world with an unracialized identity (e.g., white people can represent all of humanity, people of color can only represent their racial selves). She argues that white people

> are centered in all matters deemed normal, universal, benign, neutral and good. Challenges to this identity become highly stressful and even intolerable. Not often encountering these challenges, we withdraw, defend, cry, argue, minimize, ignore, and in other ways push back to regain our racial position and equilibrium. (p. 57)

Thus, for colleagues of color, in addition to the diversity work itself, they must also navigate the emotional landmines of white fragility so often triggered in response to diversity work.

Another unnamed logic of whiteness is the presumed neutrality of white European enlightenment epistemology. The modern university—in its knowledge generation, research, and social and material sciences, and with its "experts" and its privileging of particular forms of knowledge over others (e.g., written over oral, history over memory, rationalism over wisdom)—has played a key role in the spreading of colonial empire. In this way, the university has validated and elevated positivistic, white Eurocentric knowledge over non-white, Indigenous, and non-European knowledges (Battiste et al., 2002; Carvalho & Flórez-Flórez, 2014; Grosfoguel et al., 2016; Mignolo, 2002). These knowledge forms "inscribed a conceptualization of knowledge to a geopolitical space (Western Europe) and erased the possibility of even thinking about a conceptualization and distribution of knowledge 'emanating' from other local histories (China, India, Islam, etc.)" (Grosfoguel et al., 2016, p. 59). The decolonization of the academy requires, at minimum, an interrogation of not only the disciplinary fields and their borders but also the everyday commonsense practices of the institution itself.

In what follows, we analyze a typical faculty hiring scenario. While there may be slight variations in the process (depending on discipline and teaching- versus research-intensive campus), the core elements of the job search are predictable and stable (Perlmutter, 2017; Vick & Furlong, 2012). We focus on illustrative practices that serve to block greater diversification of academic units and thereby protect the inherent whiteness of HWCUs.

THE STEPS OF THE HIRE

When the people in power receive a mandate to search out excellence, the first place they look is to people like themselves, and too often that is also where the search ends.

—Gabriella Gutiérrez y Muhs et al., *Presumed Incompetent*

Step 1: The Job Description

Tenure-Track Position in Elementary Education

Primary responsibilities will include teaching elementary-level teacher preparation courses and other teacher education courses as needed by the unit. Required qualifications include PhD or EdD in Curriculum and Instruction or another closely related field, demonstrated excellence in teaching, and experience teaching in Grades 1–6. The ideal candidate will be adept in the use of instructional technology, be familiar with state teacher preparation standards, and be interested in joining a campus community that promotes diversity, respect, and inclusion.

In mainstream thought, it is people of color who "have" race (are racialized) and whose identities are hyphenated and marked (e.g., Black Canadian, Chinese-American) as compared to "regular" (white settler) identities that remain unnamed (e.g., you don't see white American or

Scottish-Canadian). Thus, one of the most powerful actions an academic unit can take up when beginning a hiring process is to mark the invisible aspects of dominance that are embedded yet go unnamed in the position description. The field into which a new hire is proposed is never neutral. Therefore, a call for a general position in any field is not possible. While an open job description may allow for a wider range of candidates, it also reinforces the idea that some aspects of the job are core, foundational, and thus presumed neutral, while other aspects are additional, extra, and specialized. Because specializations are necessarily more focused, they can also seem narrower and limited.

The default of privileging a presumed neutral generalist will position them as able to teach more courses in the program; we presume that candidate Bob, as a generalist elementary education graduate, can "hit the ground running" and teach several of the courses we need covering, while candidate Ali, a multiculturalist, would be great for our required diversity course but not for the general elementary education courses (such as Classroom Management or Assessment). The failure to acknowledge that everything we teach is from a particular disciplinary perspective positions Bob as a generalist and Ali as a narrow specialist. Further, it disavows the extensive work a specialist undertakes. Consider a medical analogy: A neurologist will have undergone similar training as a general practitioner as well as further study and specialization in neurology.

Whenever diversity is an add-on, we normalize whiteness rather than diversity. Curriculum, instruction, or elementary teaching are not neutral fields free of political agendas. And when there is no signal that those who wrote the job description recognize this, the message conveyed is that of the status quo. The institution is thus missing its first opportunity to recruit from the small handful of newly minted scholars who could support the institution in reaching the goals it claims to value.

Constructive Alternatives

Most traditional fields are based on old classifications and, as such, reproduce the status quo. For example, the field of multicultural education grew out of the traditional social studies field (Banks, 1993). Be forward thinking in how the disciplines have evolved and reclassify the position to demonstrate that understanding this evolution is central to the position.

Consider the following issues when writing the job description:

- *Operationalize diversity.* If the job announcement states that yours is a campus that "promotes diversity," the committee needs to set clear targets by operationalizing the term. For example, decide what explicit evidence you will use to determine that the candidate has promoted (rather than simply values) diversity. Consider diversity in terms of numbers (e.g., who is and is not there) and as an integrated perspective (more than an opinion or feeling). Ask those with specific expertise to give their thoughts on the job description and to incorporate their ideas. If the committee cannot operationalize diversity, don't use it in the job announcement.
- *Politicize traditional canonic fields.* Incorporate language into every job description that signals a critical paradigm to traditional canons. For example, "Candidates must demonstrate an ability to situate knowledge in their field in a social (cultural, historical) context" (e.g., must be able to speak to how knowledge is validated and institutionalized in their field).
- *Avoid coded language.* Avoid language that signals an uncritical ideological paradigm, such as "urban," "inner city," or "disadvantaged," or racializes all students (e.g., "Candidates are expected to explain the role of mathematical thinking in the lived race and class experiences of elementary students as well as in the teacher and school staff in the region. For example, the impact of white settler colonialism on Vancouver's racialized and Coast Salish communities, or Seattle's racialized and Duwamish communities").
- *Understand that dominant groups are always overrepresented in body and/or in ideology, particularly in disciplines seen as nonpolitical.* Given that the default of most HWCUs is an overrepresentation of the dominant groups (e.g., white people, white men [especially at higher ranks], native English speakers, nondisabled peoples), use every job description as an opportunity to name and correct the imbalance.

Step 2: The Committee Composition

Imagine two committees:

- *Committee 1.* Head of academic unit makes an announcement in the faculty meeting: "We have a new generalist line open in elementary education and need to put the committee together. In addition to those on the standing committee, we will need at least two additional volunteers from the faculty at large. At least one of the volunteers needs to be a generalist. Who would like to volunteer?"
- *Committee 2.* Head of academic unit approaches faculty member with expertise in diversity and says: "We have a new generalist line open in elementary education and need to put the committee together. I am asking you as a member of our faculty with expertise in diversity to head this process. If you are unable to, whom do you recommend I speak with?"

Which one of these approaches to the committee's composition is biased?

They both are. Despite the appearance of neutrality and an open system of participation by all members of the faculty, the first one will continue to reproduce the same outcomes because it does not intentionally act to disrupt them. Given that little progress has been made in terms of faculty diversity in many decades, interrupting status quo procedures is a critical entry point for challenging the reproduction of inequity. This includes unexamined assumptions when putting hiring committees together.

Most university committees would say they try for balance on working groups. However, balance as a working concept is often not adequately problematized. It must be contextualized. When baking, for example, a baker must balance the ratio of wet to dry ingredients. This balance is not fixed for all cases; the wet-to-dry ratio will be different if the desired outcome is pancakes versus bread. Thus, the desired outcome determines what is needed to achieve balance. Similarly, when universities strive for committees that are balanced in terms of diversity, they must consider a different set of parameters than simple equal numbers of tenured versus pretenure faculty, faculty versus students, people of color versus white people. If the organization has stated a desire to recruit and retain a faculty complement that reflects the diversity of the student body or local community, committee membership needs to reflect who can best assess a candidate's contributions to that goal.

Common committee formulas include senior administrative leaders, a subject-matter expert or two, and newer tenure-track members of the faculty. Because this is how hiring committees are typically put together in many academic units, we may assume that it is a proven successful process and that we can trust the good intentions of our peers to use their best judgments and bring forward the most qualified candidates. But as evidenced by our outcomes, these assumptions are false. Whether a department takes volunteers or votes members in, when a predetermined formula generated by the institution is used, the default is the reproduction of power; such formulas were not originally constructed to address diversity and thus cannot be relied on to achieve diversity.

As the pressure to diversify faculty has increased, the response has often been to ensure that a person of color serves on the hiring committee. Given the demographics at most institutions, there are typically one or two colleagues who are repeatedly tapped to provide "diversity cover" (Henry, 2015; Sensoy & DiAngelo, 2009). In addition to being tokenized and overworked, members of color must also deal with ongoing microaggressions (Sue, 2010) in the deliberation process and white fragility should they resist. If the racial perspective the "token" member is asked to provide is in conflict with the desires of the white members, it is most often dismissed (Henry et al., 2017). The token member eventually refuses to endure any more committees (and is seen as "difficult") or, and especially if pretenure, learns to go along to get along (which guarantees that they will continue to be tapped to provide cover rather than critique).

The following dynamics are common and problematic:

+ Members (except for token members) are presumed to be objective and neutral (well-intentioned = objective = supportive of a "balanced" approach to diversity).
+ By positioning the token member as the one to bring the racial perspective, that member is continually racialized.

+ The token member is presumed to have expertise on race and racial issues (such as racism, tracking, profiling), but only on these issues.

+ White members do not recognize that the burden on this token member to bring race perspective is occurring in a hostile (white) workplace.

+ The white assumption of a universal experience is that if the committee (or indeed, the academic unit) feels welcoming to the white members, it must feel equally welcoming to everyone.

+ If the token member actually does call out the racism in a discussion, they are often met with resistance and dismissal.

Constructive Alternatives

When putting together the committee, consider the following:

+ *Think about committee balance in terms of bodies as well as perspectives.* If your institution has the numbers, ensure that the search committee tilts to redress the racial imbalance by having members of color as the majority and, especially, in senior roles on the committee. Ensure that the colleagues who are asked to serve—including white colleagues—bring expertise in racial equity. If your department is predominantly white and no members have racial equity expertise, invite faculty members with expertise from affiliated departments to serve.

+ *Develop a response to stand by decisions that will be read by some faculty as biased.* Remind faculty that for generations the department was mostly white and male and that those members hired the first groups who set up the culture and curriculum. Be prepared to clearly articulate how your committee composition today is in line with the institution's professed diversity goals.

+ *Don't underestimate the role of the committee chair.* Make sure the person in charge has the critical understanding necessary to evaluate diversity-related questions and can advance the work of the committee with diversity as a central project. The chair should have the facilitation skills needed to redirect problematic tangents and arguments against diversity during committee discussions. Be sure that the chair will be able to present a strong case of recommendation to the power structure. If not, be firm and consider a different chair.

+ *Draw on expertise in your faculty and account for their extra service load.* Recognize diversity service by increasing release time. Ensure that those assessing job applicants have a demonstrated critical understanding of, not just a "belief in" or "commitment to," diversity. Use measures such as committee members' published work, research projects, community involvement, and professional development efforts as specific evidence of their commitment and expertise, rather than their warmth, friendliness, professed interest in the issues, or international travels.

Step 3: The "Objective" Scrutiny of the CV

As chair, in preparation for our discussion, I have gone through the applicant CVs and created a table of candidates' publications in terms of numbers, quality of journals, and grant monies. This will help us compare the candidates on fair grounds.

This vignette is based on an actual experience one of us had on a hiring committee. The committee chair (a white male) prepared for the short-listing meeting by creating an elaborate template that he saw as an impartial frame, presuming that evaluating according to the same criteria equaled evaluating fairly.

Education researchers have extensively problematized the standardized approach to assessing students (Darling-Hammond, 2014; Darling-Hammond et al., 1995; Kohn, 2000; Oakes, 2005). Further, beyond the assessment of students, assessments by students of their courses and professors shift predictably along group-based lines: (cis) male professors are rated more positively than (cis) female, white professors are rated more positively than professors of color, and courses that address privilege and racism are rated more negatively (Deo, 2015; Gutiérrez y Muhs et al., 2012; Ladson-Billings, 1996; Nast, 1999; Sensoy & DiAngelo, 2014). Further, research on implicit bias (Jones et al., 2013; Jost et al., 2009) shows that there is a large-scale social belief that peoples of color are inherently less qualified, yet implicit bias and its impact on an applicant's materials (such as teaching evaluations) are rarely ever addressed by hiring committees.

This research shows that the qualifications of candidates of color are often overscrutinized—for example, Why are their student evaluations so poor? Why are there so few grants acquired for their research? At the same time, many contributions are undervalued—for example, the extra work-load that faculty of color typically take on is not "countable" on the CV. This includes mentoring students of color and/or helping them navigate HWCUs, supporting student activist organizations and community groups (e.g., Muslim Students Association, Black Lives Matter chapter), mentoring junior faculty, and consulting with administrators on issues pertaining to particular minoritized populations. Further, candidates of color and Indigenous candidates are often asked to bear additional high-stakes responsibilities—for example, Can you serve on the vice president's advisory committee for the new Aboriginal Students Services Center? Could you consult with the president on his Asian Heritage Month speaker series? The department received a request for a speaker from the Aga Khan Community Leadership group, and the chair recommended they contact you. The pressure to accept these responsibilities is intense, because if a candidate does not agree to take them up, it is likely that the important work won't be done—or won't be done thoughtfully. All of this shadow work draws on the personal, lived, and academic expertise of scholars of color and other marginalized scholars, yet it seldom counts (or counts very little) toward career progression. Conversely, the absence of these skills and experiences is not viewed as a deficit on white applicants' profiles, as their capacity to contribute to this type of service work is rarely seen to be essential.

Constructive Alternatives

Think through the following when reviewing candidate CVs:

* *No CV is race neutral.* Is the committee tending to neutralize the CV of candidates who do not address race and to racialize those

who do? For example, committees may begin to talk about the candidate of color as being an expert on "urban" issues rather than a "general" elementary education person (We need someone who can teach and supervise our students on a range of elementary education topics, not just race).

- *Count input, not just output, in research.* Is the committee counting only candidates' output (the number of publications) and not input (the time it takes to build the relationships that grant access)? Some forms of traditional cultural knowledge are exceedingly challenging to obtain, and some are against cultural rules to disclose to outsiders, and doing so could lose the researcher future access. Consider what other evidence might be considered, such as relationships with communities and activism/advocacy work, and ask for this type of evidence to be included with the application materials for all candidates.
- *Count multilingualism as a strength, not a barrier.* Are discussions about whether or not a particular committee member can understand the speaker allowed to distract from the content? If monolingual committee members are having trouble understanding accented English, that should be considered a deficit on the part of the monolinguist, not the speaker.
- *Be aware that not all publications appear in Western indexes.* Does our assessment of publications consider the languages in which the candidate publishes? Recognize, for example, that international journals may not be indexed in your university's library.
- *Expect evidence of diversity literacy from every applicant, regardless of the field.* Is every candidate able to demonstrate a degree of diversity literacy? Consider what coursework candidates have taken. What are they writing about and who are they citing? In the context of racialized candidates, the playing field is not level, so seek criteria to include these candidates rather than eliminate them. Take as long as necessary to get it right. If you did not get candidates who could further your racial equity goals, why didn't you do well enough to attract them? If you had diverse candidates

in the pool but did not shortlist them, why not? If your long list does not include minoritized candidates, consider it a failed list and be willing to start over.

Step 4: The Interview

Interview Schedule for Dr. V. L. Stone
Elementary Education Position
Tuesday, April 7
6:00–8:00 pm   Dinner with Drs. D. Waterson and P. Lawrence (Rainy City Brewing Co. Pub and Restaurant)

Wednesday, April 8
8:30–9:30 am   Continental breakfast with dept heads (Robert Johnson Hall, Rm 110)
10:00–11:30 am   Research presentation to faculty (RJH, Rm 112)
12:00–1:30 pm   Lunch with committee members (Faculty Club)
1:30–3:00 pm   Interview with full committee (RJH, Rm 112)
3:15–3:45 pm   Meeting with Dean Swenson (RJH, Dean's Suite)

The seemingly neutral layout of a typical campus visit should be considered more critically, as it serves as the most intensive interaction between a candidate and the institutional committee. In this way, it is important to consider the concept of embodiment and how it shapes all institutional interactions.

Racial power manifests institutionally, but it is also inscribed on bodies themselves. While we often acknowledge race in the bodies of racialized others—particularly when it is perceived as a commodity that we want or need—we do not often see how whiteness, too, is embodied by a hiring committee or how it bears on racialized others who interact with the committee. Herein lies a dilemma. To continually mark the bodies of some candidates as diverse (as we too have done in this chapter) is to reify the normative power inscribed on the bodies perceived as white. While there is not currently a way around this dilemma, it can at least be diminished with attention and consciousness. One of the dynamics we can attend to is how the diverse candidate's embodiment implicitly raises both doubts and expectations for the committee: doubts about whether or not the candidate can be a person of color and also be a generalist who won't "just" be interested in race issues, and expectations that the candidate can function as a representative of the diversity the campus claims to desire. These doubts and expectations are present in the candidate's interactions with the committee, whether the committee is explicitly aware of them or not.

In addition to performing well during all parts of the interview, candidates of color must also navigate the default conditions of white normativity within the HWCU institution at large. Along with the conditions of white normativity, they also have the parallel track of their racialized experiences to attend to as they prepare for the day, what W. E. B. Du Bois (1903) termed "double consciousness." For example, Is the campus in a city or a small town? Will I be safe after hours there? Will I encounter any other peoples of color (or otherwise minoritized peoples)? What microaggressions will I face and how do I stay focused in spite of them? Do I speak openly and honestly about my work on race? Do I talk about how my identity shapes my work? Against this backdrop, well-meaning advice by a committee member to "just be yourself" does not alleviate the multilayered stress a candidate of color may feel. Indeed, it can actually increase that stress because it reveals how little the well-meaning committee member understands racial dynamics. Our point here is not that hosts should be so careful as to be distant and reserved, but that committees need to recognize their own embodiment as well as each candidate's and understand that every interaction occurs within a sociocultural and political context, no matter how benign it may appear.

While many candidates of color have a great deal of professional experience navigating white-dominant spaces, a primarily white department still has an impact on their interview experience. Every question conveys information to the candidate about the department's consciousness, or lack thereof. In an HWCU, a candidate who is of color but does not challenge racism and whiteness will more likely be seen as an asset, as unbiased and relatable (Ahmed, 2012; Henry et al., 2017). The committee will presume that such a candidate can "help" with diversity initiatives and will do so as a team player, not "pushing race" or "seeing racism/racists everywhere." In these ways the candidate will be implicitly racialized, while at the same time positioned as unbiased and "naturally" competent on issues of diversity.

Conversely, a racialized candidate who also conducts diversity-related research must manage the committee's perception that they have a single-focus expertise, which may present in such questions as: This is great, but how will you teach all the other students? How does this relate to other students?

The Diversity Question

Some institutions have a bank of questions for committees to choose from. These questions may not address racial diversity at all, leaving it up to the committee to include the discussion. The add-on nature of these questions, and that they are so often optional and thus not included at all, communicates that the capacity to understand oneself in relation to their socio-political context is not central to the department. When a question is asked, it is typically something like: How do you manage diversity in your courses? How do you support diversity, respect, and inclusion in your classes? How do you work with diverse students? Yet these questions proceed from the unmarked norm of whiteness. They do so through their presumption that the white candidate is neutral, that diversity exists outside of oneself, and that difference is something that should or could be controlled and managed. These questions also do not account for the dynamics of unequal power relations embedded in the classroom and the institution at large.

Some of the responses we have heard from candidates to these types of uncritical questions are

> "I taught in a rough inner-city school/tribal school."
> "My wife is Thai."
> "I consulted in Baghdad."
> "I'm a minority myself; I am a _____."
> "I grew up in a small town, so I understand the need to feel included."
> "I taught English in China for 2 years, so I understand feeling excluded."

These answers proceed from the unmarked norm of whiteness in their presumption that simply being near peoples of color, holding fond regard across race, experiencing marginalization in another axis of difference, or any experience of difference at all can result in constructive interventions against oppression. They also function to exempt one from complicity in systems of oppression or the further need for critical engagement.

A candidate's race plays a powerful role in how they are held accountable to engage with complexity and nuance in arguably the most complex and nuanced social problem of our time: race relations. While candidates of color are expected to be able to speak to this topic, white candidates (and white men in particular) are not only permitted ignorance but can openly profess ignorance and still be seen by an uncritical committee as honest, even charming, but certainly not unqualified (Gutiérrez y Muhs et al., 2012). In a classic example of the lack of institutional accountability for faculty diversity, an advice column in the *Chronicle of Higher Education* explained how to answer the diversity question without acknowledging that there are conditions under which a candidate might be unqualified to answer (Utz, 2017). To offer tips that presume that anyone can "pass" the diversity question with just a little preparation gained from an advice-style column reinforces the lack of institutional accountability to diversity. It also relieves the hiring committee of accountability to its institution's professed commitment to diversity; it doesn't have to see a candidate's inability to speak with nuance and complexity to this issue as reason for disqualification or endure the discomfort of standing behind the decision to disqualify a candidate based on that inability. In our experience, a candidate's response to a question on diversity has never been the determining factor in the decision. In this way, these questions simply function as cover for the committee and the institution itself, as they are rarely taken seriously. (One of us was present at an interview when a diversity-themed question was asked and two of the white male members of the committee chose that moment to get up and refill their coffee cups, while a third opened his laptop to check email.)

Constructive Alternatives

While our ads and public narratives (such as mission/vision statements) may tell candidates that our institutions are critically conscious, institutions rarely show this consciousness in action. The interview is an opportunity to do so. While most of us sitting at the hiring table will be white, if we have a critical consciousness, we are better equipped to create a welcoming and affirming climate for underrepresented candidates. If we do not have a critical consciousness, we are less likely to recruit (or retain) these candidates. So what shape are we in? If we state that we want candidates with experience in urban schools, the committee should know how to assess this experience. Again, we must be prepared to expect accountability. This means that if a committee member is not able to assess answers to diversity questions as strong or weak, then that member is simply not qualified to serve on a hiring committee at an institution that professes diversity as a core value and mission.

To be more responsive to these dynamics, consider strategies such as the following:

+ *Integrate diversity into every question in a meaningful way.* In turn, listen closely for complexity and nuance, critical reflection, humility, and self-awareness. Ask follow-up questions and hold high expectations. In so doing, it is communicated from the start that the issues are taken seriously and that faculty will be held accountable to these values. Some questions might be
    + What are some of the techniques you use to teach in a culturally responsive way?
    + Can you trace the history and key politics of your field? How has it responded to calls to move away from "great white men" and toward more inclusive/diverse scholarship?
    + You are asked to teach a general Elementary Teaching course. Who are the five to ten authors the students must read, and why? [Listen for diversity of authors in each candidate's response.]
    + How do you recruit and support racially diverse graduate students?
    + What success have you had? Challenges?
    + What role models are there in your field for nontraditional students (e.g., female students, LGBTQ+ students, Indigenous students, students of color, and students with disabilities)?

- More and more students are demanding faculty accountability on issues of race and equity. How have you responded? What areas of growth do you see for yourself?
- A group of students comes to you and says that there is racial inequity in the classroom's dynamics. How might you respond to these concerns?

- *View less formalized parts of the day as further opportunities to communicate your diversity literacy.* For example, have you asked about dietary restrictions? Is your interview occurring during an important period of faith (e.g., Ramadan, Yom Kippur)? Has there been an acknowledgment of unceded Indigenous territories to start the day and meaningful address of local protocols? What consideration has been given to accessibility within a potentially noisy space (such as a pub or large cafeteria) for candidates who might be hard of hearing, or have mobility limitations?

- *Consider which students you put in front of which candidates.* Because our field is multicultural education, during the interview process we are consistently put in front of the students-of-color groups and other activist groups on campus. Are these same student groups invited to meet candidates for all positions? If not, why? For example, consider having the elementary education candidate meet with activist students on your campus; the candidate would be pressed to demonstrate that they understood the historical impact of their field on marginalized peoples and the impact of that history on children in schools today.

- *Challenge your response to affect.* The affects (body language, facial expression, tone) that are traditionally read as neutral or friendly are de facto white cultural norms. These norms shape both how a predominantly white committee will be read as well as how that committee will read the candidates. Because the affect of white candidates will more easily match the expectations of a predominantly white committee, this candidate will appear to be a better fit over a candidate of color who might be presenting a different affect. Educate yourself on the power of implicit bias and ways to ameliorate it. Consider whether your response to a candidate is based on descriptive observations ("He didn't smile") versus evaluations ("He's not a team player"). For example, a white man who does not smile may be seen as a competent authority figure, while a woman of color who does not smile may be seen as angry and difficult to work with. Develop strategies to keep committee members alert to the reality of implicit bias.

Step 5: The Decision

I think she is great, and if we had a position that was specifically about urban schools, then she might be right for the job. . . .

Try this thought experiment: A predominantly white hiring committee with a white person as chair hires a white person. The next hire is a white person. The next hire is a white person. The next hire is a white person. It could go on for years this way, and the people who might raise a red flag are most likely only faculty of color or others working from a critical social justice framework. In fact, one of us taught in a department that went 17 years without hiring a single person of color. Now imagine that a Black person is chair of the committee, and two or more members are Black. The committee hires a Black person. Most (white) people would raise the red flag right there, but certainly they would do so if the second hire and the third and fourth hires were also Black. But when a red flag is raised on the continual pattern of white hires, justifications often surface, including

+ There just aren't many qualified people of color in this field. People of color who excel usually don't choose to go into education because the pay and status are low.
+ We did everything we could to recruit candidates of color, but they just aren't applying. We can't create people who aren't there.
+ We needed someone who can hit the ground running.
+ Are you saying we shouldn't have our jobs?

When a committee is ready to meet to vote and recommend a candidate for a position, two dominant discourses tend to emerge: fit and merit. As Ian Haney López (2015) argues, fit is the "dog whistle" of the hiring committee, or how committees signal race without explicitly naming it.

From this perspective, "candidate fit" actually means their ability to keep white people racially comfortable and their likelihood of leaving whiteness (or the status quo) undisturbed. Hand in hand with fit is the discourse of merit. These discourses and the assumptions they rest on need to be continually interrogated.

Constructive Alternatives

If, as academic institutions, we truly want to correct the existing diversity imbalance on campus, we need to develop our stamina and skills in talking about identity at every hiring decision. To do so, practice the following strategies:

- *Avoid coded discourses, such as "adding diversity."* These discourses fetishize and commodify non-white bodies. When hiring committees are considering a candidate of color, the fact that the candidate would "add" diversity to the faculty is most always talked about, yet when a white candidate is at the top of the list, the fact that that candidate would not add diversity is not talked about. Grapple openly with how every candidate will or won't contribute to your equity goals.
- *Attend to the reality of implicit bias.* If, as a hiring committee, you are all (or predominantly) white and are excited about a white candidate, ask yourselves if there might be something going on that should be grappled with. Revisit the case for the white candidate and consider how much of the case is based on descriptive qualifications ("integrates multiple perspectives in their research as evidenced by . . . ," "demonstrates commitment to equity as evidenced by . . .") rather than evaluative ones (friendly, relaxed, great sense of humor, cool style, fits in, students love her).
- *Revisit the institutional mission and vision statements.* As a committee, you should ask whether your practices and outcomes are in line with the institution's professed values. If not, then be honest about the department's unwillingness to be accountable to those values and remove any misaligned statements from marketing and other materials promoting your faculty.

◆ *Acknowledge and address power dynamics on committees.* Junior faculty are most vulnerable in their positions on committees. At the same time, they may actually be more current on research related to diversity if this is their field or they were mindful to attend to subjectivity in their research. Yet they often don't challenge their tenured/senior colleagues due to concerns about career progression. Talk openly about your positions and plan how you will mediate the power differentials. For example, the chair might explicitly state that all perspectives are necessary for a successful search and express an expectation that there will be no retaliation for disagreements. The chair should also be mindful to facilitate the discussions in an equitable way by, for example, calling for go-arounds to ensure that all voices are heard, not allowing the most powerful members to set the agenda by speaking first and most, and checking in with quieter members both inside and outside the meetings.

"YEAH, BUT . . .": COMMON NARRATIVES OF RESISTANCE

Our constructive alternatives will be challenging to operationalize, but we have to be honest in asking ourselves, Do we really want to open the gates to greater faculty diversity? If we are indeed committed, and this commitment goes beyond simply marketing the bodies of racialized students to sell our campuses as diverse, we need to be prepared to do everything differently, because everything in the institution was set up to reproduce the existing order. Thus, every step of the hiring process is an opportunity to interrupt the reproduction of racial inequity.

Here we identify common objections and explicitly speak back to them from a racial equity framework.

Won't putting diversity ahead of subject-matter expertise bring down the quality of our institution's research profile?

Diversity literacy and subject-matter expertise are not mutually exclusive, and we need to challenge the implicit bias that continually positions them as such. Further, our measures of quality must be interrogated. If we continue to base quality solely on factors such as the tier of publication, then, due to the institutional and cultural supports that exist for mainstream work, white, male, middle-class, and otherwise privileged scholars will have the equivalent of a "wind at their backs" (Kimmel, 2002) and will continue to excel by these measures, with research that does not further the cause of racial justice continuing to be elevated. Might we instead consider research that does not further the cause of racial justice to be, in fact, lesser quality research?

You're just advocating for diversity because it's your area of scholarship. Why not make math education a mandatory subject for all candidates to demonstrate expertise on?

Let us be clear. We are not advocating that diversity be put ahead of subject-matter expertise. We are advocating for an understanding that one cannot be considered to have subject-matter expertise if one cannot position their field within a socio-political context. For example, if a STEM education candidate is not able to articulate how STEM education can meet the needs of a diverse group of students, recognize that up until now it has not, and have some analysis of why that is and how it might be remedied, that candidate is not qualified in STEM education. Especially as schools become increasingly separate and unequal, we must consider this ability as integral to all positions rather than as optional, desired, but not really weighted.

We are all for diversity, but isn't privileging candidates of color over white applicants just reverse racism?

Racism is different from racial bias. While all people have racial biases, racism refers to the collective impact of that bias when it is backed by the weight of history, legal authority, and institutional control. When these dimensions are present, racial bias is transformed into racism, a system of racial oppression. By definition, racism is not fluid and cannot be wielded by individuals regardless of their racial positions; thus, reverse racism does not exist (Sensoy & DiAngelo, 2017).

Also, there is an abundance of empirical evidence that people of color are discriminated against in hiring and have been for generations and into the present (Cheung et al., 2016; Derous et al., 2016; Hasford, 2016;

Rivera, 2015). Unfounded beliefs that diversity goals require unqualified peoples of color to be hired over white people are insulting because they are based on the assumption that a person of color could not possibly have been the most qualified.

In the case of two candidates who are equally qualified but one is a person of color and the other is white and the workplace is not racially diverse, consider that the person of color is actually more qualified because they bring a perspective to the workplace that is missing.

Aren't we setting up new hires to fail if we bring them into a hostile workplace?

While this statement is meant to exhibit concern, it actually conveys acceptance of a racially hostile workplace. If we are aware enough of the racial hostility that we can make this statement, why is it being allowed to continue? Why are we not up in arms about our climate and putting all effort into changing it?

Unexamined whiteness does make for a hostile work environment for peoples of color, and support will be needed for new hires. Efforts to change the climate and support faculty of color should occur simultaneously. But while this need for support is often positioned as a deficit of candidates of color, consider all the resources put into diversity workshops for white staff. Why do we not see this need for training as a deficit of white employees? Why would we continue to hire candidates who we know will need this education? Why are we willing to wait for them to receive it, even as we know that these training sessions are only occasional occurrences and rarely ever mandatory? In fact, most faculty may not ever receive this training or respond constructively to it if they do. Why is the harm that unaware faculty perpetrate on students and colleagues in the meantime acceptable? We are in support of continual training; racial justice learning is ongoing and our learning is never finished. Still, we do not recommend hiring people with virtually no interest or foundational education.

There just aren't qualified diverse candidates out there.

Change is difficult for many, especially when the change in question is to a system that serves and privileges us. We tend to make excuses and put up roadblocks for inaction rather than take risks, be innovative, and be accountable to diversity goals no matter what challenges may emerge. In addition, there are nondiverse candidates who specialize in diversity content and can bring the critical expertise that is much needed. Students have demanded that white faculty with the skills to engage in diversity with complexity and nuance also be hired (not just well-intentioned open-mindedness, which almost all faculty will have). When we consider white candidates with these skills and perspectives, our pool opens even wider.

These are really good suggestions and thank you for raising them, but the job description was approved by senior administration and it cannot be changed. Besides, if we ask them for changes, we risk losing the position altogether.

Leadership often argues that many of the components of a search have already been approved and thus cannot be changed. While this may sound reasonable, consider what is actually being said: We developed these practices without a lens on equity. Now that we have begun to profess valuing equity, we can't change them. Of course, this is not true; institutions can and do change policies all the time. But we must have the will. Centuries of exclusionary policies will not shift without commitment and the courage to fight resistance. If we cannot demonstrate that we have this commitment through our actions and their outcomes, in good conscience we should stop making the claim that we are campus communities that promote diversity, respect, and inclusion.

CONCLUSION

Demonstrating the value of racialized and Indigenous scholars in the academy . . . means disrupting established ways of doing things and challenging normative notions of selection, appointment, and promotion.

—Frances Henry et al., *The Equity Myth*

The default of historically white institutions is the reproduction of racial inequality. From that premise comes the understanding that we cannot rest on our good intentions or self-images and expect our outcomes to change. As Frances Henry and her colleagues (2017) remind us, "For many racialized and Indigenous faculty, whose numbers have increased only slightly over the past three decades, the policies and diversity initiatives are only a foil to deflect criticism of a system that is doing little to change itself" (p. 8). Rather than exempt ourselves from the lack of change, we must consider the inevitability of our complicity. Our task, then, is to identify how our complicity is manifesting, rather than to establish our so-called openness or neutrality.

Pushing against tradition and the normative practices that have been institutionalized and function to exclude diverse faculty at every step is profoundly challenging. We are up against historic and current differentials in power, privilege, and access that are manifesting concretely (even as their existence is denied). Interrupting these processes requires that we reconsider a multitude of commonsense practices. With this in mind, we offer small steps that can be taken at each point in the academic hiring process. But first we must have the will. We ask our white colleagues to consider how a lack of knowledge, apathy, seeing oneself as "the choir" without need for specific effort, and any resentment toward this work function to hold racial inequity in place. Ideally, we understand the ongoing and lifelong struggle inherent in changing deeply embedded patterns and practices. But if we do not have the knowledge and skills that develop out of sustained intentionality rather than mere good intentions and are not actively working toward attaining them, we must not position ourselves or our programs as "valuing diversity" or "encouraging diverse candidates." To claim that HWCUs value diversity and seek a diverse faculty without fundamental changes in our processes is meaningless, though not benign.

REFERENCES

Academic Women's Association [AWA]. (2016a). The diversity gap in representation. Retrieved from https://uofaawa.wordpress.com/awa-diversity-gap -campaign/the-diversity-gap-in-representation/

Academic Women's Association [AWA]. (2016b). The diversity gap in university leadership. Retrieved from https://uofaawa.wordpress.com/awa-diversity-gap-campaign/the-diversity-gap-in-university-leadership/

Ahmed, S. (2012). *On being included: Racism and diversity in institutional life.* Duke University Press. https://doi.org/10.1215/9780822395324

Banks, J. (1993). The canon debate, knowledge construction, and multicultural education. *Educational Researcher, 22*(5), 4–14. https://doi.org/10.3102/0013189X022005004

Barker, A. J. (2009). The contemporary reality of Canadian imperialism: Settler colonialism and the hybrid colonial state. *American Indian Quarterly, 33*(3), 325–351. https://doi.org/10.1353/aiq.0.0054

Battiste, M., Bell, L., & Findlay, L. M. (2002). Decolonizing education in Canadian universities: An interdisciplinary, international, Indigenous research project. *Canadian Journal of Native Education, 26*(2), 82.

Beard, K. V., & Julion, W. A. (2016). Does race still matter in nursing? The narratives of African-American nursing faculty members. *Nursing Outlook, 64*(6), 583–596. https://doi.org/10.1016/j.outlook.2016.06.005

Bonilla-Silva, E. (2012). The invisible weight of whiteness: The racial grammar of everyday life in contemporary America. *Ethnic and Racial Studies, 35*(2), 173–194. https://doi.org/10.1080/01419870.2011.613997

Bonilla-Silva, E. (2015, November 12). The white racial innocence game. *Racism Review: Scholarship and Activism Towards Racial Justice* [blog]. Retrieved from http://www.racismreview.com/blog/2015/11/12/white-racial-innocence-game/

Brayboy, B. M. J. (2003). The implementation of diversity in predominantly white colleges and universities. *Journal of Black Studies, 34*(1), 72–86. https://doi.org/10.1177/0021934703253679

Canadian Association of University Teachers. (2010). The changing academy? A portrait of Canada's university teachers. *CAUT Education Review, 12*(1). Retrieved from http://www.caut.ca/docs/education-review/the-changing-academy-a-portrait-of-canada-rsquo-s-university-teachers-%28jan-2010%29.pdf?sfvrsn=14

Carvalho, J. J. D., & Flórez-Flórez, J. (2014). The meeting of knowledges: A project for the decolonization of universities in Latin America. *Postcolonial Studies, 17*(2), 122–139. https://doi.org/10.1080/13688790.2014.966411

Chessman, H., & Wayt, L. (2016, January 23). What are students demanding? *Higher Education Today.* Retrieved from http://www.higheredtoday.org/2016/01/13/what-are-students-demanding/

Cheung, H. K., King, E., Lindsey, A., Membere, A., Markell, H. M., & Kilcullen, M. (2016). Understanding and reducing workplace discrimination. In M. R. Buckley, J. R. B. Halbesleben, and A. R. Wheeler (Eds.), *Research in personnel and human resources management* (pp. 101–152). Emerald Group. https://doi.org/10.1108/S0742-730120160000034010

Darling-Hammond, L. (Ed.). (2014). *Next generation assessment: Moving beyond the bubble test to support 21st century learning.* Jossey-Bass.

Darling-Hammond, L., Ancess, J., & Falk, B. (1995). *Authentic assessment in action: Studies of schools and students at work.* Teachers College Press.

Deo, M. (2015). Better tenure battle: Fighting bias in teaching evaluations. *Columbia Journal of Gender and Law, 31*(1), 7–43.

Derous, E., Buijsrogge, A., Roulin, N., & Duyck, W. (2016). Why your stigma isn't hired: A dual-process framework of interview bias. *Human Resource Management Review, 26*(2), 90–111. https://doi.org/10.1016/j.hrmr.2015.09.006

DiAngelo, R. (2011). White fragility. *International Journal of Critical Pedagogy, 3*(3), 54–70.

Dion, S. D. (2009). *Braiding histories: Learning from Aboriginal peoples' experiences and perspectives.* University of British Columbia Press.

Du Bois, W. E. B. (1903). *The souls of Black folk.* A. C. McClure.

Frankenberg, R. (Ed.). (1997). *Displacing whiteness: Essays in social and cultural criticism.* Duke University Press. https://doi.org/10.1215/9780822382270

Gasman, M. (2016, September 20). The five things no one will tell you about why colleges don't hire more faculty of color: It's time for higher ed to change its ways. *The Hechinger Report.* Retrieved from http://hechingerreport.org/five-things-no-one-will-tell-colleges-dont-hire-faculty-color/

Grosfoguel, R., Hernández, R., & Velásques, E. R. (Eds.). (2016). *Decolonizing the Westernized university: Interventions in philosophy of education from within and without.* Lexington Books.

Gutiérrez y Muhs, G., Nieman, Y. F., González, C. G., & Harris, A. P. (2012). *Presumed incompetent: The intersections of race and class for women in academia.* University Press of Colorado.

Hasford, J. (2016). Dominant cultural narratives, racism, and resistance in the workplace: A study of the experiences of young Black Canadians. *American Journal of Community Psychology, 57*(12), 158–170. https://doi.org/10.1002/ajcp.12024

Henry, A. (2015). 'We especially welcome applications from members of visible minority groups': Reflections on race, gender and life at three universities.

Race Ethnicity and Education, 18(5), 589–610. https://doi.org/10.1080/13613324.2015.1023787

Henry, F., Dua, E., James, C. E., Kobayashi, A., Li, P., Ramos, R., & Smith, M. S. (2017). The equity myth: Racialization and indigeneity at Canadian universities. University of British Columbia Press.

Jones, K. P., Peddie, C. I., Gilrane, V. L., King, E. B., & Gray, A. L. (2013). Not so subtle: A meta-analytic investigation of the correlates of subtle and overt discrimination. Journal of Management, 42(6), 1588–1613. https://doi.org/10.1177/0149206313506466

Jost, J. T., Rudman, L. A., Blair, I. V., Carney, D. R., Dasgupta, N., Glaser, J., & Hardin, C. D. (2009). The existence of implicit bias is beyond reasonable doubt: A refutation of ideological and methodological objections and executive summary of ten studies that no manager should ignore. Research in Organizational Behavior, 29, 39–69. https://doi.org/10.1016/j.riob.2009.10.001

Kayes, P. E. (2006). New paradigms for diversifying faculty and staff in higher education: Uncovering cultural biases in the search and hiring process. Multicultural Education, 14(2), 65–69.

Kimmel, M. (2002, November/December). Toward a pedagogy of the oppressor: This breeze at my back. Tikkun Magazine. Retrieved from http://www.fjaz.com/kimmel.html

Kohn, A. (2000). The case against standardized testing: Raising the scores, ruining the schools. Heinemann.

Ladson-Billings, G. (1996). Silence as weapons: Challenges of a Black professor teaching white students. Theory into Practice, 35(2), 79–85. https://doi.org/10.1080/00405849609543706

López, I. H. (2015). Dog whistle politics: How coded racial appeals have reinvented racism and wrecked the middle class. Oxford University Press.

Matthews, P. A. (Ed.). (2016). Written/unwritten: Diversity and the hidden truths of tenure. University of North Carolina Press.

Mignolo, W. (2002). The geopolitics of knowledge and the colonial difference. South Atlantic Quarterly, 101(1), 57–96. https://doi.org/10.1215/00382876-101-1-57

Nast, H. J. (1999). "Sex," "race," and multiculturalism: Critical consumption and the politics of course evaluations. Journal of Geography in Higher Education, 23(1), 102–115. https://doi.org/10.1080/03098269985650

National Center for Education Statistics. (2015). Characteristics of postsecondary faculty. In The condition of education 2015 (pp. 222–225). Department of Education. Retrieved from http://files.eric.ed.gov/fulltext/ED565888.pdf

Ng, R. (1993). "A woman out of control": Deconstructing sexism and racism in the university. *Canadian Journal of Education/Revue canadienne de l'education*, 18(3), 189–205. https://doi.org/10.2307/1495382

Oakes, J. (2005). *Keeping track: How schools structure inequality* (2nd ed.). Yale University Press.

Perlmutter, D. D. (2017, June 13). Administration 101: The first-round interview. *The Chronicle of Higher Education*. Retrieved from http://www.chronicle.com/article/Administration-101-The/240318

Razack, S. (Ed.). (2002). *Race, space, and the law: Unmapping a white settler society*. Between the Lines.

Rivera, L. A. (2015). *Pedigree: How elite students get elite jobs*. Princeton University Press. https://doi.org/10.1515/9781400865895

Roediger, D. (2007). *The wages of whiteness: Race and the making of the American working class*. Verso.

Schick, C. (2000). Keeping the ivory tower white: Discourses of racial domination. *Canadian Journal of Law and Society*, 15(2), 70–90. https://doi.org/10.1017/S0829320100006372

Sensoy, Ö., & DiAngelo, R. (2009). Developing social justice literacy: An open letter to our faculty colleagues. *Phi Delta Kappan*, 90(5), 345–352. https://doi.org/10.1177/003172170909000508

Sensoy, Ö., & DiAngelo, R. (2014). Respect differences? Challenging the common guidelines in social justice education. *Democracy & Education*, 22(2). Retrieved from http://democracyeducationjournal.org/home/vol22/iss2/1

Sensoy, Ö., & DiAngelo, R. (2017). *Is everyone really equal? An introduction to key concepts in social justice education* (2nd ed.). Teachers College Press.

Smith, D. G., Turner, C. S., Osei-Kofi, N., & Richards, S. (2004). Interrupting the usual: Successful strategies for hiring diverse faculty. *Journal of Higher Education*, 75(2), 133–160. https://doi.org/10.1080/00221546.2004.11778900

Sue, D. W. (2010). *Microaggressions in everyday life: Race, gender, and sexual orientation*. Wiley.

Utz, R. (2017, January 18). The diversity question and the administrative job interview. *The Chronicle of Higher Education*. Retrieved from http://www.chronicle.com/article/The-Diversity-Questionthe/238914

Vick, J. M., & Furlong, J. S. (2012, February 1). What to expect in a second-round interview. *The Chronicle of Higher Education*. Retrieved from http://www.chronicle.com/article/What-to-Expect-in-a/130491

Ware, L. (2000). People of color in the academy: Patterns of discrimination in faculty hiring and retention. *British Columbia Third World Law Journal, 20*(1), 55–76.

We The Protesters. (2015). *The demands.* Retrieved from http://www.thedemands.org/

Wolfe, P. (2006). Settler colonialism and the elimination of the native. *Journal of Genocide Research, 8*(4), 387–409. https://doi.org/10.1080/14623520601056240

Index

About the Author

Dr. Robin DiAngelo is an affiliate associate professor of Education at the University of Washington. In addition, she holds two honorary doctorates. Her area of research is in Whiteness Studies and Discourse Analysis, tracing the ways that whiteness is reproduced in everyday narratives. She is a two-time winner of the Student's Choice Award for Educator of the Year at the University of Washington's School of Social Work. She coauthored (with Özlem Sensoy) the textbook *Is Everybody Really Equal?: An Introduction to Key Concepts in Critical Social Justice Education*, which won both the American Educational Studies Association Critics Choice Book Award and the Society of Professors of Education Book Award.

In 2011 she coined the term *white fragility* in an academic article, which influenced the international dialogue on race. Her book, *White Fragility: Why It's So Hard for White People to Talk About Racism* was released in June of 2018 and debuted on *The New York Times* Bestseller List, where it remained for over 3 years. It has been translated into 12 languages and has now been adapted for young adults. Her follow-up book, released in June of 2021, was *Nice Racism: How Progressive White People Perpetuate Racial Harm*. In 2022, she coauthored (with Amy Burtaine) *The Facilitator's Guide for White Affinity Groups: Strategies for Leading White People in an Anti-Racist Practice*. Her work and interviews have been featured in *The New York Times*, *The Guardian*, CNN, MSNBC, CBS, NPR, PBS, and the BBC, among many other forums. In addition to her academic work, Dr. DiAngelo has been a consultant, educator, and facilitator for over 20 years on issues of racial and social justice.